Building the Tatmadaw

The **Institute of Southeast Asian Studies (ISEAS)** was established as an autonomous organization in 1968. It is a regional centre dedicated to the study of socio-political, security and economic trends and developments in Southeast Asia and its wider geostrategic and economic environment. The Institute's research programmes are the Regional Economic Studies (RES, including ASEAN and APEC), Regional Strategic and Political Studies (RSPS), and Regional Social and Cultural Studies (RSCS).

ISEAS Publishing, an established academic press, has issued almost 2,000 books and journals. It is the largest scholarly publisher of research about Southeast Asia from within the region. ISEAS Publishing works with many other academic and trade publishers and distributors to disseminate important research and analyses from and about Southeast Asia to the rest of the world.

Building the Tatmadaw

Myanmar Armed Forces Since 1948

MAUNG AUNG MYOE

INSTITUTE OF SOUTHEAST ASIAN STUDIES
Singapore

First published in Singapore in 2009 by
Institute of Southeast Asian Studies
30 Heng Mui Keng Terrace
Pasir Panjang
Singapore 119614

E-mail: publish@iseas.edu.sg
Website: <http://bookshop.iseas.edu.sg>

ISEAS Library Cataloguing-in-Publication Data

Aung Myoe, Maung.
Building the Tatmadaw : Myanmar armed forces since 1948.
1. Burma—Tapma'to'.
2. Burma—Armed Forces.
3. Burma—Military policy.
I. Title.
UA854 B9A92 2009

ISBN 978-981-230-848-1 (hard cover)
ISBN 978-981-230-849-8 (PDF)

Typeset by Superskill Graphics Pte Ltd
Printed in Singapore by Utopia Press Pte Ltd

This work is dedicated to the
Department of International Relations at
the University of Mandalay

CONTENTS

LIST OF TABLES

LIST OF FIGURES

ACKNOWLEDGEMENTS

A number of people in Myanmar, Australia, and Singapore have made it possible for me to produce this book. In Myanmar, first and foremost, I am indebted to the many people who provided me with sources, gave me advice, and granted me interviews. Without their kindness, support, and encouragement, this work could not have been accomplished. They deserve to be mentioned here but would prefer to remain anonymous. They have my heartfelt gratitude and thanks. In Australia, I am particularly grateful to Ms Helen Hookey from the Strategic and Defence Studies Centre (SDSC), Australian National University. In Singapore, I would like to express my deep appreciation to Sayar Dr Tin Maung Maung Than for his encouragement and advice. Finally, but not the least, infinate gratitude and special thanks are due to my parents. Without their support, this would not have been possible.

GLOSSARY

2IC	Second-in-Command
ABRO	Army of Burma Reserved Organization
AFPFL	Anti-Fascist People's Freedom League
AG	Adjutant General
APC	Armoured Personnel Carrier
ASO	Adjutant Staff Officer
AWCS	Advanced Warning and Control System
BATD	Burma Army Training Depot
BCP	Burma Communist Party
BEDC	Burma Economic Development Corporation
BIMS	Battlefiled Information Management System
BSO	Bureau of Special Operations
BSPP	Burma Socialist Programme Party
BTF	Burma Territorial Force
BWS	Burmese Way to Socialism
C^3I	Command, Control, Communication and Intelligence
CAFTO	Chief of Armed Forces Training
CGE	Central Government Expenditure
CGSC	Command and General Staff College
CIPS	Central Institute of Political Science
CO	Commanding Officer
DDSI	Directorate of Defence Service Intelligence
DI	Defence Industries
DMT	Directorate of Military Training
DSA	Defence Services Academy

DSAS	Defence Services Administration School
DSCFS	Defence Services Combat Forces School
DSI	Defence Services Institute
DSIB	Defence Services Intelligence Bureau
DSIC	Defence Services Intelligence Centre
DSMA	Defence Services Medical Academy
DSNCOS	Defence Services Non-Commissioned Officers School
DSTA	Defence Services Technological Academy
DVB	Democratic Voice of Burma
EEZ	Exclusive Economic Zone
ELINT	Electronic Intelligence
EW	Electronic Warfare
GDP	Gross Domestic Products
GPS	Global Positioning System
GSO	General Staff Office / Officer
HIMAD	High to Medium Altitude Air Defence
IG	Inspector General
IO	Intelligence Officer
JAG	Judge Advocate General
KMT	Koumington
KNDO	Karen National Defence Organization
LAWS	Land/Air Warfare School
LIC	Low Intensity Conflict
LID	Light Infantry Devision
MAG	Military Appointment General
MANPADS	Man-portable Air Defence System
MAS	Military Affairs Security
MBT	Main Battle Tanks
MCTI	Military Computer and Technological Institute
MEC	Myanmar Economic Corporation
MIS	Military Intelligence Section
MOC	Military Operation Command
MP	Member of Parliament
MWVO	Myanmar War Veteran Organization
NBSD	North Burma Sub-District
NCO	Non-Commissioned Officer
NDC	National Defence College
NLM	New Light of Myanmar (newspaper)
NUF	National United Front
OSS	Office of Strategic Studies

OTS	Officer's Training School
PBF	Patriotic Burmese Force
PLA	People's Liberation Army (China)
QMG	Quartermaster General
QSO	Quartermaster Staff Officer
RC	Revolutionary Council
RFA	Radio Free Asia
RMA	Revolution in Military Affairs
ROC	Regional Operation Command
SAC	Security and Administrative Committee
SAM	Surface-to-Air Missile
SAO	State Administrative Organizations
SBSD	South Burma Sub-District
SEADS	Suppression of Enemy Air Defence System
SEE	State-owned Economic Enterprises
SHORAD	Short Range Air Defence
SIGINT	Signal Intelligence
SLORC	State Law and Order Restoration Council
SPDC	State Peace and Development Council
SSM	Surface-to-Surface Missile
TGE	Total Government Expenditure
TOC	Tactical Operation Command
UMEHL	Union of Myanmar Economic Holding Limited
UMP	Union Military Police
USDA	Union Solidarity and Development Association
WMD	Weapons of Mass Destration

1

INTRODUCTION

Ever since Myanmar regained its independence in January 1948, the Tatmadaw (Myanmar Armed Forces) has been crucial in restoring and maintaining law and order. It is one of the most important institutions in Myanmar politics. During the civil war of late 1940s and early 1950s, the Tatmadaw suppressed both communist and separatist insurgencies, restored law and order, and maintained peace and stability. While it had engaged in counter-insurgency operations, the Tatmadaw also had to drive foreign aggressors out of the country. However, in October 1958 as the political situation began to deteriorate to such a point that a national security crisis was imminent, the civilian government of the time, at the intervention of some senior Tatmadaw commanders agreed to transfer state power to the Tatmadaw. On 28 October 1958, the Tatmadaw formed the Caretaker Government to restore political stability and to hold general elections; it finally held general elections in February 1960 and subsequently transferred state power back to the elected government. As a political crisis had been looming large again, the Tatmadaw this time staged a military *coup d'état* in the name of the Revolutionary Council (RC) on 2 March 1962. By the end of April, the RC declared the Burmese Way to Socialism (BWS) as its nation building programme. The Tatmadaw leadership subsequently founded the Burma Socialist Programme Party (BSPP) in July 1962 to lead the socialist revolution in Myanmar. The Revolution Council rule came to an end only when a new constitution was promulgated and general elections were held to restore a constitutional government in 1974. Since January 1974, the Tatmadaw accepted the political leadership of the BSPP. Only in September 1988, did the BSPP allow Tatmadaw personnel to resign membership from the party. Then on 18 September 1988, the Tatmadaw took over the state again in the name of the State Law and Order

Restoration Council (SLORC), renamed the State Peace and Development Council (SPDC) on 15 November 1997.

Myanmar has a total land area of 667,000 square kilometres (261,228 square miles), measuring 936 kilometres (581 miles) from east to west, and 2,051 kilometres (1,275 mile) from north to south. It is situated in Southeast Asia and is bordered on the north and northeast by China, on the east and southeast by Laos and Thailand, on the south by the Andaman Sea and the Bay of Bengal, and on the west by Bangladesh and India. It is located between latitudes 09 32'N and 28 31'N, and longitudes 92 10'E and 101 11'E. The length of its contiguous frontier is 6,159 kilometres (3,828 miles) and its coastline from the mouth of the Naaf River to Kawthaung is 2,228 kilometres (1,385 miles). The total length of the Myanmar-Bangladesh boundary is 271 kilometres (168.7 miles). It consists of two parts, namely the Naaf River boundary of 64 kilometres (39.5 miles), and the land boundary of 208 kilometres (129.2 miles). The total length of the Myanmar-China boundary is 2,204 kilometres (1,370 miles); of the Myanmar-Thailand border, 2,107 kilometres (1,309.8 miles); the Myanmar-India border, 1,338 kilometres (831.8 miles); and the Myanmar-Laos border, 238 kilometres (147.9 miles). It has 29,043 square nautical miles of internal waters and 9,895 square nautical miles of territorial waters (see Table 1.1).

TABLE 1.1
Myanmar Waters

No.	*Myanmar Waters*	*Sq Nautical Mile*
A	Internal Waters (shore to baselines)	29,043.6380
B	Territorial Sea Waters (baseline to TS line)	9,895.1860
C	Contiguous Zone (TS line to CZ line)	9,879.7018
D	Exclusive Economic Zone (CZ line to EEZ line)	92,392.1250
	Total area of Myanmar waters	141,210.6508

Notes: TS = Territorial Sea
CZ = Contiguous Zone
EEZ = Exclusive Economic Zone
Source: Ministry of Defence, Myanmar.

Myanmar also has an airspace that covers both land area and territorial waters. In terms of population, it was estimated that in 2006 Myanmar had more than 52 million people. The Tatmadaw is entrusted with the defence of this land, sea, air, and people.

Despite its significant role in Myanmar, little has been made public about the defence policy and missions of the armed forces. Only in February 1999, for the first time since its existence of more than half a century, did the Tatmadaw quietly declare its defence policy and its missions. The declared policy outlined the doctrine of "total people's defence" for the Union of Myanmar. By enshrining the "*Our Three National Causes*" — non-disintegration of the Union; non-disintegration of national solidarity; and perpetuation of national sovereignty — as its national interests (later known as national ideology), the SPDC declared that its national objective is to "build a peaceful, modern and prosperous nation".[1] This is to be pursued through "twelve objectives", which are equally divided into three areas: political, economic, and social.[2] In the view of the present regime, the political objectives will lay the foundation for a disciplined, flourishing democracy in Myanmar. The economic objectives reflect the important role of the state in national economic life. Although a market economy is seen as a desirable form of economic system, its implementation will be nationalistic and somewhat socialistic. The social objectives draw extensively on an appeal to nationalism by the current regime. Through these measures, in the view of the regime, the peaceful, modern and prosperous Union of Myanmar will have a "multiparty democratic society with a market-oriented economy based on noble principles of justice, liberty and equality and will ensure the national identity and cultural traditions of all the national races".[3]

In order to pursue the national objective of building a peaceful, modern, and prosperous nation, the Tatmadaw leadership decided to transform the existing armed forces into a force that is "modern, strong, proficient and highly capable".[4] It is in this context that the Tatmadaw has defined its defence policy and the mission of the defence forces. In his speech to senior commanders in July 1997, Senior General Than Shwe explained Myanmar's defence policy and the missions of the defence forces for the first time. However, nothing was released to the public until February 1999. The document contains a lengthy discussion on the genealogy of the present-day Tatmadaw and claims that the Tatmadaw was born as a freedom fighter for national independence. It also states that "in the light of Myanmar's historical background, the geographical location, socio-economic conditions and overall situation of the region, Myanmar's national defence policy can be understood and appreciated". It continues:

> Safeguarding Myanmar's own national interest is also conducive to the building of peace, security and economic progress in the region, the salient features of Myanmar's national defence policy are:

(a) To perpetually safeguard national values concerning independence and sovereignty and prevent all acts detrimental to the three main national causes which are non-disintegration of the Union, non-disintegration of the national solidarity and perpetuation of national sovereignty;
(b) To build national defence avoiding external dependence as much as possible in striving for stability of the state, community peace and tranquility and prevalence of law and order based on the strength of national forces within the country and with the armed forces as [the] pivot, combining the strength of auxiliary defence forces;
(c) To valiantly and effectively prevent interference in our internal affairs[,] deploying various ways and means while avoiding interference in the internal affairs of other nations; and
(d) To employ a defence system that gives priority to world peace, regional tranquility in accord with the five principles of peaceful co-existence.

In connection with the defence policy, the Tatmadaw declared its missions, which are:

(a) To build a strong, capable and modern Tatmadaw[,] involving the auxiliary forces in order to dutifully work for the materialization of our three main national causes: non-disintegration of the Union, non-disintegration of the national solidarity and perpetuation of national sovereignty;
(b) To form a modern people's defence system for national defence and security involving the entire citizenry[,] based on internal forces without depending on foreign elements;
(c) To abide by the provisions of the state constitution and to safeguard the new nation that will emerge according to that constitution for sustained development;
(d) To train and develop a strong defence force which possess [sic] [a] military, political, economic and administrative outlook in order to participate in the national political leadership role in the future state; and
(e) To always carry in the fore and safeguard the twelve objectives of the state in order to see the further burgeoning of the noblest and worthiest of worldly values such as justice, liberty and equality to guarantee [the] security of national economic [sic] interests and freedom and security of citizens.

The document states that, in keeping with the principles of non-alignment and peaceful coexistence, which have been the basic tenets in moulding its security policy, Myanmar never takes sides with contending parties, but tries its best to maintain friendly relations with all countries, and particularly, with neighbouring countries. It states, "Myanmar has never allowed and never will allow the stationing of foreign forces on its soil against the interest of a neighbouring country" and "has no security cooperation agreement with any country". Believing that "the strength of the nation lies within", the document claims that "Myanmar has not taken part in any joint military exercise with foreign armies and its military posture is purely defensive", and its defence policy is basically self-reliant. However, it does not give threat perceptions, doctrine and strategy, force structure, armament, and training; in fact, there is no official document released for public consumption.

Here, although some aspects may be irrelevant to the Tatmadaw, I would like to give a brief overview of the conceptual framework for analysing military capability. In analysing the military capability of a nation, it is important to look at military doctrine and strategy, organizational structure of the armed forces, armament or weapon acquisition, and military leadership and training regimes; whether they could produce firepower, protection, mobility, and so on. They are usually in line with the principles of war accepted in each and every individual military force. Here, the "principles of war" mean fundamental ideas and rules that set the standard for victory in the war. They encompass not only principles, but also fundamentals, factors, maxims, laws, and elements of war. While "military doctrine" is defined as fundamental principles by which the military forces or elements thereof guide their actions in support of national objectives — authoritative but requiring judgment in its application — "military strategy" is the art and science of employing the armed forces of a nation to secure the objectives of national policy by application of force or the threat of force.[5] To some, strategy is "the art of the general".[6] Almost every military has its own accepted principles of war and, on the basis of a threat environment, it defines, adopts, and follows a particular military doctrine and strategy. The principle of war provides general guidance for the conduct of war at the strategic, operational, and tactical levels. These principles help the military in planning, preparing, and waging armed combat. They also help the military organize, equip, and train the troops. In line with the principles of war, the military formulates and applies certain military doctrine and military strategy. In spite of new developments in military technology and war-fighting methods, scholars argue that the fundamentals in the battlefield have remained relatively unchanged since the beginning of the twentieth century. There is of course, a rapid growth in the reach, lethality, speed, information-gathering potential, and so on of armies. However, these new developments in military technology still require the application of combined arms, cover and concealment, tightly integrated suppressive fire and manoeuvre, and defence depth and reserves in regular conventional war. Indeed, they have actually increased their importance. They are key factors in determining the military capability of an armed force.

Air power is another important aspect of military capability in modern armed forces. An air force generally needs to perform three broadly defined missions: air superiority; air mobility; and air combat support missions. In detail, these will include defensive and offensive counter air operation, close air support, airborne early warning and control, air interdiction or surgical air strike, electronic warfare, air reconnaissance and surveillance, anti-submarine warfare, anti-surface ship operations, strategic airlift, strategic bombing, suppression of enemy air defence, tactical air transport and mobility, combat search and rescue, and so on. Depending on the type of missions and degree of effectiveness or competence in performing these missions, an air force could be judged as an air power or not. John Warden III, a modern air power theorist, argued that "no country has won a war in the face of enemy air superiority, no major offensive has succeeded against an opponent who controlled the air, and no defense has sustained itself against an enemy who had air superiority".[7] This statement could be disputed especially in the context of asymmetric or irregular warfare. To Warden, air superiority is the first goal and all other operations must be subordinated to its attainment, with an exception that close air support is absolutely necessary for the ground campaign.[8] Robert Pape, however, argued for the importance of strategic or interdiction bombing in winning a war.[9] It is not for me here to debate who is right about the air power theory, but just to make a point about the importance of air power in modern warfighting. Air power could be both tactical and strategic. Tactical air power implies the use of aircraft and other air power components to operate in conjunction with, and in relations to, the operation of military forces on land or on sea. It is designed and employed to undermine the enemy's military capabilities in the battlefield. Strategic air power, on the other hand, involves the use of aircraft independently of the surface force for the purpose of destruction, disruption, and dislocation of the enemy war-waging machine in its totality, so as to degrade the enemy's overall capabilities to wage war and/or increase the costs of waging war to an unacceptable level.

Air superiority is achieved when there is "a degree of dominance in the air battle of one force over another which permits the conduct of operations by the former and its related land, sea and air forces at a given time and place, without prohibitive interference by the opposing force".[10] A high degree and continuous state of "air superiority wherein the opposing air force is incapable of effective interference" is generally considered as air supremacy.[11] It is also known as air dominance. Air superiority, therefore, involves retaining the initiative and freedom of action of all elements of one's own military power in the face of hostile air power, while denying it to the enemy. Air superiority is perhaps the surest way of providing for air defence of friendly ground and naval forces and safeguards their freedom for action and manoeuvre. To attain and maintain a desired degree of air superiority, the air force needs to conduct counter air operations which are designed to destroy or negate enemy aircraft and missile, both before and after launch. Counter air operations include both offensive and defensive missions. Offensive Counter-Air Operation is "an operation mounted to destroy, disrupt, or limit the enemy air power as close to its source as possible" whereas Defensive Counter-Air Operation is the "all defensive measures designed to detect, identify, intercept, and destroy or negate enemy forces attempting to attack or penetrate the friendly air environment".[12] Counter-air operations could be conducted as air-to-air and air-to-ground wars. Another important element for achieving air superiority is the Suppression of Enemy Air Defence System (SEADS) that is both hard- and soft-kill. For this purpose, an air force needs air superiority fighters, interceptors, ground attack aircraft, multi-role fighter, and helicopter gunship.

But it is important to understand that air superiority or air supremacy could last only as long as enough air effort is devoted to it.

Air Mobility is another important aspect of an air power. Air transport operation, both strategic airlift and tactical airlift, using fixed-wing and helicopter, play a key role in modern warfare. Airborne Operation, another aspect of air mobility, is also vital in the modern-day battlefield. Combat support missions can enhance the effectiveness of other air power missions as they constitute a force multiplier. The missions cover operations of Advanced Warning and Control System (AWCS), Electronic Warfare, Surveillance and Reconnaissance (including maritime patrol), the Command, Control, Communication and Intelligence (C^3I), and In-flight refuelling. Air combat support involves attacking ground targets from air, especially military installations, economic, and industrial zones. Strategic offensive primarily concerns strategic bombing and surgical air strike against high-value targets. Air interdiction and close air support come under tactical offensive. While tactical interdiction is confined to areas and targets close to the battlefield, strategic interdiction implies penetration deep into hostile territory. Close air support is provided for the friendly force in the battlefield. Both anti-submarine warfare and anti-surface ship operations fall under the category of maritime strike. This mission is taken against the hostile naval force. Pre-emptive and surgical air strikes have increasingly become attractive in modern warfare.[13]

Another aspect of military capability is naval power. Naval capability could be assessed on the basis of the different naval platforms (surface ship, submarines, and aircraft) and weapon systems (mines, guns, torpedoes, cruise missile). Most navies maintain a balanced mix of fleet platforms and weaponry as modern naval warfare becomes multidimensional. Two important pillars of a navy are to affect events on land and to control use of the sea. A navy could be classified based on its operations: open or high seas, coastal waters and straits, littoral waters or in-shore waters, off-shore waters, and inland waters. Moreover, depending on the size and nature of the fleet, geographic reach, function and capability, access to high-grade technology, and reputation, a navy could generally be classified as a global navy or regional navy or coastal navy. A global navy or major naval power will have functions of strategic deterrence, power projection, sea control, naval diplomacy, national security and constabulary, and humanitarian assistance. But a regional navy lacks strategic deterrence and has only limited power projection and sea control capabilities. Coastal navies have only limited sea control even over their own waters, but have a certain degree of sea denial, and capability to engage in national security and constabulary missions and humanitarian assistance within their waters.[14]

In terms of naval operations, the highest priority is the command of the sea. Thus, a navy could project military power into the sea, for the purpose of sea and area control, and from the sea, in order to influence events on land. The most important goal of naval forces is perhaps to ensure sea control, broadly defined as a guarantee that the sea can be used freely, and that the enemy is limited to fugitive use. A navy can utilize the sea without significant opposition from the enemy. In many cases, sea control is transitory; often the area controlled is limited. Below sea control is sea denial, in which neither side can use the sea fully. Sea control is the ability to maintain use of the sea, which, in turn, usually means keeping an enemy's attackers from sinking friendly ships. Power projection refers to the ability to attack land targets, either with weapons, which may be carried by aircraft, or by landing troops. Aircraft carriers could be described as power projection assets, while frigates or patrol aircraft, as sea control assets. The offensive use of the carrier exemplifies an important truth: sea control and power projection can be two aspects of the same thing. Depending on a number of factors, some navies seek only sea denial, or local or temporary sea control. The power projection method of gaining sea control combines two tactics: decisive battle and attack at source. Convoy is a better-known sea control strategy. In a sense, it is a form of the decisive battle strategy. Convoy offers a series of battles of annihilation on a small scale. Carrier battle group could be regarded as a gigantic convoy, combining the most attractive targets with the deadliest counter measures. Convoy is effective only if there are enough escorts, and the number of escorts is set not by the strength of the opposing force, but rather by the number of convoys that must be protected.[15] Sea denial is preventing an opponent from using the sea without attempting to establish local sea control. The submarine is perhaps the most prominent naval platform. A navy's effectiveness also depends on its ability to conduct sea surveillance.

There are a number of books and articles on the history of the Tatmadaw, particularly for the period before Myanmar's independence in 1948, which shed light on the formation and political orientation of the Tatmadaw.[16] Before the early 1990s, a few scholars have contributed to the study of the Tatmadaw. Most of the books, edited volumes, and articles are about the involvement of the military in politics, civil-military relations, and the performance of the "military regime".[17] There were only a few publications on the military, or security matters as such.[18] However, since the early 1990s, there has been a resurgence of academic interest in Myanmar. Many books and articles on Myanmar in general, and the Tatmadaw in particular, came out in the 1990s. Various aspects of the Tatmadaw have been studied. The most notable area of study has been the performance and the political role of the military.[19] Yet many of them fail to reflect the complexity of the situation. Another area of study is the counter-insurgency aspect of the Tatmadaw, in relation to various insurgencies in Myanmar.[20] A few scholars deal exclusively with the military capabilities of the Tatmadaw,[21] and strategic and national security issues of Myanmar.[22] There are also a number of theses on the Tatmadaw, but, to the best of my knowledge, none of these is on military capabilities.[23]

Here, I would like to draw attention to the works of Andrew Selth, who is also known to some observers and analysts in Myanmar as William Ashton, and is a long-term "Myanmar Watcher". He has written a volume of articles and working papers on the Myanmar armed forces. He is probably the only scholar so far to give serious treatment to purely military matters of the Tatmadaw, such as armament, procurement, and combat capabilities. Drawing "entirely on open sources" with "no official status or endorsement", Andrew Selth divided his empirically rich monograph titled, *Transforming the Tatmadaw*, the first of its kind in studying the Tatmadaw, into eight chapters. By focusing on "the expansion and modernization of the armed forces", Andrew Selth did indeed fill some of the gaps in the existing literature. The monograph begins with an introduction that explains the difficulty of the study, and lays out the aim and objectives of the monograph. It is followed by the defence expenditure of the Tatmadaw. Three subsequent chapters discuss force modernization of army, navy, and air forces. While chapter six discusses the debate about the alleged possession of "exotic weapons" by the Myanmar armed forces, the following chapter highlights the political and security imperatives influencing the Tatmadaw's security perceptions. His last chapter is essentially a recapitulation of his findings and conclusion. Despite all these expansion and modernization programmes, Andrew questioned the military capabilities and professionalism of the Tatmadaw, given the fact that the Tatmadaw has been facing a number of critical issues such as intra-military rivalry,[24] an image problem, and the ethnic composition of the forces. In his second book on the Myanmar military, by revealing *Burma's Secret Military Partners*, Andrew elaborates on the arms sales and transaction between Myanmar and four major "secret partners", namely Germany, Singapore, Israel, and Pakistan. Selth concludes that the secret military partners "play a significant role in the country's internal affairs in the face of considerable pressure for fundamental political and economic changes in Myanmar".[25] In short, both books by Andrew Selth concern themselves primarily with the expansion and modernization of the Myanmar armed forces. However, Andrew argued that "the SLORC has devoted so much of Burma's resources to the armed forces for purely domestic political reasons. All the regime's rhetoric aside, the rapid expansion and modernization of the armed forces after 1988 seems to have been based primarily on the fear that it might lose its monopoly of political power".[26] Based on his previous works, Andrew produced a book titled *Burma's Armed Forces: Power without Glory*, which is organized into twelve chapters. Many chapters are reproduced from his previous works. The book begins with a historical background geopolitical setting. It is followed by chapters on defence policies and threat perceptions and structure and organization. The fourth chapter is on recruitment, training and doctrine. He devotes a chapter to military intelligence. In chapter six, Selth discusses the economic dimension of armed forces building. Chapters seven, eight and nine are on army, navy, and air force. Within each chapter, he discusses organization and armament. In chapter ten Andrew investigates the alleged possession of Weapons of Mass Destruction (WMD) by the Tatmadaw. Chapter eleven is on the current state or status of the Tatmadaw, while the last chapter examines the political aspect of the Tatmadaw in Myanmar's democracy movement. Andrew places the Tatmadaw into a broader political context. His assessment of the Tatmadaw's transformation remains basically the same; it is for domestic political reasons. But he argues that the transformation has made the Tatmadaw an institution in power, but without glory.

To commemorate the golden jubilee of the Myanmar Armed Forces in 1995, the Tatmadaw began to produce a series on the official history of the Tatmadaw. By 2008, the Tatmadaw has produced eight volumes in the series, which cover the period up to 1997. A ninth volume is on its way. The manuscripts for the first three volumes, covering up to 1948, were prepared in the early 1960s and kept in the military archive. Only in 1994 and 1995 did these manuscripts finally surface as books for the general public. The Defence Services Historical Research Institute was assigned to produce more volumes on the history of the Tatmadaw. Therefore, three more volumes were produced in successive years: volume four for 1948–62; volume five for 1962–74; and volume six for 1974–88. Despite questionable arguments about the genealogy and historiography of the Tatmadaw, these books contribute to the better understanding of the Tatmadaw, especially in terms of its self-projected political role. These volumes also reveal arms procurement, military operations, and the structural expansion of the Tatmadaw. Yet, none of them discusses the military capability or combat readiness of the Tatmadaw. However, when the last two volumes — for 1988–93 and 1993–97 — came out, the structure of the books was completely changed; there was nothing about force modernization, such as arms procurement or expansion of the command structure. The last two volumes were merely the compilation of so-called nation building (actually infrastructure building) activities carried out by the Tatmadaw during the SLORC/SPDC period from all published sources. In recent years, a number of military officers have published their memoirs and shed some light on certain aspects of the Tatmadaw. But, again, they did not touch on force modernization in any historical period of post-colonial Myanmar.[27]

This work is based on my working papers published by the Strategic and Defence Studies Centre (SDSC) in Canberra; these papers are widely referred by scholars interested in the Tatmadaw. Here, I would like to argue that while the internal armed security threat to the state continues to play an important role, it is the external security threat that has given more weight to the expansion and modernization of the Tatmadaw since 1988. I would also argue that, despite its imperfections, the Tatmadaw is in the process of transforming itself from essentially a counter-insurgency force into a conventional one. Moreover, in order to understand the military capabilities of the Tatmadaw, it is equally important to look beyond its force modernization. This work examines the military capabilities and studies four aspects of the Tatmadaw in historical perspective, in contrast to existing works on state security and security perceptions in Myanmar: military doctrine and strategy, organization and force structure, armament and force modernization, and military training and officer education. It is neither comprehensive nor exhaustive, yet I sincerely hope that it will fill some of the gaps in the literature on the Tatmadaw.

Notes

1 Senior General Than Shwe's speech on the 54th Anniversary of Armed Forces Day, 27 March 1999.

2 The four political objectives are: stability of the State, community peace and tranquility, prevalence of law and order; national reconsolidation; emergence of a new enduring State Constitution; and building of a new, modern, developed nation in accord with the new State Constitution. The four economic objectives are: development of agriculture as the base and all-round development of other sectors of the economy as well; proper evolution of the market-oriented economic system; development of the economy, inviting participation in terms of technical know-how and investments from sources inside the country and abroad; and, the initiative to shape the national economy must be kept in the hands of the State and the national peoples. The four social objectives are: uplifting of the morale and morality of the entire nation; uplifting of national prestige and integrity and preservation and safeguarding of its cultural heritage and national character; uplifting of the dynamism of patriotic spirit; and uplifting of health, fitness, and education standards of the entire nation.

3 Ministry of Information, *Myanmar Today* 1, no. 2 (May 1998): 15.

4 Senior General Than Shwe's speech on the graduation of the first intake of the Defence Services Institute of Technology, 11 April 1999.

5 U.S. Department of Defence, *Dictionary of Military Terms* (Pennsylvania: Stackpole Books, 1995), pp. 126, 242.

6 B.H. Liddell Hart, *Strategy*, 2nd revised ed. (New York: Meridian Printing, 1991), p. 322.

7 John A. Warden III, *The Air Campaign: Planning for Combat* (New York: Pergamon-Brassey's, 1989), p. 10.

8 Ibid.

9 Robert Pape, *Bombing to Win: Air Power and Coercion in War* (Ithaca and London: Cornell University Press, 1996), p. 46.

10 This information come from "lecture notes" used among air force officers. Regretably, no reference is made to original sources.

11 Ibid.

12 Ibid.

13 Ibid.

14 Geoffrey Till, *Seapower: A Guide for the Twenty First Century* (London: Frank Cass, 2004).

15 Norman Friedman, *Seapower as Strategy: Navies and National Interests* (Annapolis, Maryland: Naval Institute Press, 2001).

[16] Dorathy H. Guyot, "The Burma Independence Army: A Political Movement in Military Garb", in *Southeast Asia in World War II: Four Essays*, edited by Josef Silverstein (New Haven: Yale University, 1966); J.C Lebra, *Japanese Trained Armies of Southeast Asia: Independence and Volunteer Forces in World War II* (Hong Kong: Heinemann, 1977); Maung Maung, *Burmese Nationalist Movements 1940–1948* (Edinburgh: Kiscadale, 1989).

[17] Josef Silverstein, *Burma: Military Rule and Politics of Stagnation* (Ithaca: Cornell University Press, 1977); F.K: Lehman, ed., *Military Rule in Burma since 1962* (Singapore: Maruzen Asia, 1981); Moshe Lissak, *Military Roles in Modernization: Civil-Military Relations in Thailand and Burma* (London: Sage Publications, 1976); Lucian Pye, "The Army in Burmese Politics", in *The Role of the Military in Underdeveloped Countries*, edited by J.J. Johnson (Princeton: Princeton University Press, 1962); Robert H. Taylor, "Burma", in *Military-Civilian Relations in South-East Asia*, edited by Zakaria Haji Ahmad and Harold Crouch (Singapore: Oxford University Press, 1985); Robert H. Taylor, *The State in Burma* (Hawaii: Hawaii University Press, 1987); Jon A. Wiant and David I. Steinberg, "Burma: The Military and National Development", in *Soldiers and Stability in Southeast Asia*, edited by J. Soedjati Djiwandono and Yong Mun Cheong (Singapore: Institute of Southeast Asian Studies, 1988).

[18] Robert Taylor, "Government Response to Armed Communist and Separatist Movements: Burma", in *Government and Rebellion in Southeast Asia*, edited by Chandran Jeshurun (Singapore: Institute of Southeast Asian Studies, 1985); Robert H. Taylor, "Burma: Defence Expenditure and Threat Perceptions", in *Defence Spending in Southeast Asia*, edited by Chin Kin Wah (Singapore: Institute of Southeast Asian Studies, 1987); Robert H. Taylor, "Burma: Political Leadership, Security Perceptions and Policies", in *Leadership Perceptions and National Security: The Southeast Asian Experience*, edited by Mohammed Ayoob and Chai-Anan Samudavanija (Singapore: Institute of Southeast Asian Studies, 1989).

[19] Mya Maung, *Totalitarianism in Burma: Prospects for Economic Development* (New York: Paragon House, 1992); Christina Fink, *Living Silence: Burma under Military Rule* (London: Zed Book, 2001); Robert H. Taylor, ed., *Burma: Political Economy under Military Rule* (London: Hurst & Company, 2001); David I. Steinberg, *Burma: The State of Myanmar* (Washington D.C: Georgetown University Press, 2001); Mary P. Callahan, "Building an Army: The Early Years of the Tatmadaw", *Burma Debate*, vol. IV, no. 3, July/August 1997; David I. Steinberg, "Burma/Myanmar: Under the Military", in *Driven by Growth*, edited by James W. Morley, revised edition (Singapore: Institute of Southeast Asian Studies, 1999); Robert H. Taylor, "The Evolving Military Role in Burma", *Current History*, March 1990; Robert H. Taylor, "The Military in Myanmar (Burma): What Scope for a New Role?", in *The Military, the State, and Development in Asia and the Pacific*, edited by Viberto Selochan (Boulder: Westview Press, 1991); Josef Silverstein, "Burma's Struggle for Democracy: The Army against the People", in *The Military and Democracy in Asia and the Pacific*, edited by R.J. May and Viberto Selochan

(Bathurst: Crawford House, 1998); Mary P. Callahan, "Cracks in the Edifice?: Military-Society Relations in Burma since 1988", in *Burma/Myanmar: Strong Regime, Weak State?*, edited by Morten B. Pedensen, Emily Rudland and R.J. May (Adelaide: Crawford House, 2000); Mary P. Callahan, "Burma: Soldiers as State Builders", in *Coercion and Governance: The Declining Political Role of the Military in Asia*, edited by Muthia Alagappa (Stanford, California: Stanford University Press, 2001); Andrew Selth, "The Future of the Burmese Armed Forces", in *Burma/Myanmar: Strong Regime, Weak State?*, edited by Morten B. Pedensen, Emily Rudland and R.J. May (Adelaide: Crawford House, 2000); Robert H. Taylor, "Change in Burma: Political Demands and Military Power", *Asian Affairs*, vol. 22, no. 6, June 1991; Robert H. Taylor, "Myanmar: Military Politics and the Prospects for Democratisation", *Asian Affairs*, vol. 29, part I, February 1998.

20 Martin Smith, *Burma: Insurgency and the Politics of Ethnicity* (London: Zed Books, 1991); Michael Fredholm, *Burma: Ethnicity and Insurgency* (Westport, Connecticut: Praeger, 1993); Bertil Lintner, *Burma in Revolt: Opium and Insurgency since 1948* (Boulder: Westview Press, 1994).

21 Desmond Ball, *Burma's Military Secrets: Signals Intelligence (SIGINT) from 1941 to Cyber Warfare* (Bangkok: White Lotus, 1998); Andrew Selth, *Transforming the Tatmadaw: The Burmese Armed Forces since 1988* (Canberra: SDSC, 1996); Andrew Selth, *Burma's Secret Military Partners* (Canberra: SDSC, 2000); Andrew Selth, "Burma's Intelligence Apparatus", *Intelligence and National Security*, vol. 13, no. 4, Winter 1998.

22 Tin Maung Maung Than, "Burma's National Security and Defence Posture", *Contemporary Southeast Asia*, vol. 11, no. 1, June 1989; Tin Maung Maung Than, "Myanmar: Preoccupation with Regime Survival, National Unity and Stability", in *Asian Security Practice: Material and Ideational Influences*, edited by Muthiah Alagappa (Stanford: Stanford University Press, 1998); Tin Maung Maung Than, "Myanmar: Myanmar-ness and Realism in Historical Perspective", in *Strategic Cultures in the Asia-Pacific Region*, edited by Ken Booth and Russell Trood (London: Macmillan Press Ltd., 1999); Andrew Selth, "Burma and the Strategic Competition between China and India", *The Journal of Strategic Studies*, vol. 19, no. 2, June 1996; Mohan Malik, "Sino-Indian Rivalry in Myanmar: Implications for Regional Security", *Contemporary Southeast Asia*, vol. 16, no. 2, September 1994; Mohan Malik, "Myanmar's Role in Regional Security: Pawn or Pivot?", *Contemporary Southeast Asia*, vol. 19, no. 1, June 1997.

23 Mary P. Callahan, *The Origins of Military Rule in Burma*, Ph.D. thesis (Ithaca: Cornell University, 1996); Chao Tzang Yawnghwe, *Ne Win's Tatmadaw Dictatorship*, MA thesis (Vancouver: University of British Columbia, 1990); Maung Aung Myoe, *The Counterinsurgency in Myanmar: The Government's Response to the Burma Communist Party* (Canberra: Australian National University, 1999).

24 In terms of intra-military rivalry, Andrew Selth draws attention to six areas:

(1) tension between moderates and hardliners over domestic political issues; (2) tension between senior commanders over the policy issue of the degree of Chinese influence; (3) resentment and antagonism between the (often younger) officers in active service in the field, and those officers assigned to more comfortable administrative or political duties in rear areas; (4) tension between those officers who appear to owe their promotions primarily to their ties with former President Ne Win, and those who have followed a more professional career path; (5) tension between those with different backgrounds in training; and (6) antagonism between the army and the two other services.

25 Andrew Selth, *Burma's Secret Military Partners* (Canberra: SDSC, 2000).

26 Andrew Selth, *Transforming the Tatmadaw*, pp. 153–54.

27 For example, these memoirs included books by Colonel Khin Maung Thaung, Colonel P. Kyaw Han, Brigadier General Than Tin, Colonel Thaung Wai, Colonel Thura Tun Tin (former Prime Minister), Lieutenant General Chit Swe, Major General Hla Myint Swe, and Colonel Ko Lay.

2

MILITARY DOCTRINE AND STRATEGY

This chapter primarily discusses the historical development of the military doctrine and strategy of the Tatmadaw since Myanmar's independence in 1948. It sets out both security perceptions and policies, charting developments in each against the situation at the time, and also notes the contributions of the leading actors in each period. The Tatmadaw has gone through three phases of doctrinal developments. In the initial period, doctrine focused on the method of coping with foreign invasion; the second period saw the development of counter-insurgency doctrine and the formulation of the concept of total people's war; in the third period the Tatmadaw modified its people's war doctrine to meet modern conditions.

FIRST PHASE OF THE DEVELOPMENT OF MILITARY DOCTRINE

Since independence day in January 1948, the armed forces of the Union of Myanmar, the Tatmadaw, have been combating a number of insurgencies throughout the country. The insurgencies of both right- and left-wing groups, such as the Karen National Defence Organisation (KNDO) and the Burma Communist Party (BCP), were so strong in the late 1940s that the Myanmar Government[1] was described in the international media as the Rangoon (Yangon) government. Various communist and separatist insurgencies in Myanmar were so widespread that the government of the time admitted that "large section[s] of the countryside was under complete domination of the insurgents". Only from the early 1950s was the Tatmadaw able to recapture and reassert its control over some important cities. However, the rural areas were still very much under the control and influence of various insurgents. This internal armed security threat to the state has long overshadowed the security perception of the Tatmadaw, in terms of doctrine, force structure, armament, and training. In the meantime, as the communists came to power in China in 1949, remnants of the Kuomintang (KMT) troops under General Li Mi moved into Myanmar and used the frontier as a springboard for attack against the People's Republic of China, which, in turn, became an external threat to national security in Myanmar.

The first military doctrine for the Tatmadaw was formulated in the early 1950s, when the security situation of the Union had improved markedly, but it focused on methods of coping with foreign invasion, rather than suppressing insurgency. Despite the fact that internal security operations continued to preoccupy the Tatmadaw's operational priority, the first military doctrine was surprisingly for external defence. As a General Staff officer at the War Office, Lieutenant Colonel Maung Maung, the most important architect of the doctrine, studied all the factors that were likely to influence the military doctrine of the Tatmadaw. There were at least two factors that could have influenced Maung Maung's thinking. One was his strong anti-Communist belief and the other was his desire to improve his own image.[2] With little or no combat experience, Maung Maung was essentially an armchair strategist at the War Office. Taking the situation of the time into consideration, he thought that communist China was an immediate threat, and, being fascinated by the writings on armoured warfare, he drew up a defence plan based on conventional warfare, with large divisions, armoured brigades, tanks, and motorized war. Mass mobilization for the war effort was an important element of the plan.

Maung Maung's doctrine was based on the strategy of strategic denial. The objective was to contain the offensive of invading forces at the border for at least a couple of months, while waiting for the arrival of international forces. He expected the kind of police action by international forces under the United Nations' banner that took place on the Korean peninsula. However, the conventional strategy under the concept of total war was seriously undermined by the lack of an appropriate command and control system, a proper logistical support structure and training regime, sound economic and technological resources, and efficient civil defence organizations.

The doctrine was tested for the first time in an operation against the KMT in February 1953, codenamed "*Naga-Naing* (နဂါးနိုင်)" [Victorious Dragon]. Badly executed under unfavourable terrain and a lack of resources, the operation was a complete and humiliating defeat for the Tatmadaw, and was subsequently nicknamed '*Naga-Shone* (နဂါးရှုံး)' [Defeated Dragon]. Maung Maung argued that the defeat was partly due to the media coverage and excessive publicity given to the operation. He pointed out that newspapers, such as *The Nation*, carried reports detailing the training and social background of the commanders who would lead the operation. The KMT commanders could easily guess the nature of the operation by reading newspapers. The operation thus lost the element of surprise.[3] Colonel Saw Myint, who was second-in-command of the operation, also talked about the long lines of communication and about excessive public relations designed to prove that the support of the people was behind the operation.[4]

Despite its failure, the Tatmadaw continued to rely on this doctrine until the mid-1960s. However, the doctrine was under constant review throughout the period and, with some modifications, gained some success in the anti-KMT operations of the late 1950s.[5] The annual Tatmadaw conference, known as the Commanding Officers' (COs') conference, was the place to discuss military doctrine and strategy. Beginning in 1956, discussion on military doctrine and strategy became an important part of the annual Tatmadaw conference. At the 1957 Tatmadaw conference, General Ne Win stressed the importance of military education, along with moral and psychological warfare courses. He announced that the Tatmadaw would open a National Defence College in the near future to catch up with advances in military science. Furthermore, he ordered a review of the courses offered at the Command and General Staff College and other training schools.

Although the military doctrine and strategy that emphasized positional warfare was somewhat applicable in fighting the KMT and insurgencies such as the KNDO and the BCP up until the mid-1950s, it became increasingly irrelevant and unsuitable in the late 1950s as the insurgents changed their strategy from regular conventional to irregular guerrilla warfare.[6] At the 1958 Tatmadaw conference, held at Meikhtila, Colonel Kyi Win submitted a report on a new military doctrine and strategy. In the opening paragraph of his 124-page report, Kyi Win stated that "the Tatmadaw did not have a clear strategy to cope with communist insurgents".[7] It was true that although the Tatmadaw had some experience of guerrilla warfare, it had little knowledge of anti-guerrilla or counter-insurgency warfare. His report detailed several pitfalls of past military operations, and provided recommendations:

> In countering an insurgency with political and military objectives, it is not appropriate to apply conventional warfare. It [the Tatmadaw] will not have sufficient time to use conventional tactics while the enemy is on "hit and run".[8]

Colonel Kyi Win further argued that since the "hit and run" (guerrilla) warfare did not have a concept of positional defence, it was best for the Tatmadaw to adopt a military doctrine and strategy based on unconventional warfare. He also argued that military doctrine should have a political dimension, and his study included details of the BCP's organizational set-up.[9] Kyi Win's recommendations were overshadowed by discussion of the Tatmadaw's immediate task of running the country in the name of the Caretaker Government; nevertheless, the Tatmadaw started developing an appropriate military doctrine and strategy for Myanmar.

SECOND PHASE OF THE DEVELOPMENT OF MILITARY DOCTRINE

The drafting of a new military doctrine and strategy began with a survey of people's attitudes towards the Tatmadaw and the nature of its operations.[10] Special attention was given to the suppression of insurgency. It was a common view among the commanders of the time that unless insurgency was suppressed, foreign interference would be highly probable. The Tatmadaw leadership was very much concerned with the linkage of external to internal problems.[11] By the late 1950s, the Tatmadaw leadership was fully aware of various insurgent groups seeking external assistance. The KNDO, for example, sought arms from the KMT and even considered coordinated operations against the Tatmadaw. The BCP, according to the Tatmadaw, received instructions from the Chinese Communist Party. The Tatmadaw commanders knew that some BCP members had received political and military trainings in China. Counter-insurgency, therefore, became the core of the new military doctrine and strategy. At the 1959 Tatmadaw conference, the General Staff Office reported on the advantages and disadvantages of the Tatmadaw's counter-insurgency operations. The advantages were:

(1) year-round operations by the Tatmadaw left the insurgents dispersed;
(2) the village defence system interrupted the insurgents' organizational activities;
(3) cooperation from police and civil servants;
(4) coordination between the Tatmadaw's tactical moves and militias; and
(5) it was good psychological warfare.[12]

The disadvantages were:

(1) poor public relations;
(2) inaccurate and poor combat intelligence;
(3) poor information security;

(4) troops were prone to being ambushed;
(5) the Tatmadaw was weak in military tactics (in counter-insurgency warfare); and
(6) it was weak in gathering strategic intelligence.[13]

Beginning in 1961, in accord with the decision reached at the General Staff Office, the directorate of military training took charge of not only the training programmes for its officers and rank and file, but also the study and research of national defence planning, military doctrine, and strategy for both internal and external threats. This included reviews of international and domestic political situations, studies of the potential sources of conflict, collection of information for strategic planning, and defining the possible routes of foreign invasions.[14]

At the 1962 Tatmadaw conference, the General Staff Office reported that it had drafted a document on the principles of anti-guerrilla warfare and had begun teaching this in training schools.[15] A year later, at the 1963 Tatmadaw conference, representatives from regional commands presented their views on counter-insurgency operations. Their presentations could be summarized as follows:

- insurgents were taking refuge in the boundary area between different regional military commands;
- there was no coordination between different commands;
- the Tatmadaw had no time to rest, but insurgents could do so when hiding;
- the Tatmadaw had to deploy most of its troops for garrison duty and securing lines of communication and had little chance to annihilate insurgents;
- the Tatmadaw suffered heavy casualties in insurgents' ambushes;
- there was no national-level military doctrine and defence plan;
- each command had to initiate its own local operations;
- there was no proper deployment of troops (each troop or battalion had its own characteristics);
- the Tatmadaw needed reserve battalions;
- involvement of troops in local administration (Security and Administrative Committee) halved attention to operations;
- training for counter-insurgency warfare was inadequate; and
- the Tatmadaw was still influenced by conventional warfare doctrine with a tendency to total war.[16]

Field commanders also complained that emphasis on development tasks rather than on the maintenance of law and order in counter-insurgency posed a major problem. When comparing the Caretaker Government with the RC Government, the former gave priority to the maintenance of law and order and stability, whereas the latter focused on development, and argued that without proper security arrangement and with administrative deficiencies, development projects were consequently disrupted.[17] They complained that they could not concentrate their resources and energy on counter-insurgency and they had the heavy workload of running the local administration at various levels required under new administrative structure. It was also a marked departure from the Caretaker Government period when only a handful of senior officers were involved in the government at the ministerial level. To overcome this manpower shortage and as the new administrative system of "Security and Administrative Committee (SAC)" was considered necessary to enhance the state-building process, the Tatmadaw leadership decided to expand the Tatmadaw by forming new battalions or through a recruitment drive. A report submitted by the General Staff Office in 1963 stated that the Tatmadaw no longer engaged in operations designed for territorial gain. But it faced a new kind of fighting — insurgents were fighting from the villages. The report said:

> It is difficult to distinguish insurgents from villagers. If we cannot distinguish insurgents from villagers, we will suffer. We will always face the insurgents having the upper hand in operations. It is necessary to step up organisational activities in villages. Whenever a section of the Tatmadaw is sent to a village, it should be assigned not only to security and intelligence gathering but also to public relations tasks.[18]

In the process of formulating a new military doctrine in 1964, the General Staff Office's report spelt out the three potential enemies and laid out recommendations on strategy. The potential opponents were: internal insurgents, historical enemies with roughly an equal strength, and enemies with greater strength. Although no clear indication was given to a particular country, we can easily guess the sources of threat.[19] The report recommended:

> In suppressing insurgencies, the Tatmadaw should be trained to conduct long-range penetration with a tactic of continuous search and destroy. Scouting, ambush and night-time warfare are important parts of anti-guerrilla warfare. It is also important to win the people's support in fighting.

> For countering an enemy with equal strength, the Tatmadaw should fight a conventional warfare under total war, without giving up an inch of its territory to the enemy.
>
> For a more powerful enemy, the Tatmadaw should engage in total people's war, with a special focus on guerrilla strategy.[20]

The 1964 Tatmadaw conference in July 1964 was an important landmark in shaping a new military doctrine and strategy. Brigadier San Yu, then Vice-Chief of Staff (Army), declared that it was time for the Tatmadaw to review the existing military doctrine and consider a new one if necessary. A new military doctrine should bring the Tatmadaw and the people together in fighting insurgency.[21] Commodore Thaung Tin, then Vice-Chief of Staff (Navy), proposed a new military doctrine. In his report, Commodore Thaung Tin surveyed the political situation in the post-Second World War period, the political situation of Myanmar, the order of battle and military doctrine of the Tatmadaw, and possible forms of warfare in Myanmar. It also discussed counter-insurgency strategies and tactics, training programmes for militias, and military education.[22]

There were two basic themes in the discussions of this period. One was counter-insurgency; the other was preparation to fight a foreign invasion, in case the war in Indochina spilled over the border. To combat insurgency, the COs realized that they must do something to "deny the water to the fish", and compared their counter-insurgency campaigns with "the buffalo swimming in the pond of water hyacinth".[23] To combat foreign invasion, commanders discussed the feasibility of introducing the "people's war" doctrine. However, the people's war could also be used in counter-insurgency operations.

To prepare for the transition to people's war, a delegation led by Lieutenant Colonel Thura Tun Tin was sent to Switzerland, Yugoslavia, Czechoslovakia, and East Germany in July 1964 to study the organizational structure, armaments, training, territorial organization, and strategy of people's militias. On its return, the delegation submitted a report entitled "Studies Relating to the People's Armed Forces" in January 1965. A research team was also formed to study the defence capabilities and militia formations of neighbouring countries. On 10 June 1964, a document entitled "Survey of the Situation for Training Tatmadaw and People in Accordance with People's War Doctrine" was submitted to the General Staff Office. It recommended that the Tatmadaw and the people should be trained for the "people's war" and made ready by 1970. For training purposes, it recommended the establishment of a "People's Defence College", a "People's Staff College", "People's Militias and Civil Servant Training Schools (senior) (intermediate) (junior)", and

"People's Militias Basic Training Schools". Before the whole plan could be implemented, the Central School of Public Servants was established in Phaungyi as an immediate measure. It also recommended the transformation of the Tatmadaw from a force for fighting conventional warfare into one to fight a "people's war", by running training programmes and launching a campaign to educate the general public about the doctrine.[24]

In relation to the "people's war", the Directorate of Training and Planning prepared a document entitled "Training Plan for People's War". The plan recommended:

> … If the Union of Myanmar wants to be relieved from fear of pressure and interference from powerful neighbouring countries, it is necessary to have a million well trained soldiers even in peace time and a capability to mobilise five million armed militias in time of emergency. All the basic military education must be taught in peace time.[25]

Considering the size of Myanmar's population at the time (25 million), it was recommended that 5 per cent of the population be trained and maintained as a regular force and 25 per cent of the population be trained and put on reserve as militia: the militias must be ready for combat within 72 hours of mobilization. This training plan was designed to incorporate the concepts of "total war" and "people's war". It included a recommendation for compulsory two-year national service for a certain age group (yet to be decided).[26] However, this mass mobilization plan never materialized.

The 1964 Tatmadaw conference had also discussed the formation of people's militias as a practical step to implement the "people's war" doctrine. The Directorate of Training and Planning, under the Ministry of Defence, submitted a draft proposal on "Facts in Relation to the Training of People's Militias". The significance of this document was the link between the "people's war" doctrine and counter-insurgency. The document revealed that, as of 23 December 1964, the Tatmadaw (Kyi), or army, had a total of 4,417 officers and 118,598 enlisted personnel, including 787 civilians (1:26.85); the Tatmadaw (Yay), or navy, had 306 officers and 5,795 enlisted personnel (1:18.9); and the Tatmadaw (Lay), or air force, had 323 officers and 5,877 enlisted men (1:18.2). This was just ten per cent of the recommended number of regular troops. For the time being, it was recommended that each soldier had to train ten civilians to become militia. But it was recognized that over-ambitious militia mobilization could do more harm than good.

One of the most important recommendations of the proposal was that '*Sit-Kyaung-Gyi-Ngar-Kyaung*' (စစ်ကြောင်းကြီးငါးကြောင်း) [five columns] be used to liquidate the insurgents before the nationwide militia training programme began. These "five columns" were political, social, economic, defence (military), and public management. In essence, this was a counter-insurgency strategy based on multidimensional warfare.[27] It was reasoned that unless the insurgency was eliminated, the militia programme would be ineffective and even dangerous. Another document, entitled "The Tatmadaw and the People's War", was prepared to explain to the rank-and-file why such a doctrine and strategy was necessary and what was to be done.[28]

The 1964 conference also discussed improving troop discipline and public relations, in order to make the military doctrine and counter-insurgency strategy effective. Troop discipline and public relations had been a huge problem since the early 1950s. At the 1952 COs' conference, General Ne Win warned that some officers and non-commissioned officers did mischievous things to the people, damaging the Tatmadaw's image. He cited an incident in Taungoo where some officers, in the name of the Tatmadaw, seized not only abandoned vehicles, but also cars with owners, and later sold them.[29] A report submitted to the 1963 Tatmadaw conference stated that rank and file soldiers must be educated to understand that the Tatmadaw was a national armed force that should protect the socialist economy and the people. It must also make it known that public cooperation and participation in counter-insurgency operations was essential. In essence, the report emphasized improved public relations between the rank-and-file and the people.[30] Colonel Tin Oo from the South West Command observed that insurgents in the Ayarwaddy Delta were better at winning villagers' support than the Tatmadaw. The BCP insurgents even treated wounded villagers compassionately, sent them to the vicinity of hospitals, and gave them money for expenses. The General Staff Office report said:

> … as the people were made unhappy and miserable (by the Tatmadaw troops), they brought in insurgents to fight the Tatmadaw troops. As a result, there were high casualties in operations. It is found that when the people would no longer bear such maltreatment, they asked insurgents to protect them and fight against the Tatmadaw… Since we have plenty of examples, it is better to fight the insurgents with organisational means rather than with manpower [troops] and weapons. To the best of our ability, we should neutralise the people so that they will not support the insurgents, let alone developing [sic] the people's willingness to support us.[31]

Finally, General Ne Win told the COs: "in the Delta, insurgents were doing good things while our men were doing all the bad things". He also mentioned that similar reports had been received since 1958.[32] Also in 1965 and 1966, there were reports of abuse of power by soldiers in some areas. At the 1966 Tatmadaw conference, the Vice-Chief of Staff, Brigadier San Yu, spoke out about the maltreatment of villagers by soldiers. For example, some older villagers were given harsh punishment and some villagers were publicly humiliated during operations and militia programmes.[33]

Nevertheless, by 1965 the concept of "People's War" was formally accepted as the military doctrine for the Tatmadaw. With the advent of the "People's War" concept, the doctrine was popularized in various military publications, for all levels; this included a poem written by a renowned Myanmar author in late 1960s and the poem was printed on the Independence Day anniversary facilitation cards. The poem runs: "How superior the tactics of war; how potent the weapons! without gathering in; the heart of the people; without relying on; the strength of the people; the sword edge will shatter; the spear will bend."[34] Another famous poem quoted in the cards is an extract from '*Nandithena-Pyo*' (နန္ဒိသေနပျို့) written by an eighteenth century Myanmar scholar on the Myanmar art of war. It said: "In towns and villages of near or far; along the journey during the march; without willingness by the owner; never think of taking away; a branch of leaves or a stalk of vegetable; a sheet of thatch or a node of bamboo."[35]

The people's war doctrine in counter-insurgency operations was first locally tested in the Central Command area from January to March 1966, but without detailed procedures. People's militias were formed in the area known to the BCP as '*Myit-Phya-Dae-Tha-Taing*' (မြစ်ဖျားဒေသတိုင်း) [watershed region]. The combination of "five columns" was used in crushing BCP insurgents in the Katha, Pinlebu, Banmauk, Maw Like, and Phaung Pyin districts.[36] The regional commander deemed the operation a success. Later, the strategy was tested in localized operations in other regional commands. The people's militia programme had not been formalized at this stage, nor had central planning or standard operating procedures. The first test of the "people's war" under the direct supervision of the General Staff Office was undertaken in "Operation Alinyaung" in the Central Command area in early 1966. Based on lessons from this operation, the 1966 Tatmadaw conference decided to improve the fighting, organizational, and administrative capacities of the Tatmadaw, which were the pillars of the counter-insurgency operations.[37] In addition, a curriculum for the people's militia training programmes, for both military personnel and civilians, was drawn up.

A dominant theme of discussions at the 1968 Tatmadaw conference in connection with the "people's war" doctrine was the '*Phyet-Lay-Phyet*' (ဖြတ်လေးဖြတ်) [four cuts] strategy as counter-guerrilla strategy: to cut food supply to the insurgents; to cut protection money from villagers to the insurgents; to cut contacts (intelligence) between the people and the insurgents; and to make the people "cut off the insurgent's head" (meaning, involving the people in fighting, particularly the encirclement of insurgents).[38] The strategy was, in fact, one of base denial, relying on non-combat measures to support anti-guerrilla warfare under the "military column" of the overall counter-insurgency strategy. An officer stated that preparation for a "people's war" could be carried out simultaneously with counter-insurgency operations. Sharing his knowledge of the insurgents' strategy and tactics, he said:

> In strategic terms, insurgents [primarily the BCP] avoid any decisive battle because of their weakness in strength [in numbers and armament]. They wage a protracted war to buy time to increase their fighting capability while making the Tatmadaw weak in moral and physical terms. They also exploit the changing international situation.
>
> In essence, the insurgents are waging a protracted war based on guerrilla warfare ... They operate by relying on people's support. It is evident that villages are becoming insurgent strongholds and hideouts. They infiltrate villages and breed hardcore cadres. Through these hardcore cadres they control the villages. Then in the next stage, these villages are turned into base areas. It is very difficult for our troops [the Tatmadaw] to operate in these areas.[39]

The officer further said that insurgents gained the element of surprise, had better intelligence, relied on maintaining a high tempo in manoeuvres, and applied mobile defence. He also said that insurgents used the famous Chinese communist tactics of guerrilla warfare.[40]

In relation to counter-insurgency strategy, the COs discussed tactics — what the North Vietnamese would call communists "putting fish on the chopping board".[41] It was recognized that the arrest of insurgent cadres (hardcore) was crucial; accurate intelligence was vital; annihilation was essential (not territorial occupation); and tactical independence was important in the lower levels of command (section and platoon). Liquidation of all insurgents and preparation for a "people's war" for national defence, in accordance with the Tatmadaw's military doctrine, were the elements of the long-term project. For the short term, the liquidation of communist insurgency in lower and central Myanmar was the most immediate and important task.[42]

By 1968, operational and regional priorities had been decided. To secure an insurgent-free delta was paramount in winning the war against the communist insurgents. The new doctrine and strategy focused on consolidation of an operational base, rather than chasing the insurgents. It was a tough decision for the Tatmadaw leadership, in the face of a new communist front in the northeast border region, apparently backed by Chinese Communists. At the operational level, the Tatmadaw had engaged in two different forms of wars. While it primarily applied the "four-cut" strategy in counter-insurgency warfare in lower and central Myanmar, the Tatmadaw used a combination of mobile-conventional and guerrilla warfare in the Northeast border area. Air support, aerial stifling, bombing, and artillery fire were common. Trench warfare was a vital part of the military strategy. Until late 1970s, the Tatmadaw was essentially on a defensive position in the border region. The anti-Chinese riots and diplomatic war between Myanmar and China in late 1967 aroused nationalist sentiments among the Myanmar public. Many people, even within the Tatmadaw, were emotionally motivated to engage with what they saw as a foreign-backed communist insurgency. Nevertheless, at the 1968 Party Seminar, General Ne Win urged people to be tolerant about what was happening on the border, although he admitted that the Tatmadaw had suffered heavy casualties.

The new military doctrine of "people's war", and the strategy of counter-guerrilla warfare for counter-insurgency and guerrilla warfare for foreign invasion, were designed to be appropriate for Myanmar. The doctrine flowed from the country's independent and active foreign policy, total people's defence policy, the nature of perceived threats, its geography and the regional environment, the size of its population in comparison with those of its neighbours, the relatively undeveloped nature of its economy, and its historical and political experiences. A "people's war" is generally defined in Myanmar as a just war to achieve victory for a just cause and belief by mobilizing man, material, and morale of the entire people through the five columns of political, economic, social, military and administrative management as solid basis. The doctrine was based on "*Du-Thone-Du*" (ထုသုံးထု) [three masses]: population, time, and space,[43] and "*Pamana-Lay-Yat*" (ပမာဏလေးရပ်) [four strengths]: manpower, material, time, and morale.[44] However, the doctrine did not develop concepts of either strategic denial or a counter-offensive capability in defence against foreign invasion. It relied almost totally on irregular warfare, such as its guerrilla strategy to counter any form of foreign invasion. The overall counter-insurgency strategy included not only elimination of insurgents with the "four-cut" military strategy as the counter-guerrilla strategy, but also the building of a "white area" and "hardcore area" as well. An essential element in the Tatmadaw's counter-insurgency strategy was a balanced approach that encompassed "search and destroy", "heart and mind", and "clear and hold".

To implement the new military doctrine and strategy, the Tatmadaw introduced special training programmes for military personnel at "command training centres" at various regional commands, for a year from 1 April 1968. Tactics suitable for counter-guerrilla warfare were taught, with special emphasis on ambush and counter-ambush, counter-insurgency weapons and tactics, individual battle initiative for tactical independence, commando tactics, and scouting. Battalion-size operations were also practised in the South West Command area. The new strategy and tactics proved to make troops less prone to insurgent ambush than their predecessors.

At the 1969 Tatmadaw conference, General Ne Win summarized the development of the "people's war" doctrine in the following terms:

> At the 1962 Tatmadaw conference, it was unanimously decided by the commanders to build the present Tatmadaw into a National Tatmadaw or People's Tatmadaw which will defend the Socialist economic system. At the 1964 Tatmadaw conference, it was decided, for the future generations, to lay down basic principles of "people's war" suitable for the Tatmadaw which is necessary not only for effective defence of national independence and sovereignty but also for the building of a socialist economic system. At the 1966 Tatmadaw conference, there was discussion and plans were drawn to improve the military, organisational and administrative efficiencies of the Tatmadaw. Then, at the 1968 Tatmadaw conference, there was discussion of how to implement the "people's war" doctrine.[45]

The 1969 Tatmadaw conference also discussed plans for national service. As a result, when a new constitution was promulgated in 1974, Articles 170 and 171 of the 1974 Constitution called for basic military training and national services for the citizen. Article 170 stated that "every citizen shall be under a duty to protect and safeguard the independence, sovereignty and territorial integrity of the Socialist Republic of the Union of Burma and it was a noble duty". Then Article 171 called for every citizen to, in accordance with law, (a) undergo military training, and (b) undertake military service for the defence of the state. However, this was never implemented in Myanmar.

The "people's war" doctrine was formally endorsed at the first party congress of the BSPP, held in 1971.[46] Throughout successive party congresses, the BSPP laid down "complete annihilation of the insurgents as one of the tasks for national defence and security" and called for "the liquidation of insurgents through the strength of the working people as the immediate objective".[47] In essence, the new military doctrine and strategy, as far as the counter-insurgency aspect was concerned, ensured the dominant role of the Tatmadaw at national-level policy-making.

Meanwhile, for the successful implementation of the "people's war" in counter-insurgency operations, the Tatmadaw has since 1966 taken the formation of people's militia organizations seriously. The first people's militia organization was formed in Phaung Pyin in 1966 with a group of twenty hardcore members. The encouraging result of the militia organization in Phaung Pyin led to an introduction of people's militia organizations on a larger scale. At the twenty-third anniversary of Tatmadaw Day (1968), the then Deputy Commander-in-Chief Brigadier General San Yu stated that the "entire population must be mobilized under the people's war doctrine and strategy for the national defence".[48] The 1968 Tatmadaw conference discussed the introduction of people's militia organizations when considering the "people's war" doctrine and "four-cut" strategy. Lieutenant Colonel Kyaw Win from the Southwest Command suggested the formation of residential militias in the first stage, and mobile militias at a later stage, under the leadership of the BSPP.[49] In terms of regional priority, Lieutenant Colonel Hla Shwe from the Central Command set the following criteria:

(1) villages significant and supportive in total eradication of insurgency;
(2) villages under strong party [BSPP] influence and presence of BSPP cadres;
(3) villages with 'People's Peasants Councils'; and
(4) villages where a Tatmadaw outpost or police station was present.[50]

He suggested that residential militias be assigned village security and intelligence gathering functions, in coordination with the Tatmadaw.

Another important discussion at the conference concerned the politicization of the militia organizations. Again, Hla Shwe stated:

> In mobilizing peasants for militia organizations, the principles should be based on the ideology of the BSPP. ... Because, it is vital to have an ideological conviction in fighting protracted warfare in the manner of "People's War"... It is also because the war has to be fought in both military and ideological terms.[51]

In accordance with the decision reached at the 1968 Tatmadaw conference, the Directorate of Military Training issued a set of guidelines the same year. Despite the success stories of the people's militia organizations, the concept was not formally endorsed by the ruling party and the state until 1971.

In 1968, the Directorate of Military Training issued a directive for the training of people's militias. It recommended detailed instructions for formation, training, and duties of the militias. To be successful in maintaining strong and reliable militia troops in the long term, the directive stated, cooperation and coordination among the BSPP, the Tatmadaw, and the People were needed. There were four bases on which militias should be formed: under the leadership of the BSPP cadres, through grassroots-level organizational activities of BSPP cadres, by effective coordination of the "Five Columns", and through heartfelt support from the people to the five columns.[52] It recommended that militias be formed in areas controlled by the BSPP and the government.

At the first party congress in 1971, the Central Organizing Committee of the BSPP submitted a political report in which a recommendation on the "people's war" doctrine and training programmes was included. This process was elaborated in a document entitled "Formation of People's Militias Organization in Consistence with the Prevailing Situation", issued by the BSPP Central Committee in November 1972. It declared:

> In some military command areas, People's Militias (Residential) were formed in villages, wards, factories and offices under the leadership of the BSPP and the Tatmadaw. Some of them were organized into People's Militias (Mobile) as the situation required. They were participating in the military column (of the five columns) together with the Tatmadaw. Although the People's Militias were to be formed on a nationwide scale, as the situation [dictated], anti-insurgent groups and local defence forces [(ကာကွယ်ရေး) *Kar-Kwe-Ye*] were organized in some areas.[53]

The document covered organizational activities, formation, command, control and communication, training, armament, duties, discipline, and logistic support of the militia organizations. Some of the recommendations were:

- to form two types of militias (residential and mobile);
- to form mobile militias on an *ad hoc* basis, drawing troops from residential militias of villages and wards;
- not to form militias at township level at the present time [village and ward only];
- to form anti-insurgent groups in the areas with no strong government presence;
- not to expand the *Kar-Kwe-Ye*, but to turn them into anti-insurgent groups first and then to people's militias; and

– to place militia organizations under the security and administrative committee.[54]

In accordance with the BSPP document, the General Staff Office issued a document entitled "Implementing People's Militia Programme" (24 January 1973), instructing regional military commands.[55]

In order to carry out the plan for a "people's war", the Directorate of People's Militias and Public Relations was established on 23 January 1973, under the Ministry of Defence, by incorporating the Education Department, Directorate of Burma Territorial Force, and Department of Public Relations.[56] Thus, from 1973, the People's Militias Organization was under direct command of the Tatmadaw. At the regional command level, the people's militias and public relations activities were placed under the General Staff (G) Department. It included the formation, armament, and training of people's militias; formation and armament of anti-insurgent groups; building white areas and hardcore areas; and maintaining security in command areas.

About the same time, under the leadership of the BSPP, the War Veteran Organization was formed in December 1975. It was not only an organization for the welfare of the veteran, but also a reserve force for the national defence. Moreover, the BSPP began to introduce basic military training for youth. The BSPP mobilized Myanmar youth into three different groups on the basis of age, namely Teza Youth, Shesaung Youth, and Lanzin Youth. In accordance with Article 14 (E) of the Lanzin Youth Organizing Committee, the BSPP offered a number of courses for youth. In various training programmes, basic military drill is taught. In some cases, such as the "Marine Youth" and "Aviation Youth" programmes, training involved the handling of small arms during a ten-week summer training programme. Beginning in the 1979 summer vacation, a pilot project for military training (without weapons) was introduced in the Thanlyin and Kyaukse townships. The next year, the programme was introduced in Taunggyi and Pathein.[57] However, this programme appeared to stop in the late 1980s.

In the meantime, since the mid-1960s, the Tatmadaw introduced a three-phase counter-insurgency warfare plan. Phase one transforms a "black area" into a "brown area", that is, transforms an area controlled by insurgents, but where the Tatmadaw operates, to a Tatmadaw-controlled area where insurgent operates. The second phase is to transform from "brown area" into "white area". In this phase, the area will be cleared of any insurgent activities. The final phase is to transform it into a "hard-core area". In phase one, the objective is to dislodge insurgent troops, capture insurgent strongholds and bases, and introduce a strong presence of government security forces. In this phase, the most common and primary form of fighting is conventional warfare with anti-guerrilla warfare as a secondary form. In phase two, mopping up operations and organizational activities are important. Anti-guerrilla warfare and zoning operations are common while regional development programmes are designed to win hearts and minds of the local population. In phase three, more organizational works are necessary and the government forms pro-government militia units for both counter-insurgency and for overall national defence. In lower and central Myanmar, the Tatmadaw applied the "four-cut" strategy and people's war doctrine. By the late 1970s, the Tatmadaw declared that lower and central Myanmar became "white-areas" and "hardcore-areas". As insurgency in central and lower Myanmar was wiped out, the Tatmadaw began to concentrate its efforts on the Northeast border region. In 1979, for the first time, the Tatmadaw initiated a large-scale offensive against the BCP. However, only in the mid-1980s, did the Tatmadaw break the military stalemate with the BCP. Then, it began to give much more attention to counter-insurgency operations, targeting ethnic insurgencies. More operations were conducted with greater intensity against Kachin, Shan, Mon, and Kayin insurgents. The capture of the Pajo and Narphaw strongholds of the Kachin insurgents, and the Mawpokay stronghold of the Kayin insurgents, were well publicized. In all these operations, since the "four-cut" strategy was quite irrelevant, the primarily form of warfare was a conventional one.

It appeared that the "people's war" doctrine was applied mostly in counter-insurgency operations, since Myanmar did not face any direct foreign invasion throughout the period. However, the Tatmadaw leadership never lost sight of the need to prepare for war against foreign invasion. In 1985, the then Vice-Chief of Staff, Lieutenant General Saw Maung, reminded his commanders at the Command and General Staff College that:

> You know very well about the concept of people's war. In Myanmar, out of nearly 35 million [people], the armed forces (army, navy and air force) have about two hundred thousand [personnel]. In terms of percentage, it is about 0.01 per cent. It is impossible to defend our country with only this handful of troops … Therefore, what we have to do in the case of foreign invasion is to mobilise people in accordance with the people's war doctrine. For [the] defence of our country, the entire population must be involved in the war effort. So also is the case in counterinsurgency. Remember, the support of the people will dictate the outcome of the war.[58]

Despite the recommendation to build up an armed force of about a million personnel for peacetime, the Tatmadaw had barely reached about 200,000 troops by early 1988. About 184,000 army personnel were spread out among 168 infantry battalions and support corps. These infantry battalions were put under nine territorially organized commands and seven centrally controlled light infantry divisions. Regional commands were assigned to form and train people's militias. See Table 2.1.

TABLE 2.1
The Growth of Tatmadaw Manpower

Year	*Army*	*Navy*	*Air Force*	*Total*
December 1964	122,228	6,101	6,200	134,529
May 1974	138,480	6,655	6,633	151,768
June 1981	163,700	7,419	6,546	177,665
June 1984	173,655	7,724	6,892	188,271
April 1988	184,029	8,065	6,587	198,681

Source: Tatmadaw Organizing Committee, BSPP.

THIRD PHASE OF THE DEVELOPMENT OF MILITARY DOCTRINE

The third phase of doctrinal development came soon after the military takeover and formation of the SLORC in September 1988. The Tatmadaw leadership reviewed the existing military doctrine and strategy and decided to modernize its armed forces. This probably reflected the fear of direct foreign invasion or invasion by proxy. The state-owned media had cited from time to time the presence of a U.S. naval fleet in Myanmar's territorial waters during the 1988 political upheaval as evidence of an infringement of Myanmar's sovereignty. The regime was also concerned that foreign powers might help insurgents on the Myanmar border to develop formidable armed forces that would challenge the new regime in Yangon. Moreover, the Tatmadaw leadership believed that various political organizations that proliferated in the post-1988 political upheaval and military takeover had actively sought foreign assistance, in the form of interference or intervention, to destabilize or overthrow the incumbent regime. These perceived threats further strengthen the siege mentality of the Tatmadaw commanders. This new threat perception, which was formerly insignificant under the nation's isolationist or self-reliant foreign policy, led the Tatmadaw leadership to review the defence capability and doctrine of the Tatmadaw.

Soon after the SLORC takeover, the regime declared three main national causes: non-disintegration of the Union, non-disintegration of national solidarity, and the perpetuation of national sovereignty. Threats are generally defined by the regime as those actions designed to challenge the three main national causes. Threat perceptions involve not only an external power interfering in an existing insurgency or domestic political conflict, but also such a power promoting domestic political conflict as an excuse for interference.

As the perception of the threat of foreign interference became greater, the Tatmadaw leadership decided to modernize the Tatmadaw in both material and doctrinal terms. This was evidenced by the purchase of a number of anti-aircraft guns and nearly sixty tanks in 1989–90.[59] In his speech to commanders in October 1988, General Saw Maung said:

> Our basic military doctrine since the time of our independence was not to make aggression against any other country but to defend our own country. Whatever the political system is in the country, the military strategy of our country is the people's war. The people's war is not only to counter the [sic] foreign invasion, but also to suppress the [sic] insurgency. One of the most important points to remember in applying [the] people's war strategy is the need to use conventional warfare at the last stage when complete eradication of insurgency is the objective. You cannot ignore conventional warfare.
>
> As experience of suppressing insurgency has grown, commanders tend to forget the point that conventional warfare should be applied. It is wrong to think that conventional is irrelevant in counter-insurgency warfare. Principles and rules of conventional warfare are always important in any form of warfare.[60]

His remark somewhat reflected the influence of Mao's strategic thinking among the senior commanders. The Bamar (Burmese) version of Mao Zedong's selected military writings was one of the most widely read books among officers in the 1960s and 1970s, along with Lin Piao's *People's War* and Che Guevara's *Guerrilla Warfare*. The Maoist strategy has three stages: strategic defensive, strategic stalemate, and strategic offensive. The primary form of fighting in the final stage (strategic offensive) is large-scale mobile conventional warfare. However, General Saw Maung reminded the commanders not to lose sight of the people's war doctrine:

> In every war, the people's support is vital. It is important not to forget the point that victory or defeat in a war depends largely on the support of the

> people. It is necessary to plan ahead for people's war. While suppressing insurgency, [commanders should] learn the experience of mobilisation and training of people's militias and prepare for people's war. We need to draw up a nation-wide mobilisation, training and command and control system for people's militias and people's war.[61]

Another important measure in reshaping the military doctrine was the combined arms and joint services exercises. Joint Services Military Exercises (Army, Navy, and Air Force) in 1995 and 1997 and Combined Arms Exercise (Infantry, Armour, and Air Force) in 1998 could be seen as a modification of the existing "people's war" doctrine; at the exercises, Senior General Than Shwe officially called the Tatmadaw's military doctrine as "people's war under modern condition". These exercises, according to some sources, involved more than 30,000 troops under five light infantry divisions, over one hundred 76-mm, 105-mm, 120-mm, and 155-mm field artillery, nearly 300 armoured carriers and tanks, about six squadrons of aircraft, and about thirty naval craft. Although it was a top-secret matter, the movement and mobilization of large numbers of troops was hardly a secret from the local population. The exercises were designed to introduce strategic denial and counter-offensive capabilities to the existing "people's war" doctrine. It was also reported that during the exercises some people's militias and auxiliary forces, such as members of the Auxiliary Fire Brigade, the Red Cross, and the Union Solidarity and Development Association (USDA), were mobilized. These forces were trained for guerrilla warfare and rescue missions. The exercises revealed that the purpose of such a counter-offensive was to counter low-level foreign invasion.[62] According to the doctrine, should the standing conventional force fail to defeat an invading force in the beachheads or landing zones, resistance would be organized at the village, regional, and national level to sap the will of the invading force. When the enemy's will had been sapped, its capabilities dispersed and exhausted, and sufficient force had been mustered, a counter-offensive would be launched to drive the invader from Myanmar.

The acquisition of new weapons, radar, and electronic intelligence equipment to boost national air defence; of new aircraft for air superiority; and of new naval craft to provide blue-water capability; could well be argued to have a legitimate defensive purpose. In essence, the military doctrine and strategy is arguably a "people's war under modern conditions", with limited strategic denial and counter-offensive capabilities for conventional warfare. In this light, at the graduation ceremony of the third batch of trainees of the National Defence College, Senior General Than Shwe reminded senior military officials that:

> the most important thing in the national defence is the support of the entire people. As the nation is to adopt the doctrine and strategy of "People's War", as long as we are able to implement the doctrine of "People's War Under Modern Condition", whatever situation we are facing, we believe that we shall be able to defend the state and nation.

The concept of "people's war under modern conditions" is apparently a borrowed idea from the People's Liberation Army (PLA). One of the key features of the "people's war under modern conditions" is the growing importance of weaponry. A relatively well trained and equipped regular professional force will be able to conduct conventional warfighting, based on the joint services and combined arms warfare. The essence of modern condition is to change the military posture from passive defence to active defence. Here, active defence means that instead of luring enemy forces deep into a hardcore area for annihilation in an earlier stage, as denoted in the strategic defensive strategy, the Tatmadaw will firmly stick to positional defence in order to weaken the invader's offensive, and then wage (counter) offensive campaigns with concentrated and combined forces; therefore, it is important to build up firepower for positional defence at the border. The "people's war under modern conditions" is in a way a preparation for the limited regional war scenario. In the "people's war under modern condition", instead of the traditional three masses (manpower, time, and space), there are four masses and the new one is the "cyber" mass; that reflects modern warfare which has five dimensions, namely, land, sea, air, space, and cyberspace.

In the meantime, with regard to the internal armed security threat, there has been a changing perception on counter-insurgency warfare. Junior commanders are more keen to introduce concepts of low-intensity conflict (LIC) than the decade-old "four-cut" and "people's war" doctrine and strategy in counter-insurgency operations. Yet for the time being, it appears that the "four-cut" strategy as the counter-guerrilla strategy, and the "five-column" approach remain cornerstones of the counter-insurgency warfare at the official level. However, the Tatmadaw also applied conventional firepower based warfighting with close air support and ground attack by the air force, in offensives, on insurgents' strongholds along the Myanmar-Thai border. What is important for the Tatmadaw is to gain the initiative in the counter-insurgency operations; thus, it adjusted its warfighting method in accordance with the those of the insurgents.

In recent years, special attention has been given to the implication and impact of the Revolution in Military Affairs (RMA) on the Myanmar Armed Forces. The Tatmadaw is in the process of learning what the RMA is and how to respond creatively to such a development within the context of "people's war under modern condition". The Tatmadaw has shown some enthusiasm in learning, applying, and encountering RMA as part of its efforts for force modernization and military strategy. The leadership has surely realized that the information age has arrived, and technological breakthroughs have profoundly altered the way that warfare will be conducted. The military leadership is convinced that the doctrine of "people's war under modern condition" is still valid and appropriate for the Tatmadaw and Myanmar, and under present circumstances, there is no reason to digitize its armed forces. But the leadership certainly understands that it is important to learn RMA and modern military science and technology for defensive purpose. At a passing out ceremony of the Officers' Training School in June 1995, Commander-in-Chief (Army), General Maung Aye, said: "as the [sic] technology progresses, strategies tactics and weapons become more and more advanced, and the Tatmadaw must train its troops to be capable and skillful in advanced military technology in accordance with the national needs".[63] From time to time, he passed similar messages to Tatmadaw personnel. In August 2000, at the passing out ceremony of the No. 28th Intake of the Under-Officer Course, General Maung Aye said:

> In the 21st century, information technology is being used on a broader scale to make the world communication system faster and closer. In the age of globalization, it is necessary for you to be capable of keeping up with developments in modern science and technology for the sake of national security and defence. You need to be innovative and [show] initiative, to be ingenious and be skilled in modern command and control systems... You need to be well-versed in high-tech weapon system[s] and be endowed with three capabilities [military, organizational and administrative]. You need to build yourselves up as leaders prepared to face modern warfare.[64]

At the 54th Anniversary of Armed Forces Day (27 March 1999), Commander-in-Chief of the Defence Service, Senior General Than Shwe remarked:

> In order to be a Tatmadaw which is capable of defending a peaceful, modern and prosperous nation, it is essential to be modern, strong and highly capable... To be a "modern, strong and capable Tatmadaw" is our objectives [sic]. For realization of this objective, I would like to

> urge you to strive unswervingly, step by step, from the individual to the high organizations, enhancing your capabilities. It is necessary for you, Comrades, to acquire knowledge in science and technology. Only then will you be able to utilize, in keeping with the times, advanced military science and sophisticated weaponry.[65]

Although there was no way to procure modern military equipment and platforms, it appeared that the Tatmadaw was interested in building up its electronic counter measure and information warfare capability. Senior General Than Shwe reminded his commanders to be aware of the developments in military science and technology and urged them to find appropriate measures to cope with them. He said:

> The main tenets of modern warfare are the capability in pre-emptive strike, initiative, deep strike and synchronization. As a result of development[s] in technology and electronics, weapons have become more destructive. Firepower has become massive, accurate and effective. Weapons are delivered for faster and longer range. Intelligence equipments [sic] become highly sophisticated. Thanks to information technology, dissemination of information has become very fast and more information is available. As always, there are ways to counter these developments. *Electronic equipments [sic] can be countered with electronic counter-measures and electronic deception.*[66]
>
> Military science and technologies are advancing so fast that a name Revolution in Military Affairs has to be coined. In the present time, weapons based on data processing are being used. Manoeuvre, firepower, protection and leadership are *sine qua non* for combat power. The advantage of modern warfare is the use of electronic technology. In the field of command, control, communication and intelligence, information and digital technologies are being applied. *Electronic warfare is to be waged and to be countered with electronic counter intelligence/measures and counter sabotage. The engineering officers of the Tatmadaw need to work in cooperation (to cope with the advances in military science and technology).*[67] (Italics is mine)

In connection with the RMA, it appears that the Tatmadaw has undertaken a number of studies on electronic and information warfare. Detailed studies on various aspects of war were done on "Operation Desert Storm", the "Kosovo War", and "Afghanistan War". Several articles related to the RMA and modern military science and technology appeared in the Journal of Military Affairs [(စစ်ပညာရှာနယ်) *Sit-Pyin-Nya-Gyar-Nae*].[68] The army research bureau also produced several reports on the same subject. In this context, the Defence Services Academy introduced a computer science degree for its cadets. Moreover, several officers were sent abroad for training in electronic and information warfare. To some observers, the Tatmadaw is interested in learning the Battlefield Information Management System (BIMS) and training its officers for aerial reconnaissance, intelligence database, tracking with the Global Positioning System (GPS), the Command, Control, Communication, and Intelligence (C^3I), and visualization.

Nevertheless, the military leadership is fully aware of the limitations of the war-fighting capability of the Tatmadaw when it comes to external threats. Thus, although it builds up firepower for the positional warfare at the border and eventual counter offensive, it also prepares to fight an asymmetric war in facing a powerful enemy. By looking at the articles in various publications by the Tatmadaw, one can glean that the military leadership understands the modern warfighting method of effect-based operations and airpower in parallel attacks or inside-out attacks; but what it wants is more time to prepare for resistance. In the asymmetric warfare, also known as 4th Generation War (4GW), the fundamental principle for the military leadership, is what Mao Zedong called "you fight your kind of war and I will fight mine [你打你的，我打我的 — ni da ni de, wo da wo de]." Senior military commanders are also familiar with the concept of "Unrestricted Warfare" put forward by the People's Liberation Army of China. In this light, the Tatmadaw considers defence-in-depth necessary.

Therefore, training manuals produced by the Tatmadaw continue to emphasize guerrilla warfare. Most of the fundamentals of guerrilla warfare reflected Mao Zedong's strategic thinking. The most important thing in guerrilla warfare, as stated in the manual, is the fact that guerrillas and people must be just like fish and water. Guerrillas (fish) have to swim in the people (water). The Tatmadaw adopted Mao's famous 16-character poem and other Mao teachings, such as "the enemy advances, we retreat; the enemy camps, we harass; the enemy tires, we attack; and the enemy retreats, we pursue", "strike the hollow, avoid the solid", "if they don't come, we are not afraid; if they come we disappear; if they go back, we return" and "when they concentrate, we disperse; when they disperse, we concentrate; fast mobilize, fast assault, and fast retreat". Moreover, it also takes note that preserving men by losing territory will preserve both men and territory, whereas preserving territory by losing men will lose both men and territory. In this context, it is possible to conclude that the Tatmadaw will be engaging any foreign aggression with guerrilla warfare and tunnel warfare if strategic denial fails.

While learning the RMA and its impact, the Tatmadaw is taking necessary measures for the "people's war". It appears that the Tatmadaw is interested in guerrilla warfare and tunnel warfare, which are indeed closely intertwined. Some Myanmar military analysts argued that tunnel warfare is to deal with fluid warfare and to cope with fluid battlefield characteristics. Though the tunnels are vulnerable to modern bombs and missiles, such as GBU-28 "Bunker Buster" or BLU-82 "Daisy Cutter", they are considered effective in a war against an adversary of roughly equal power using conventional weapon. Several types of tunnels, such as the civil defence tunnel, air defence tunnel, industrial complex tunnel (to keep the war machine running), and command post tunnel, can be built to save manpower, ammunition, and centre of gravity from being destroyed. But there are several limitations to tunnel warfare.

The mission of the Tatmadaw, according to the declared policy, is to prepare a total people's defence. To fulfill this mission, the political role of the Tatmadaw is assured in the future state structure. The Union Solidarity and Development Association (USDA), Auxiliary Fire Brigade, Myanmar Police Force, and Red Cross Association are organized as auxiliary forces of the Tatmadaw [(ညီနောင်တပ်ဖွဲ့) *Nyi-Naung-Tatphwe*]. Moreover, the Tatmadaw also brings non-governmental organizations (Myanmar Medical Association, Myanmar Maternal and Child Welfare Association) under its umbrella, through patronage, for national defence. In recent years, wives and dependent children of military and police personnel have been required to undergo basic military training for a certain period of time. In some cases, the training has included operating anti-aircraft guns and artillery. In the Northern Command area, for example, the families of military personnel are formed into "National Force Corps" [(ပြည်သူ့စွမ်းအားရှင်အဖွဲ့) *Pyithu Swan-Arh-Shin-Aphwe*] or "Reserved Strength for National Defence". Through the UDSA, the Tatmadaw reintroduced the "Marine Youth" and "Aviation Youth" programmes. It was reported that between 1994 and 1997, a total of 1,675 youths took basic and advanced training under the "Aviation Youth Programme". In a similar way, a total of 2,609 youths were trained under the "Marine Youth Programme" between 1995 and 1998. These programmes usually take two months and take place during the summer vacation.

In recent years, special attention has been given to the Myanmar War Veteran Organization (MWVO). Soon after the SLORC came to power, the government enacted the War Veterans Law as well as rules and regulations on 10 August 1989 with Law No. 17/89. It was aimed at reform within the War Veterans Organization.[69] However, it appeared that only in 1998 did the SPDC or the Tatmadaw gain control over the organization. The

SPDC formed the Myanmar War Veterans Organization (MWVO) Central Organizing Committee with thirty-five members on 21 October 1998, "with the participation of in-service military personnel, as War Veterans are required to maintain their perpetual contact with the Tatmadaw and to realize the goals of MWVO in accord with the developing and changing political and economic systems of Myanmar".[70] It was firmly placed under the Adjutant General Office of the Ministry of Defence. In accordance with the five tasks designated by Senior General Than Shwe, namely the national political task; national defence and security task; the economic task, the public service task; and the welfare task, and "to stand firmly as a consolidated reserve force of the nation endowed with strength and reputation",[71] War Veterans Organizations at the basic levels were formed in March 1999. It was reported that 3,010 retired military officers and 88,162 retired military personnel of other ranks were organized under 313 township organizations, 64 districts, and 17 state and division supervisory organizations.[72] It appears that war veterans are classified into three different categories. Those who are under forty-five years of age and still in good health are regarded as active national servicemen. They are called for basic tactical training from time to time. In time of emergency, they will be required to discharge frontline duties. Those who are between forty-five and fifty-five are grouped as active reserve. They will be called in for non-combat duties in time of emergency. Those who are above fifty-five are not required for military service, but for civil defence and organizational activities.

At the first nation-wide conference of MWVO held in June 2001, Senior General Than Shwe stated:

> You comrades must be in line with the Tatmadaw and must accept the leadership of the Tatmadaw. In confronting the internal and external threats, you must come under the command of the Tatmadaw and work for the national defence and security. It is necessary for war veterans who live among the people to prepare for defence of the State together with the entire people. For national defence and security, you have to discharge your duties in [the] respective areas of your residence.

To keep in line with the Tatmadaw's ideological orientation, the Directorate of People's Militias and Public Relations, of the Ministry of Defence, conducted courses on national politics and national defence and security for MWVO members. Topics included global political developments and prospects, developments and prospects in East Asia, Southeast Asia and South Asia, the developments in the neighbouring countries and their possible effects on Myanmar, strengthening of the belief and conviction based on national politics in order to safeguard Our Three Main National Causes, reformation of organizations to enable the nation to effectively use her forces in times of emergency.

CONCLUSION

Despite its historical continuity, the present military doctrine and strategy requires the members of the Tatmadaw to perform a number of new missions. In the face of the collapse of the one-party state, the doctrine makes the Tatmadaw directly responsible for mass mobilization. A new training regime has also been introduced, to train the Tatmadaw to be capable of fighting a conventional war under the existing "people's war" doctrine.

In terms of military doctrine, as discussed above, the Tatmadaw has gone through three phases of development. Beginning with conventional mechanized war in the 1950s, the Tatmadaw eventually adopted the doctrine of "people's war". Though it had never lost sight of the external threat, the Tatmadaw perceived insurgency as the most serious security threat to the state and nation. In this context, during the second phase of the doctrinal development, the Tatmadaw laid down the firm foundation for counter-insurgency warfare, based on the "four-cut" strategy and "five-column" approach. This remains the cornerstone of the Tatmadaw's counter-insurgency strategy. In the late 1980s, as the threat perception became more external, the Tatmadaw reviewed and modified its doctrine to "people's war under modern condition", by introducing strategic denial and counter-offensive capability. While the Tatmadaw continues to train its troops in anti-guerrilla warfare for counter-insurgency, it has been taking necessary measures for "guerrilla warfare" and "tunnel warfare" to deal with external threat. It appears that the Tatmadaw is also interested in new areas of warfare, such as electronic warfare and information warfare. Despite all these new developments, the doctrine of the "people's war under modern condition" will remain with the Tatmadaw for years to come.

Notes

1. In fact, the government even lost control over a suburb of Yangon.
2. Maung Maung, along with some officers, was captured by the Karen Insurgents in February 1949 and became a prisoner for about two years until he was rescued by a Tatmadaw commando in late 1951. This incident damaged his reputation as a senior military commander among Tatmadaw officers, especially Japanese trained officers.

3 Tape Recorded (TR) 44 (1–4), interview with Brigadier Maung Maung (retired), 17 July 1991, Defence Services Historical Museum and Research Institute (DSHMRI), Myanmar.

4 Interview with Colonel Saw Myint (retired), 5 July 1996, Yangon.

5 Operation Bayin Naung, Operation Sin Phyu Shin, Operation Yan Gyi Aung, and Operation Mekhong were well known for success.

6 In the early days of insurgencies, the KNDO and the BCP applied conventional warfare, involving artillery fire, tanks, and armoured carriers. For the nature of the fighting, see မိုမိုတာရောစန်၊ *မုန်တိုင်းကိုမမှုအံတုလေသော်* (ရန်ကုန်၊ မြဝတီစာပေ၊ ၁၉၉၄) [Momotaro-San, *In Defiance of the Storm* (Yangon: Myawaddy Press, 1997)]; ဗိုလ်မှူးကြီးဟောင်းတင်မောင်၊ *တိုင်းပြည်ကနန မုန်တိုင်းကထန်ထန်* (ရန်ကုန်၊ စာပေလောက စာအုပ်တိုက်၊ ပဉ္စမအကြိမ်၊ ၁၉၉၉) [Ex-Colonel Tin Maung, *Feeble Nation; Severe Storm* (Yangon: Sarpay Lawka, 5th printing, 1999)]; တပ်ကြပ်မောင်ထူး၊ *အောင်ဆန်းသူရိယလှသောင်း* (ရန်ကုန်၊ အားမာန်သစ်စာပေ၊ ဒုကြိမ်၊ ၁၉၉၉) [Tatkyat Maung Htoo, *Aung San Thuriya Hla Thaung* (Yangon: Armanthit Sarpay, 2nd printing, 1999)].

7 Clarified Document (CD) 993, Military Strategy and Tactics in Counterinsurgency (Colonel Kyi Win), DSHMRI, p. 1.

8 Ibid.

9 Ibid.

10 CD. 105 (14), Report submitted by the General Staff Office at the 1959 Tatmadaw Conference, DSHMRI.

11 For more detail, see Tin Maung Maung Than, "Myanmar: Myanmar-ness and Realism in Historical Perspective", *Strategic Cultures in the Asia-Pacific Region*, edited by Ken Booth and Russell Trood (New York: St. Martin's Press, 1999).

12 CD. 105 (14), Report submitted by the General Staff Office at the 1959 Tatmadaw Conference, DSHMRI.

13 Ibid.

14 CD. 879 (2), Report of the General Staff Office at the 1963 Tatmadaw Conference, DSHMRI.

15 CD. 341 (2), Report submitted by the General Staff Office at the 1962 Tatmadaw Conference, DSHMRI.

16 CD. 879 (1), Discussion on "G,A,Q" matters from the military commands and the speeches of the Chief of Staff at the 1963 Tatmadaw Conference, DSHMRI.

17 Ibid.

18 Ibid.

19 It is a common view among the Myanmar people that Thailand is a historical enemy with roughly equal strength, and China is an enemy with greater strength.

20 CD. 880 (10), Report of the General Staff Office at the 1964 Tatmadaw Conference, DSHMRI.

21 CD. 880, Records of the 1964 Tatmadaw Conference, DSHMRI.

22 Ibid.

23 When a military column went into an area, insurgents simply disappeared and everything was calm. Soon after it left, the insurgents reappeared.

24 Document Registered (DR) 9692, A Brief History of the Directorate of Military Training, DSHMRI.

25 Ibid.

26 Ibid.

27 Under this strategy, military operations would be followed by socio-economic development projects (building schools and bridges), with the BSPP organizing activities, and civil administration. People's militias were formed and trained for village defence. After some time, the area under operation would become a "white area", where there are no more insurgents, and later a "hardcore area". It involved mass mobilization. Public relations activities were vital in this strategy, which required the cooperation of various government departments (as recommended at the 1959 Tatmadaw conference).

28 DR. 9692, A Brief History of the Directorate of Military Training, DSHMRI.

29 CD. 351, The Minute of COs Conference held on 21 July 1952, DSHMRI.

30 CD. 931, Comparative Analysis of the Military Operations in 1962 and 1963, DSHMRI.

31 CD. 879 (1), The 1963 Tatmadaw Conference, DSHMRI.

32 Ibid.

33 CD. 882(3), Speech of the Vice-Chief of Staff (Army) at the 1966 Tatmadaw Conference, DSHMRI.

34 အောင်သင်း၊ "မျိုးဆက်သစ်တို့တိုးတက်ရစ်ဖို့" ၊ *ဈေးကွက်ဂျာနယ်* (အမှတ် ၄၆၀၊ ၃ မတ် ၂၀၀၆) စာ - ၁၂၊ ၁၅ [Aung Thin, "Myo-zet-thit-doe Toe-tet-yit-boe", *Zaygwet Journal*, no. 460 (3 March 2006): 12, 15.] (လုံကိုသို့ထား၊ ဓားကိုသို့ရုတ်၊ စစ်ဆုတ်စစ်တက်၊ အဘက်ဘက်တွင်၊ သွက်လက်သေခြာ၊ ကျွမ်းကျင်ပါလည်း၊ ပြည်သူ့နလုံး၊ မသိမ်းကျုံးသော်၊ ပြည်သူ့ခွန်အား၊ မကိုးစားသော်၊ ဓားသွားလည်းကြေ၊ လုံသွားခွေအံ့။).

35 Nandithena Pyo, Verse no. 44 (မြို့ရွာကျေးသီး၊ ခရီးတစ်ခွင်၊ ဥစ္စာရှင်က၊ ကြည်လင်မြတ်လေး၊ မပေးမစွန့်၊ သစ်ညွန့်တစ်ခက်၊ ဟင်းရွက်တစ်နွယ်၊ သက်ကယ်တစ်ပျစ်၊ ဝါးတစ်ဆစ်မျှ၊ သူ့ပစ္စည်းအား၊ မပြစ်မှားနှင့်).

36 Anon., "People's War Doctrine and the Members of the People's Armed Forces – 1", *Journal of the People's Armed Forces*, 1, vol. 25, no. 3 (15 March 1988): 13–14. From this experience, the Tatmadaw leadership planned to draw up a detailed procedure.

37 CD. 882, The 1966 Tatmadaw Conference, DSHMRI.

38 Directorate of Defence Services Intelligence, History of Insurgency, pp. 29–30.

39 CD. 883 (1), Discussion from the Regional Command HQs at the 1968 Tatmadaw Conference, DSHMRI.

40 Ibid.

41 William J. Duiker, *Sacred War* (New York: McGraw Hill, 1995), p. 153.

42 CD. 883 (1), Discussion from the Regional Command HQs at the 1968 Tatmadaw Conference, DSHMRI.

43 The concept of "mass" is known in Myanmar strategic literature as '*Du Hnit Sitsinye*', meaning operation *en mass*. The three "*masses*" are the mass of people (the entire physically and mentally fit adult population is mobilized), the mass of space (the entire country is the battlefield), and the *mass* of time (the entire period is fighting hours).

44 These four elements of strength will be mobilized.

45 CD. 884, Records of the 1969 Tatmadaw Conference, DSHMRI.

46 Burma Socialist Programme Party, *The 1971 First Party Congress* (Yangon: BSPP Press, 1971).

47 Ibid.

48 အမည်မပါ၊ "နိုင်ငံတော်ကာကွယ်ရေးသည် အရေးကြီးသည်" *ပြည်သူ့တပ်မတော်စာစဉ်* (အတွဲ ၁၆၊ အမှတ် ၂။ ၁၅ ဖေဖော်ဝါရီ ၁၉၇၉) [Anno, "National Defence is Important", *Pyithu Tatmadaw Sarsin*, vol. 16, no. 2, 15 February 1979].

49 CD. 883 (1), Discussion from the Regional Command HQs at the 1968 Tatmadaw Conference.

50 Ibid.

51 Ibid.

52 Directorate of Military Training, Directive for People's Militias – 1, p. 4.

53 Central Committee, BSPP, "Formation of People's Militias Organization in Consistence with the Prevailing Situation", p. 4.

54 Ibid., pp. 14–15.

55 DR. 8479, A Brief History of the Directorate of People's Militias and Public Relations and the Units under it.

56 Ibid.

57 အမည်မပါ၊ "လူငယ်နှင့်အခြေခံစစ်ပညာသင်တန်း" *ပြည်သူ့တပ်မတော်စာစဉ်* (အတွဲ ၁၇၊ အမှတ် ၁၂။ ၁၅ ဒီဇင်ဘာ ၁၉၈၀) [Anno, "Youth and Basic Military Training", *Pyithu Tatmadaw Sarsin*, vol. 17, no. 12, 15 December 1980].

58 Lieutenant General Saw Maung's speech at the closing ceremony of No. 37 Batch of Command and General Staff College, 14 June 1985.

59 Apparently anti-aircraft guns and tanks are of little use in counter-insurgency warfare.

60 General Saw Maung's speech on the occasion of the graduation of No. 39 Staff College, 28 October 1988.

61 Ibid.

62 With a more powerful enemy, the nature of warfare would most likely be a "total people's war", in which the Tatmadaw would fight hand-in-hand with militias and the people.

63 DR. 10704, General Maung Aye speech at the graduation parade of 91 Intake, 23 June 1995.

64 General Maung Aye's speech at the graduation parade of 28 Teza, 25 August 2000.

65 54th Anniversary of Armed Forces Day Speech, 27 March 2001.

66 43rd DSA Passing out Parade Speech, 6 April 2001.

67 3rd DSIT Graduation Parade, 9 April 2001.

68 For example, a Brigadier General discussed the fundamentals and dynamics of battle command. His article discussed the importance of agility, initiative, depth, synchronization, versatility, flexibility, judgment, intuition, empathy, adaptation, creativity, integration, and will in the battle command. [See *Journal of Military Affairs*, vol. 34, no. 2 (May 2000): 18–30.]

69 It is important to note that some members of the War Veterans Organization (WVO) actively participated in the 1988 demonstration. Various statements were issued in their names. Moreover, some WVO members joined the political parties. Another problem with the WVO was that those who remained in the central committee level were very much senior and former commanders of the SLORC/SPDC chairman and members. This made the SLORC/SPDC ineffective in taking control.

70 *Kyemon Newspaper*, 6 June 2001.

71 *Kyemon Newspaper*, 7 June 2001.

72 Township Supervisory Committees are still to be formed in the eleven townships, namely Jangyang, Lahe, Manphant, Pangyang, Nahpan, Panwaing, Mongmaw, Mangtung, Laukkai, Kongyun, and Mongyang, and the District Supervisory Committee is still to be formed in Laukkai District.

3

ORGANIZATION AND FORCE STRUCTURE

This chapter discusses how a weak, small, and disunited Tatmadaw in Myanmar has emerged into a considerably strong, large, and more or less united one, with a dominant role in Myanmar politics. In the process of building a strong and united Tatmadaw, any split along the lines of racial background, organizational origin, and political affiliation was resolved; the gap between staff and field officers was bridged; and competition between intelligence officers and field commanders was settled. Unity of the officer corps was further maintained by giving a fair share of senior command positions to graduates of different schools of training. Since the late 1960s, open split within the Tatmadaw had been more or less eliminated and the occasional factional struggle was managed, sometimes at a considerable cost, to maintain institutional unity. However, despite its growth in force structure the Tatmadaw remained an army of infantry battalions.

BUILDING UNITY WITHIN THE TATMADAW

At the time of Myanmar's independence in 1948, the Tatmadaw was weak, small and disunited. Cracks appeared along the lines of racial background, political affiliation, organizational origin, and different services. Its unity and operational efficiency were further weakened by the interference of civilians and politicians in military affairs, and the perception gap between staff officers and field commanders. The most serious problem was the tension between Karen officers, coming from the British Burma Army, and Bamar officers, coming from the Patriotic Burmese Force (PBF).[1] For the ex-PBF members, those who served in the British Burma Army were regarded as *Kyesar Sittha*, soldiers serving foreigners for a living, whereas they regarded themselves as *Myochit Sittha*, soldiers serving their own people out of patriotism. Generally, ex-PBF officers regarded officers from the ex-British Burma Army (mostly Karen, Kachin, and Chin, as well as Anglo-Indian and Sino-Burman) as "Pro-West", "Pro-British", or "Rightists".

In accordance with the agreement reached at Kandy in September 1945, the Tatmadaw was reorganized by incorporating the British Burma Army and the PBF. The officer corps was also shared by the ex-PBF officers and officers from the British Burma Army or the Army of Burma Reserve Organization (ABRO). The British also decided to form what were known as "class battalions", based on ethnicity. There were fifteen infantry battalions at the time of independence. Among them, only four were made up of the former members of the PBF.[2] Furthermore, influential positions within the "War Office" and commands were manned with non-former PBF officers.[3] It was the same in the other services of the Tatmadaw, such as military engineers, supply and transport, ordinance, and medical services. The navy and air force were also in the hands of ex-ABRO officers. Although Bo Letya, the then Minister for Defence, was a member of the "Thirty Comrades"[4] and a founder of the PBF, he was regarded by the ex-PBF officers as "Rightist". This situation made the ex-PBF officers feel that they were undermined by minority representation in the Tatmadaw.[5]

The most important and immediate thing for the ex-PBF officers was to get rid of the "Rightists" in general and Karen officers in particular.[6] They were disappointed with what they called the "Karenization of the Tatmadaw". They believed that unless they could get rid of the Karens and "Pro-West Stooges", their existence in the Tatmadaw would be jeopardized. When Major Chit Myaing[7] complained about the Karen dominance in the Tatmadaw to Bo Letya, the latter replied that he purposely let it happen simply because Karens were apolitical and professional, unlike the former PBF members. In addition to this situation, the ex-PBF officers were unhappy with the "scorched earth" and "slash and burn" tactics used by the Karen troops in counter-insurgency operations.[8] Major Chit Myaing finally complained about the situation to Bo Letya at the commanding officers' (COs') meeting on 1 June 1948. The majority of the participants at the COs' meeting were ex-PBF officers.[9] At first he was alone in attacking the "Rightists". During the recess, he was able to persuade Brigadier Ne Win on to his side. In the afternoon, the meeting became a heated discussion. The COs strongly criticized politicians for failure to reach a political settlement with the Communists and restore law and order. As the commanders' criticism of the politicians for allowing political chaos to develop was strident, Bo Letya challenged that if the military commanders could restore peace and end the communist insurgency, they could try to do so.

Therefore, beginning from June 1948, the former PBF commanders had been discussing a plan for leftist unity. It was also a plan to prevent the "Rightists" from getting the upper hand in the control of the state in general, and the Tatmadaw, in particular. They formed, with the consent of the government, the "Nine-Man Tatmadaw Committee for Leftist Unity" to find political solutions to the crisis.[10] The COs and the second-in-commands (2-ICs) were among the committee members.[11] The Tatmadaw Committee tried to restore peace in the country. It worked on the "Leftist Unity" programme. However, as a large portion of the People's Volunteer Organisation (PVO), known as Yebaw-Phyu, went underground on 16 July 1948, the political and security situation further deteriorated. The Tatmadaw Committee also became defunct as personal rivalry arose among the members.[12] In late July 1948, the government issued an order that Brigadier Ne Win, who was in Yangon for the COs' conference, return to the headquarters of the North Burma Sub-District (NBSD) as early as possible. But the ex-PBF commanders wanted him in Yangon. Due to strong and persistent demand from the commanders,[13] Brigadier Ne Win was finally appointed Vice-Chief of Staff on 1 August 1948.[14]

Taking advantage of this fluid political situation, the National Security Council (controlled by General Smith Dun, U Hla Tun Aung, Lieutenant Colonel Saw Shisho, Brigadier Saw Kyar Doe, and U Tin Htut, all of whom were regarded by the ex-PBF members as "Rightists") decided to disarm the battalions manned with ex-PBF members. When Colonel Zeya and Lieutenant Colonel Ye Htut discovered this plan, they tried to counter it by raising a coup. They wooed U Thein Pe Myint, a prominent Communist, to lead their movement. They also persuaded General Ne Win to side with them.[15] At this point, General Ne Win argued that if a military coup were organized under present circumstances, relying only on a handful of troops, the National Security Council and other security forces controlled by the "Rightists" would call on international assistance to crush it.[16]

However, the coup plan was somehow uncovered by the "Rightists". When Major Chit Myaing, the then 2-IC from No. 3 Burma Rifles, met Brigadier Aung Thin, the then commander of the South Burma Sub-District (SBSD), on the evening of 9 August 1948, the latter asked about the plan and tried to confirm the news. But Major Chit Myaing denied any knowledge of the coup. He then rushed back to his battalion and informed Colonel Zeya, Lieutenant Colonel Ye Htut, and U Thein Pe Myint about his meeting with

Brigadier Aung Thin. He made it clear that he did not want to see his fellow officers suffer at the hands of the "Rightists". Early next morning, although he did not encourage the coup, Major Chit Myaing asked his troops to line up and he then let them decide whether to remain with him or follow their CO, Lieutenant Colonel Ye Htut. He also promised not to pursue an attack within seventy-two hours. Almost a quarter of the members of No. 3 Burma Rifles went underground. At about 5 a.m., Major Chit Myaing reported to General Ne Win about the coup, which had now turned into a mutiny. Major General Ne Win remarked, "Good. Now we know who is black and who is white." Then they went to U Nu's residence to inform him of the mutiny.[17]

Due to the political affiliation of some members of the officer corps, mostly former PBF members, the pro-communist faction of the Tatmadaw mutinied on 10 August 1948. No. 1 Burma Rifles and some troops from No. 6 Burma Rifles also went along with the mutineers. The mutiny further weakened the ex-PBF officer faction within the Tatmadaw. Under these circumstances, the "Rightists" tried to marginalize the ex-PBF commanders and prevent them from utilizing other security forces. The ex-PBF commanders were now surrounded by both communists and pro-communists on one side, and the "Rightists" on the other. They realized that their existence was in jeopardy and were shocked when they learnt that Bo Letya had suggested that U Nu appoint U Tun Hla Aung and U Tin Htut, both "Rightists", as Inspector General of Police and Inspector General of the Union Auxiliary Forces respectively — two possible important sources of support for the ex-PBF officers. On 16 August 1948, both of them were given the rank of brigadier.[18] About the same time, some Karen battalions of the Union Military Police (UMP) captured cities in lower Myanmar, ushering in a full-scale insurgency.[19] Within a couple of months, more and more towns were captured by the Karen National Defence Organisation (KNDO) and the Karen UMP battalions. On 28 November 1948, Sama Duwa Sinwa Naung, a Kachin leader, informed Prime Minister U Nu that Karen leaders were persuading Kachins to cooperate with them. Only then did U Nu consider the situation serious, and ordered General Ne Win and Major Aung Gyi to form Burma Territorial Force (BTF) battalions by the end of January 1949 at the latest.[20]

On 31 January 1949, a COs' conference was held for the last time under the leadership of Karen officers.[21] It was attended mostly by non-Bamar commanders. Bamar officers were blamed for the politicization of the Tatmadaw. Meanwhile, as the Karen uprising had become serious, the government decided to disarm Karen battalions. At that time, No. 1 Karen Rifles and No. 2 Karen Rifles were already in revolt and only No. 3 Karen

Rifles in Mandalay remained to be disarmed. Senior Karen commanders were given leave for an unspecified period on 1 February 1949. Karen soldiers were disarmed and detained in Army Rest Camps in Mandalay and Yangon.[22] Lieutenant General Ne Win was appointed Chief of Staff of the Tatmadaw the same day. The "Rightists", most importantly, the Karens, were removed from the Tatmadaw leadership. However, the ex-PBF officers faced serious insurgency by both Karens and Communists, and they had barely 2,000 armed personnel at hand to confront much larger forces.[23] Unity within the Tatmadaw became vital for the survival of the ex-PBF members. Nevertheless, the Tatmadaw leadership was now mostly in the hands of ex-PBF officers. They were also supported by most of the non-Karen soldiers, particularly Chin officers, from the British Burma Army.

In the post-Karen leadership, the ex-PFB officers tried to bridge the gap between officers with different organizational origins and different branches of the defence services. This job was made much easier as the remaining forces within the Tatmadaw worked hand-in-hand for their survival during the darkest hours of post-colonial Myanmar history. Gaps between Bamar, Kachin, Chin, and Shan, and gaps between the army, navy, and air force, were narrowed. Yet it was also important to prevent outside interference in the Tatmadaw in order to keep institutional unity and to prevent any further split along the lines of political loyalty, promoted by the politicians, based on patron-client relations. Furthermore, the Tatmadaw had to limit civilian interference in Tatmadaw affairs, both in internal matters and at the policy-making level, in matters such as procurement and budget allocation. At the 1950 COs' conference, held on 20 January 1950, General Ne Win opened a discussion on how to distribute ranks equally among the ex-ABRO officers, ex-PBF officers, and national minority officers. This was apparently an attempt to topple civilian interference in the promotion of some officers.[24]

The COs also complained about the wider policy decisions of the government, such as a plan to restore the road and railway between Yangon and Mandalay without prior consultation with them on proper security arrangements.[25] Besides, the ex-PBF officers felt that while they were fighting for an ideal of social revolution, struggling against destructive forces from both left and right, the politicians were deviating more and more from the promised goal of a socialist state for Myanmar. The politicians were increasingly seen as careerists and opportunists. Colonel Chit Myaing mentioned in an interview that while the military commanders were sacrificing lives for the country, the parliamentarians were drawing salaries in Yangon, without even considering how to restore law and order and local administration in the recaptured territories.[26]

The best way to keep civilians from meddling in the Tatmadaw's internal affairs and to bridge the gap between different services of the Tatmadaw was to reorganize the "War Office". In the old "War Office", navy and air force were independent of the army, and cooperation between the services was weak (see Figure 3.1). Reorganization could not only bring about a new division of labour between soldiers and civilians, but also contribute to operational efficiency. As soon as General Ne Win became the Chief of Staff, he discussed a plan to reorganize the "War Office", which was officially opened on 8 May 1948, under the Ministry of Defence and managed by a War Office Council chaired by the Defence Minister. The "War Office" had not been functioning properly. The "General Staff Office" had not been sufficiently staffed and the chain of command had been weak. General Ne Win asked the "General Staff Office" (G), the "Adjutant General Office" (A), the "Quartermaster General Office" (Q), and the Corps[27] to submit

FIGURE 3.1
The Tatmadaw Command Structure, 1948

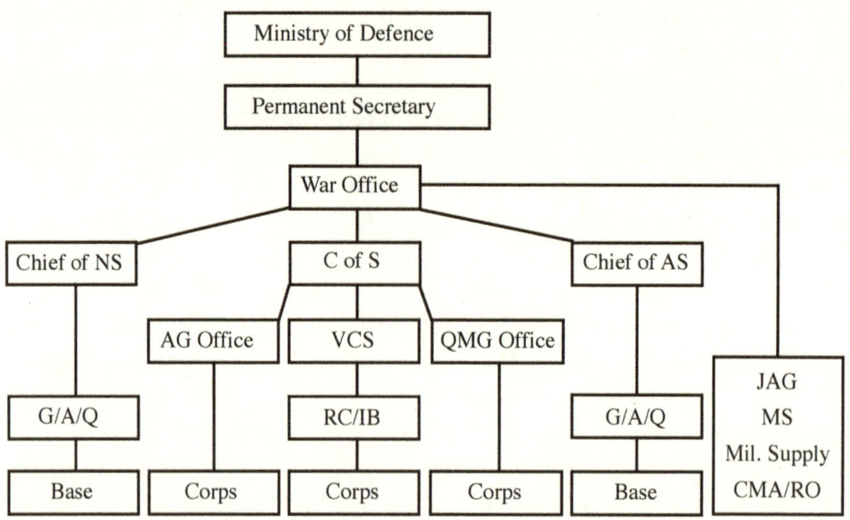

Notes:
C of S = Chief of Staff; VCS = Vice-Chief of Staff; Chief of NS = Chief of Naval Staff; Chief of AS = Chief of Air Staff; AG = Adjutant General; QMG = Quartermaster General; RC/IB = Regional Command/Infantry Brigade; CMA = Central Military Account; RO = Record Office; G/A/Q = General Staff/Adjutant/Quartermaster matters; MS = Military Secretary; JAG = Judge Advocate General.

recommendations for a new War Office set-up. On 23 May 1950, the "Plan for Reorganization of the War Office" was produced.[28] Three months later, since it was a long process and the pressure for effective military operations against both insurgents and foreign aggressors (Kuomintang or KMT) was mounting, General Ne Win issued an order to consider a new plan for the army only. He authorized Lieutenant Colonel Aung Gyi to form a Military Planning Staff (MPS) to come up with immediate recommendations.[29] On 1 September, a draft proposal for a War Office Council (Army) was ready for discussion.[30] The proposal included the transformation of the "War Office" into a Ministry of Defence, with greater financial authority and administrative power. It also suggested the formation of the "National Defence Committee", the "Executive Committee of the Defence Services Council", and the "Defence Services Councils".[31] The proposal was discussed at the 162nd Cabinet meeting held on 25 January 1952 and it was decided to establish a new War Office structure.[32] The return of Lieutenant Colonel Maung Maung (who was captured by the KNDO on 19 February 1949 and rescued by a commando unit on 21 August 1951) to the War Office as General Staff Officer Grade-I (GSO-I) for staff duty, commonly known as GSO-I (SD), on 4 October 1951, brought a new direction and new strength to the Military Planning Staff. From September 1951, Lieutenant Colonel Maung Maung was involved with the MPS.[33]

The MPS became more active and effective when U Ba Swe became Defence Minister; he was very close to ex-PBF commanders. At the second meeting of the War Office Council, held from 7 to 10 April 1952, U Ba Swe gave the green light to transforming the War Office into the Ministry of Defence. Meanwhile, Lieutenant Colonel Maung Maung was transferred to No. 1 Brigade on 26 May 1952. On 5 June, a new committee was formed with Colonel Kyaw Win (Adjutant General), Lieutenant Colonel Aung Gyi (GSO-I), U Maung Maung (Joint Secretary), and Lieutenant Commander Barbar. Missions were sent to various countries to study their War Office set-ups. Finally, on 19 September, it was decided at the Defence Services Council to transform the "War Office" into the Ministry of Defence.[34] Yet this became official only on 1 October 1956 (see Figure 3.2).

The new Ministry of Defence introduced a new division of labour. The National Defence Committee was formed with the Prime Minister as chairman, and the Ministers of Defence, Home Affairs, Foreign Affairs, and one or two other ministers as members. The Chief of Staff of the Defence Services was an advisory member. It was a sub-cabinet or a war cabinet. It was responsible for broader policy formulation. The Defence Services Council (DSC) was formed as well, with the Defence Minister as chairman, the Chief

FIGURE 3.2
The Tatmadaw Command Structure, 1958

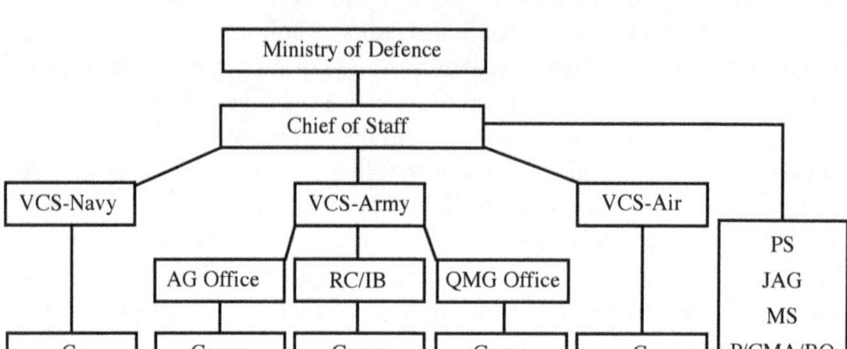

Notes:
VCS = Vice-Chief of Staff; AG = Adjutant General; QMG = Quartermaster General; PS = Permanent Secretary; JAG = Judge Advocate General; MS = Military Secretary; RC/IB = Regional Command/Infantry Brigade; CMA = Central Military Account; RO = Record Office; P = Procurement (Military Supply); G = General Staff.

of Staff of the Defence Services, the Vice-Chiefs of Staff of army, navy, and air force, the Adjutant General (AG), the Quartermaster General (QMG), the Parliamentary Secretary, and the Permanent Secretary for Defence as members. This body deals with the Tatmadaw's internal affairs. In essence, through this process the Tatmadaw leadership had greatly reduced civilian control over defence matters and brought the navy and the air force directly under the Chief of Staff. Thus, the Chief of Staff had become the most powerful person in the Tatmadaw.[35]

About the same time a marathon COs' conference was held in January and February 1950. General Ne Win brought all the field commanders and senior staff officers to the discussion table. It was the longest COs' conference in the history of the Tatmadaw. General Ne Win spoke of the lack of cooperation between the field commanders and the staff officers at the War Office. Complaints coming from the field commanders were about shortages of personnel and ammunition, and deficiencies in training and welfare. They discussed the problem of command, control, communications and intelligence (C^3I) as well.[36] These kinds of "G,A,Q" matters were not uncommon in the annual COs' conferences. In 1951, General Ne Win reminded the field commanders that the inexperienced and understaffed War Office could not manage to fulfill all the needs of the field battalions and asked for some understanding for the staff officers. He further mentioned that although shuffling appointments between field and staff officers could bring mutual understanding, this would be a cause of suffering for both.[37] The 1951 COs' conference also discussed operational efficiency and integrated the command structure of the UMP, Police Force, People's Guerrilla Forces, and other paramilitary forces. Although no details were made available, discussion also covered how to handle suspected Communists within the Tatmadaw and how to treat captured and surrendered Communists.[38]

Beginning from the 1953 COs' conference, the Prime Minister and Defence Minister were invited to address the COs. The 1954 COs' conference was held in Maymyo and, for the first time, officers from the navy and air force were also invited. General Ne Win pointed out that it was necessary to eliminate the competition among different branches of the defence services. Another important point that General Ne Win made in his speech was the need of a guiding ideology for the Tatmadaw.[39] By 1954, the ex-PBF officers were in control of both field and staff positions, and many were very much concerned about communist infiltration into the Tatmadaw. Brigadier General Kyaw Zaw was suspected of having an affiliation with the BCP and was watched by some commanders.[40] When Colonel Kyi Win captured some documents at the headquarters of the Burma Communist Party (BCP) in central Myanmar in 1956, which cast doubts and suspicion on Brigadier Kyaw Zaw, he subsequently requested the War Office to take appropriate actions. General Ne Win discussed this matter with regional and brigade commanders, including Kyaw Zaw, on 27 September 1956, during the annual COs' conference.[41] General Ne Win promptly recommended that the Defence Minister dismiss the suspected brigadier. This matter was discussed among U Ba Swe, Thakin Chit Maung, U Hla Maung, and General Ne Win. Finally, Brigadier Kyaw Zaw was dismissed in February 1957.[42] About fifty years later, Kyaw Zaw admitted that he did have contact with the BCP.[43]

By mid-1958, the ruling Anti-Fascist People's Freedom League (AFPFL) had split into two factions, "Clean AFPFL" (led by U Nu and Thakin Tin) and "Stable AFPFL" (U Ba Swe and U Kyaw Nyein). This had major repercussions in the Tatmadaw. As the "Stable" faction retained the majority of AFPFL members of parliament (MPs), the "Clean" faction wooed Nationalities MPs and the MPs from the National United Front (NUF), with offers, promises, and compromises.[44] Most of the NUF members were the aboveground Communists who were strongly suspected by the Tatmadaw of having links with the outlawed BCP. With the support of forty-four MPs from the NUF and thirty-two Nationalities MPs, the "Clean" faction remained in power for a few more months.[45] Within the Tatmadaw, many senior officers were close to leaders of the "Stable" faction. Furthermore, the Tatmadaw leadership was disappointed with the "Clean" faction's compromise with the Communists. The Tatmadaw leadership decided to take pre-emptive action, fearing that Communists, both aboveground and underground, might get an important role in future politics,[46] and also being concerned about the possibility of a coup against the Tatmadaw being raised by the "Clean" faction, using some police forces and UMP battalions.[47] This concern was apparent especially among the field commanders, who were disappointed with the way their comrades in Yangon were handling the issues.[48] Some of the commanders manoeuvred their troops and the situation became explosive. Finally, on 24 September, Colonel Aung Gyi and Colonel Maung Maung from the Ministry of Defence went to see Prime Minister U Nu and discussed the situation, hinting at the possibility of a military coup, which led to the transfer of power to the Tatmadaw. The Caretaker Government was thus formed with General Ne Win as Prime Minister on 28 October 1958. The initial mandate of six months for the Caretaker Government to maintain law and order and then to hold general elections was further extended by one more year. As a result, general elections were finally held in February 1960. However, some senior officers were found guilty of bias, in favour of the "Stable" faction, in the election. In this connection, eleven senior commanders were dismissed, forced to retire, or transferred to civilian posts in 1961.[49]

There were some other explanations offered for this move, ranging from a coup plot against General Ne Win to differences on policy matters. To some observers, it was crisis management. A strained relationship had existed between the field officers and the staff officers. The underlying cause of the problem was the rise of staff officers to prominent positions within the Tatmadaw leadership, at the expense of field commanders. The situation was further complicated by the lack of rotation between the two. Since the early 1950s, field commanders had held the view that, while they were fighting, staff officers were enjoying an easy life in the capital and controlling policy-making. No doubt, as field commanders did not have a high regard for them, staff officers tried to impress them with national-level policy-making. In fact, the new set-up for the Ministry of Defence benefited staff officers. In the period following the War Office restructure, staff officers rose to prominent positions, especially Colonel Aung Gyi and Colonel Maung Maung. The worst came when the position of the Vice-Chief of Staff (Army) was opened and filled with Colonel Aung Gyi as brigadier in April 1959, rather than with one of the field commanders. Colonel Maung Maung was also promoted to brigadier within the Ministry of Defence. As they became more and more powerful in their areas, and influential among the troops, field commanders began to challenge the staff officers. The unity of the Tatmadaw became questionable. The removal of influential field commanders in 1961 solved the problem in the short term.

The rivalry between field commanders and staff officers was finally settled in the mid-1960s through a pattern of promotions which favoured the field commanders. Without proper field service or frontline duty, an officer could not reach higher positions. One could not even become a colonel. It became more common that positions such as Vice-Chief of Staff, Adjutant General, Quartermaster General, Appointment General, and Inspector General were filled with field commanders. Even at the regional command and Light Infantry Division (LID) levels, only officers with 'G' background were promoted to senior command positions. Only GSO-I (lieutenant colonel) could become commander of Tactical Operation Command (TOC) and beyond. Promotion of ASO-I (lieutenant colonel) and QSO-I (lieutenant colonel) to command positions was extremely rare.

In building unity within the Tatmadaw, the Tatmadaw leadership took the issue of infiltration by foreign intelligence organizations into its own officer corps and ranks seriously. This resulted in the end of their military careers for most of the Myanmar military attachés.[50] To the best of my knowledge, only two military attachés have been reinstated to command positions since the 1970s. One of these was Colonel Chit Swe. He was the Myanmar military attaché in Moscow. Later, in 1978, he was promoted to commander of No. 77 LID. He became the chief of the Bureau of Special Operations-2. Another was Colonel Win Zaw Nyunt. He was the Myanmar military attaché in Tokyo. At the end of his tour of duty, he was posted as deputy commander of the Eastern Command. He was promoted to commander of No. 99 LID in August 1988. But his life as the commander was short-lived; barely five months later, he was transferred to a civilian post.

Furthermore, the Tatmadaw was also cautious about the formation of cliques within the institution and took serious action against it. The first wave of purges within the Tatmadaw since the 1962 military coup came in 1976–77. In 1976, some senior and junior officers were dismissed in connection with an alleged attempt to assassinate the leaders of the Burma Socialist Programme Party (BSPP), formed on 4 July 1962.[51] Even before the assassination or coup attempt in July 1976, the then Chief of Staff General Tin Oo was dismissed on 6 March 1976 in connection with his wife allegedly breaking the rules and regulations laid down by the BSPP for spouses of senior commanders by accepting numerous bribes. Some observers speculated that the real reason would be his increasing popularity among the rank-and-file that could have threatened Ne Win's position. Later, he was implicated for the alleged withholding of information concerning the assassination attempt and sentenced to seven years imprisonment on 11 January 1977. Again in November 1977, another five senior commanders were removed from command for the alleged formation of a clique within the Central Committee of the ruling BSPP.[52] To some observers, the purge was masterminded by the then Military Intelligence Chief Brigadier Tin Oo in the wake of declining Ne Win popularity within the BSPP. At the third party congress held in February 1977, according to some observers, Ne Win's ranking fell from first to third and he was very angry; therefore, Tin Oo immediately looked into the matter and began to restore Ne Win's undisputed chairmanship. Hence, a purge was carried out in November by convening an emergency session of the BSPP congress.

The second wave of purges came in 1983. This could be traced back to the late 1960s, particularly to the rise of Colonel Tin Oo (known as MI Tin Oo). As the director of the Directorate of Defence Services Intelligence (DDSI) was merely a colonel, the Office of Military Assistance to the Chairman of the State Council was opened within the Ministry of Defence on 12 August 1974, with the rank of brigadier.[53] Colonel Tin Oo was promoted to this position. According to some sources, since 1981, soon after U Ne Win decided to give up the presidency, Brigadier Tin Oo, who became Joint-Secretary of the BSPP, started building his own power base, using the intelligence apparatus (of which he was in charge for more than a decade). As a result, a line of division appeared among the senior field commanders and intelligence officers. The situation became apparent when the Vice-Chief of Staff (Army) post was vacant in late 1981. Several rounds of negotiations produced no agreement. Finally, at the intervention of U Ne Win, the deadlock was resolved by appointing Major General Tun Yi, representing field commanders, as Vice-Chief of Staff (Army) and Major General Tin Sein, representing the intelligence officers, as Deputy Defence Minister. Despite this settlement, the situation had worsened and the unity of the Tatmadaw was in danger. Finally, the whole intelligence clique was purged in early 1983. Those with the rank of major and above within the intelligence set-up were forced to retire, those with the rank of captain and below were transferred to the infantry, and a very few junior officers were kept on to maintain the office. The purge was not without a price. There was series of security failures and the most prominent case was the bombing of Martyr Mausoleum in Yangon by Korean agents during the state visit of South Korean President Chan Doo Hwan on 9 October 1983. Later, a new batch of field officers was brought in to take over the intelligence apparatus. In this way, unity within the Tatmadaw was restored by the mid-1980s. The third wave of purge came in 2004 and I will discuss it in some detail later.

Another aspect of building unity within the Tatmadaw was ideological or political indoctrination. The growth of communist revolutionary warfare and a general fear of communism helped develop in the Tatmadaw what Alfred Stepan would call the "New Professionalism" in its approach in counter-insurgency operations.[54] Beginning from 1951, the Tatmadaw had been considering the expansion of its role beyond the traditional domain of defending the country from external aggression and the newly acquired role of suppressing insurgency. It had placed great emphasis on socio-economic development of the country. At the 1952 COs' conference, the COs discussed economic development planning, democratization of local administration, health and education services, land reform, agricultural productivity, and transportation and communication. Many of these discussions embraced the socio-economic development of rural society.[55] Colonel Saw Myint noted that the Tatmadaw needed to consider all these aspects as communist propaganda was very appealing to villagers.[56] The Tatmadaw leadership argued that it was necessary to arm itself with ideological weapons, not only to defeat communist insurgency, but also to prevent the infiltration of Communists into the Tatmadaw. The lack of capacity to carry out socio-economic programmes led the Tatmadaw to develop an ideology and institutions to train its officers. The Tatmadaw's ideology was based largely on Buddhism, Nationalism, and Marxism. Since Marxism had emerged as an important part of nation building in Myanmar after the Japanese Occupation (1942–45), the Tatmadaw embraced it.[57] This was, in fact, one of the very important factors that contributed to the prolonged dominance of the Tatmadaw in the politics of Myanmar. In early 1960s, there were strong indications that the Tatmadaw leadership believed that a Marxist or Socialist-oriented regime was a historical necessity in Myanmar. With some Marxist elements at the core of the Burmese Way to Socialism, the Tatmadaw was able to neutralize the aboveground leftist political forces, draw support from prominent leftist leaders, and, in their view, project itself as a revolutionary force that could fulfill the socialist wishes of post-colonial Myanmar; thus, its political role was justified both within and outside the Tatmadaw.

According to the Tatmadaw, there have been eight stages in its ideological development up until now. The first two stages are regarded as pre-ideological. The first stage roughly covered the period of the Burma Independence Army and the Burma Defence Army (1941–43), during which national independence and political freedom were major objectives. The second stage began with the formation of the AFPFL and ended with independence (1944–48). During this period, the Tatmadaw's ideological formulation was based on the attainment of national independence, the establishment of a democratic state, and the implementation of socialism. The third and fourth stages were periods of rethinking and reassessing national ideology. The Tatmadaw defined the third stage (1948–55) as the "period of ideological gestation", and the fourth stage (1956–57) as the "period of thorough study and discussion of the ideology for the defence services". The statement issued at the 1959 COs' conference outlined that:

> Ever since their Conference of 1956 the Commanding Officers in the Defence Services have all thoroughly studied and discussed the National Ideology which must be the ever-fixed guiding star of the Defence Services.[58]

In accordance with the decision of the 1956 COs' conference, U Saw Oo and U Chit Hlaing, two prominent ideologists with leftist orientation, were appointed to the Department of Education and Psychological Warfare to study and formulate the Tatmadaw's ideology. These two persons were the masterminds of declarations of the Takmadaw, such as "The National Ideology and the Role of the Defence Services" and "The Burmese Way to Socialism" (BWS).

The fifth stage of ideological development came with the declaration of "The National Ideology and Our Pledge" at the Meiktila COs' conference held on 21 October 1958. The Tatmadaw called it the "first phase of ideological development". The document was heavily influenced by socialist ideology. This was the first time the Tatmadaw in the post-independence period had an ideological orientation to legitimize its political role. A year later, at the 1959 COs' conference, the sixth stage of ideological development (or the second phase, according to the defence services) was inaugurated with a statement titled "The National Ideology and the Role of the Defence Services". This document, in which the military attempted to project its image as an important political institution, stated major socio-political objectives. The seventh stage of ideological development culminated in the Tatmadaw's endorsement of "The Burmese Way to Socialism". In the face of what the Tatmadaw leadership believed to be the disintegration of the union, the Tatmadaw raised a military coup on 2 March 1962 and formed the Revolutionary Council. Within a couple of months, it declared a nation building programme, known as "The Burmese Way to Socialism". The 1962 COs' conference was fully occupied with the discussion of the BWS. Finally, the document was signed and approved by the commanding officers present at the conference. It was later released to the public.

With the formation of the Revolutionary Council in March 1962, the Tatmadaw's position was changed from "Praetorian Army" to "Revolutionary Army". In the period between 1962 and 1988, the Tatmadaw had been the backbone of the socialist revolution led by the Burma Socialist Programme Party. During these years, following the military coup in 1962, the Tatmadaw's role and attitude was to build a socialist society with a socialist economic system in Myanmar.[59] However, after the Revolutionary Council's rule came to an end, the Tatmadaw's role was restricted to acting under the leadership of the BSPP and it was governed by the party. Nevertheless, the Tatmadaw was portrayed in the media, throughout this period, as the backbone of the social revolution in Myanmar. The terms "under the leadership of the Burma Socialist Programme Party", "in accordance with the guidance of the different levels of People's Council", and "with the cooperation of the People's Armed Forces" (Tatmadaw) were heard frequently in the daily lives of Myanmar's people during the period from 1974 to 1988. After the fall of the socialist regime, followed by a series of anti-government demonstrations in 1988, the Tatmadaw changed its role and attitude to ensuring the "non-disintegration of the union, non-disintegration of unity, and perpetuation of national sovereignty". This is the eighth stage of its ideological development. It is claimed by the Tatmadaw that these three objectives have been with the institution ever since the days of its formation.

One of the organizations that helped institutionalize the Tatmadaw's ideology was the National Defence College. The college was designed to train both military personnel and civilians to perform duties consistent with the national interest and the changing international political, security, and economic environment. Although the college was founded in early 1955 within the Southern Command, it was not formalized until 24 November 1958. A pilot course was opened for twenty-nine senior officers in August 1957. The course included the Tatmadaw's ideology, socio-economic programmes, and military doctrine. A regular course at the college was designed for an academic year and there were also some short-term courses and refresher courses. Various ministers and heads of government departments also lectured the trainees on their respective functions. However, after the military coup in 1962, more institutions were introduced to indoctrinate both civil servants and military personnel. The most important institution was the "Central Institute of Political Science" (CIPS) run by the BSPP. Others were the training centres at the various regional military commands.

To have a correct ideological orientation and clear political outlook, the BSPP claimed, every Tatmadaw member must study the "System of Correlation of Man and His Environment", the party's official ideology. Tatmadaw personnel were sent to ideological orientation courses [(တပ်တွင်းပညာပေး) *Tattwin Pyinnyapay*] at both the Regional Command Training Centres and the CIPS. These discussion sessions [(တပ်တွင်းဆွေးနွေးပွဲ) *Tattwin Swe-nwe-pwe*] were organized once a month at the battalion level and once a week at the company, platoon, and section levels. The discussion was based largely on the articles appearing in the "Journal of Ideology" [(သဘောတရားရေးရာစာစောင်) *Tabawtayaryeya Sarsaung*], the "Lanzin Journal" [(လမ်းစဉ်သတင်းဂျာနယ်) *Lanzin Thatin Journal*], and the "Pyithu Tatmadaw Journal" [(ပြည်သူ့တပ်မတော်စာစဉ်) *Pyithu Tatmadaw Sarsin*].[60]

In the period following the 1962 military coup, the BSPP developed a new model for civil-military relations. Although the model was similar to that of the Communists, the BSPP did not create the post of political commissar.[61] This relationship became clearer in the post-1974 period, when the Revolutionary Council transferred power to the BSPP. The Tatmadaw was fully politicized and every officer had to be a member of the BSPP. The BSPP had the Tatmadaw Party Committee, which was formed with three to seven Central Committee members. The Tatmadaw Party Committee organized the Tatmadaw Organizing Committee with five to seven members, who were appointed by the Party's Central Committee. The Tatmadaw Organizing Committees were formed at various levels, ranging from Ministry of Defence down to battalion and unit level, such as military hospitals.[62] The COs were usually full-fledged party members. They were the chairmen of the Party Organizing Committees of the respective battalions and units. However, they were subordinate to the chairmen of the "Township Party Units", about which they were not happy. However, after the 1985 general election, more military officers were appointed as chairmen of Township Party Units.

Despite these efforts to convince Tatmadaw personnel that they were revolutionaries, many junior officers in the 1980s felt uneasy about the "revolution". But they refrained from open criticism, as their career advancement would then be in jeopardy. For senior officers, such as those with the rank of colonel and above, the BSPP had developed a system of opportunities through patronage, which created an avenue to prominent positions within the Tatmadaw and the government, and allowed access to sacred resources. Gaining access to this Soviet-style *nomenklatura*,[63] or what Djilas would call "a new class",[64] ensured the loyalty of the Tatmadaw personnel to the ruling party[65] and prevented splits within the Tatmadaw. As a result, the officer corps was united behind its Chief of Staff and was loyal to the BSPP to the very last moment in the political chaos of 1988. Even the military coup against the BSPP was raised only after the BSPP permitted the Tatmadaw members to withdraw their party membership. The socialist era was ended by the coup raised on 18 September 1988. In essence, the convergence of the Tatmadaw's ideological orientation with nation building in Myanmar, as well as the projection of the image of being the backbone of the social revolution, were major factors that contributed to the dominance of the Tatmadaw in Myanmar politics.

In the post-1988 period, analysts of Tatmadaw affairs have focused on two themes. One is the possibility of a split between intelligence officers and field commanders. The other is the split between the two different schools of military training. Andrew Selth, a Myanmar specialist, wrote:

> There have also been persistent reports of suspicion and rivalry between the graduates of Burma's prestigious Defence Services Academy (DSA) at Maymyo and the Officer Training School (OTS) at Hmawbi. There has always been a degree of competition, but in Burma these differences were made much worse by the 1976 plot against Ne Win. Although led by a OTS graduate, this plot was seen to have sprung from members of a particular DSA class. For a long time this view led to a reluctance by the Tatmadaw leadership to appoint DSA graduates to senior positions. As veteran Burma watcher Bertil Lintner has pointed out, this discrimination was something which itself led to further tensions within the Burma Army officer corps, as one career stream was seen to be given priority for promotions over the other.[66]

In order to understand the officer corps of the Tatmadaw, we need to look at the share of graduates from different training schools in the officer corps. This will help show whether or not there is a split between the OTS and DSA officers. An important point missing in the writing of scholars on Myanmar is the ratio between the two. In 1959 and 1960, out of 805 commissioned officers (excluding Young Officer Course — YOC officers, medical officers, nursing officers and Long Service Commissioned officers), only sixty-five were from the DSA. It was about a 1:11 ratio or eight per cent of the officers. It was the same ratio in 1965.[67] If we count the ratio of officers between the two schools, DSA officers are over-represented in the command and general staff positions. In 1988, among the nineteen members of the SLORC, three officers were from the DSA. If we consider only army officers, the DSA officers shared eighteen per cent of the SLORC. When the SLORC was reorganized and named State Peace and Development Council (SPDC), DSA graduates shared almost fifty per cent of the SPDC membership.[68] The evidence is abundantly clear that there is no discrimination against the DSA graduates in promotion.[69] In fact, among 164 senior commanders appointed between September 1988 and February 2008, 107 were from the DSA, 45 from the OTS, and the rest 12 from Teza (officers with different training background) (see Figure 3.3).[70]

FIGURE 3.3
Division Commanders and their Training Backgrounds (September 1988–February 2008)

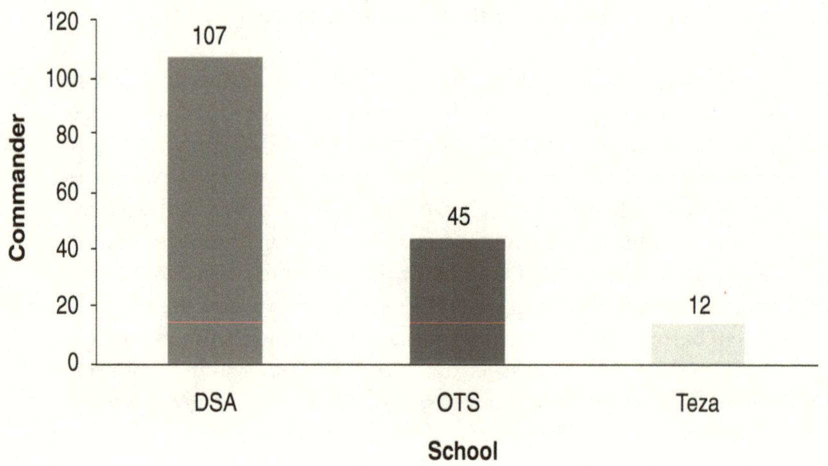

Even if we look at the training school background among division level commanders in recent years (see Figure 3.4), one can find a fair distribution of officers, considering the number of recruitments, age limitation, and survival rate.

Another area of discussion on the Tatmadaw in the post-1988 period is the split between intelligence officers and field commanders. In the early 1990s, several news reports appeared in the foreign media about the rise of intelligence officers and the conflict between intelligence officers and field commanders. In late 1992 and early 1993, Myanmar analysts watched closely to see who was going to take the second-to-top job, Commander-in-Chief of Defence Services cum Commander-in-Chief (Army) — either Lieutenant General Maung Aye or Lieutenant General Khin Nyunt. The post was vacant for five months and finally Lieutenant General Maung

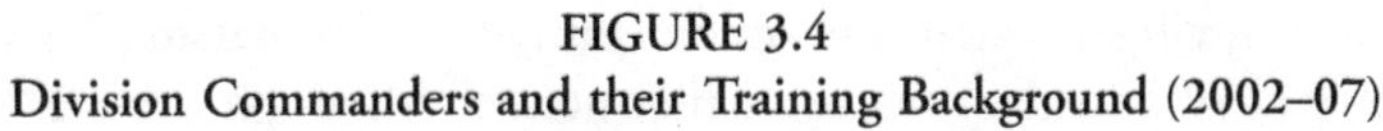

FIGURE 3.4
Division Commanders and their Training Background (2002–07)

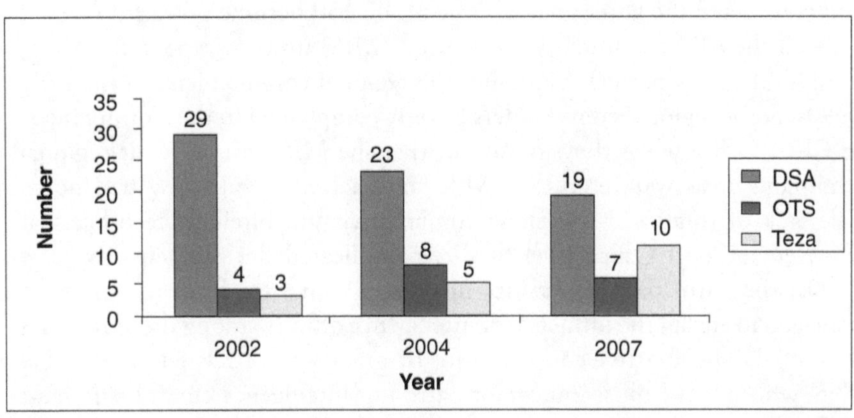

Aye was promoted and appointed, keeping the tradition of favouring field commanders. For Lieutenant General Khin Nyunt, the Office of Strategic Studies (OSS) was created.[71] In the Tatmadaw command structure, the OSS chief ranks fifth, after the Commander-in-Chief (C-in-C) of the Defence Services, the Deputy C-in-C of the Defence Services cum C-in-C (Army), C-in-C (Navy) and C-in-C (Air Force). The OSS is known as a military think-tank. Many foreign analysts see Chief of Staff Lieutenant General Tin Oo following Commander-in-Chief General Maung Aye during tours as a sign of alliance against the OSS chief. What they do not realize is that, being the Chief of Staff cum Chief of Bureau of Special Operations (BSO), Lieutenant General Tin Oo is responsible for overseeing the troops and he has to answer to the Commander-in-Chief (Army). This is clear from the command structure. It is a common arrangement that the Chief of Staff is responsible for "G" matters, the AG is responsible for "A" matters and the QMG is responsible for "Q" matters. Commanders of regional command HQs, LIDs, Military Operation Commands (MOCs) and Regional Operation Commands (ROCs) are loyal to all their superiors and there is little evidence of alliances against others within the Tatmadaw. The infantry-intelligence tension, however, did not lead to an open split in the Tatmadaw. The appointment of Colonel Kyaw Win [later Major General], the right hand man of Senior General Than Shwe, as the deputy director of intelligence in 1995 was the beginning of the long process of resolving the infantry-intelligence tension which centred on the personality of the intelligence chief and the institutional structure. Although the DDSI was theoretically under the General Staff Office, the former acted independently and considered the latter its rival. The DDSI had become powerful when it ordered the Military Intelligence Section (MIS) units to report directly to the DDSI Headquarters, bypassing the regional commanders, in the early 1990s. Some regional commanders bitterly complained to the Commander-in-Chief Office when they found out that the MIS units in their regional command areas were equipped with fax machines while they had none. The lack of rotation between senior infantry and intelligence officers at the General Staff Office level further complicated the problem. By early 2000s, the Tatmadaw leadership, most of whom were from the infantry, managed to curtail the influence of intelligence officers among the Tatmadaw personnel. The abortive coup attempt by grandsons of retired General Ne Win, who was the most important patron of intelligence chief, Lieutenant General Khin Nyunt, marked the beginning of the end of the intelligence faction. By the early 2004, to further marginalize General Khin Nyunt and his intelligence officers, the Tatmadaw leadership forced General Khin Nyunt to give up his position as chief of intelligence. Although he did not seem to be pleased with the idea, he agreed to give up the position by the end of 2004. Having realized that he would be marginalized from the command structure, General Khin Nyunt began to raise his profile by engaging in public relations activities. In international media, General Khin Nyunt was increasingly projected as a reformer or softliner; senior infantry commanders were offended by this portrayal of General Khin Nyunt as a softliner and Senior General Than Shwe as a hardliner. Moreover, the repeated contention by the diplomatic community and some scholars that General Khin Nyunt was "the wise guy" in the regime had seriously undermined his position within the regime. For example, a scholar on Myanmar, David Steinberg, reportedly portrayed General Khin Nyunt as "*the person* in the top tier of the junta with knowledge of and exposure to international affairs and information"[72] or "*the senior guy* who did know what was going on in the world".[73] Of course this is not true; the Army has its own research unit and senior commanders did receive reports on various international issues several times a day. His failure to share whatever credits he gained in public relations or to defend other top leaders in the regime had alienated Senior General Than Shwe and Vice Senior General Maung Aye. General Khin Nyunt never came out to publicly state that the policies and programmes that he had been implementing were that of the regime or with the blessing of the top leadership; this, in the view of some senior commanders, violate the principle of collective leadership and collective responsibility. Moreover, the DDSI officers were widely known for corruption and abuse of power, even threatening their fellow officers in infantry. Senior infantry commanders resented the lack of respect even from junior intelligence officers, violating the military code of conduct. A captain in the intelligence corps never cared about a colonel in the infantry. The commanding officer of local intelligent battalion, a major, behaved as if he was of equal power as the regional commander, a major-general, in that region. By early 2004, the top leadership in the Army was thoroughly convinced that they had to do something to resolve this infantry-intelligence tension at all levels of the command structure. When Senior General Than Shwe asked General Khin Nyunt to relinquish his position as Chief of DSIB in early 2004, many officers in the Tatmadaw realized that the days of the intelligence officers were numbered. Meanwhile, Senior General Than Shwe was angry over General Khin Nyunt's insubordination as the latter refused to take disciplinary action against corrupted intelligence officers being investigated and found guilty by Inspector General Office; this had effectively led to the dramatic fall of General Khin Nyunt and the intelligence corps.[74] Finally, on 19 October 2004, General Khin Nyunt was arrested, and since then the entire intelligence corps was purged and reorganized; it was the third wave of purge in the history of the Tatmadaw. Now, the Military Affairs Security (MAS), the successor of DDSI, is firmly under the General Staff Office and the Chief of Staff. Unlike its predecessors, now the chief of MAS comes from among regional commanders and with a one-step higher promotion, from major general to lieutenant general. Moreover, at the regional command level, the MIS units are under the direct control of the regional commander through the GSO-I (Intelligence). The new appointment system and structural adjustment are clearly designed to address the infantry-intelligence tension.

Another topic for discussion in connection with the unity of the Tatmadaw since 1988 is the relations between senior commanders in Yangon and powerful regional commanders. As a result of insurgencies, the regional commanders were given a wide range of powers for military mobilization. In the pre-1988 coup period, although regional commanders were chairmen of their regional party committees, they were subjected to various party committees at the central level, such as party discipline and organizing committees, and other organs of the state, such as council of state, council of ministers, council of justice, and council of attorneys. These bodies had some form of restraint on military authority. Although the regional commanders were chairmen of their respective party regional committees, their ranking within the party hierarchy was not in the influential circle. In those days, regional commanders were usually promoted to be ministers and members of various state organs.

The coup on 18 September 1988 changed the political status of the regional commanders and displaced the "checks and balances" system. From being one of the members of the party central committee, a regional commander became a member of the SLORC, the highest state organ made up of nineteen senior commanders. This generated far-reaching consequences for the Tatmadaw leadership. For the first time since 1974, the regional commanders enjoyed enormous power: they became supreme authorities in their respective regions. Economic power further supplemented the political and military power of regional commanders. In the early years of the SLORC rule, about three years, due to the incapacity of central authorities — ministers in this case — to oversee and supervise industries and offices in the area outside Yangon, some of the ministries rendered their authority to the regional commanders. Regional commanders were authorized to run government factories and stores, in their respective command areas.[75] They could also make use of state resources under their control as they saw fit, such as building hotels or watch towers. This decentralization of political, military, and economic power into the hands of regional commanders gave them immense power. Thus, regional commands became somewhat like autonomous regions.

Nevertheless, power was recentralized in Yangon in 1992 when all the regional commanders (of 1988), except one, were posted to Yangon as cabinet ministers. First, on 5 March 1992, Major General Myint Aung from the Southwest Command was promoted to Adjutant General at the Ministry of Defence. He was concurrently appointed as Minister for Agriculture. On the same day, Major General Mya Thin from Western command was transferred to Yangon and appointed Minister for Cooperatives. On 20 March, Major General Myo Nyunt from Yangon Command became Minister for Religious Affairs. In the meantime, on 23 April 1992, Senior General Saw Maung was replaced with General Than Shwe as commander-in-chief. This move was allegedly masterminded by U Ne Win and carried out by Major General Khin Nyunt, the then DDSI chief. In this move, Major General Khin Nyunt, being a key player, strengthened his position significantly. As a protégé of U Ne Win, he came out as the most influential figure in the regime; but, he was aware that regional commanders posed serious challenges to his position. Since 1989, some regional commanders had been unhappy with Major General Khin Nyunt and his DDSI units; they bitterly complained about his arrogance. General Than Shwe also appeared not to be happy with Major General Khin Nyunt's arrogance and spectacular rise, but he was helpless to do anything at that time; therefore, his position was to stay above the factional struggle between some regional commanders and Major General Khin Nyunt. At the same time, General Than Shwe also realized that regional commanders were too powerful, but he needed them, for the time being, to balance Major General Khin Nyunt. By then, some regional commanders were notoriously corrupted. It was now time for Major General Khin Nyunt to remove these commanders from their power bases and to marginalize them from the command structure by appointing ministerial posts. Apparently with the approval of General Than Shwe, by October 1992, other regional commanders, except Major General Maung Aye from Eastern Command, were brought to Yangon as ministers. Major General Myo Nyunt from the Yangon Command was another exception, but he was insignificant as he once told his colleagues that the Yangon commander was merely a *Pyar-Tar* [(ပြာတာ) peon] while other regional commanders were *Yar-Zar* [(ရာဇာ) king]. Some observers believed that there were some forms of manoeuvre by Major General Khin Nyunt in this promotion exercise. First, with the exception of Major General Myint Aung, who was officially entitled to the rank of lieutenant general, all regional commanders received honorary promotions as lieutenant generals with no official positions within the Defence Ministry. Both Major General Maung Aye and Major General Myo Nyunt were promoted too as lieutenant generals, though their positions as regional commanders were just for major generals. Major General Khin Nyunt also received a lieutenant general promotion as chief of OSS. Second, as insisted by senior commanders at the Ministry of Defence and some regional commanders, Major General Khin Nyunt had to accept that Major General Maung Aye remained as regional commander and within the command structure, but the position of Deputy Commander-in-Chief of Defence Services cum Commander-in-Chief of Army was to be left vacant (for about five months). Lieutenant General Maung Aye was finally appointed as Deputy Commander-in-Chief of Defence Services cum Commander-in-Chief of Army on 27 March 1993.

After their appointment as ministers, some regional commanders brought their close associates and colleagues to their ministries. Thus, for example, the Ministry of Agriculture was nicknamed "Ministry of Southwest Command" and "Ministry of Trade", "Ministry of Central Command". The ministerial appointments had weakened their authority and influence in their former regional command areas. Lack of coordination among various ministries became apparent as former regional commanders acted independently; hence, ministers became Chief Executive Officers (CEOs) of corporate giants. They built up their economic power bases with their own cronies. Meanwhile, Lieutenant General Maung Aye was promoted as the Deputy Commander-in-

Chief of Defence Services cum Commander-in-Chief of Army, in line with the tradition of giving the position to an infantry commander. At the Ministry of Defence, when the Vice-Adjutant General position became vacant, Lieutenant General Khin Nyunt manoeuvred to place his protégé Colonel Than Tun, deputy director of DDSI, in that post to counterbalance Lieutenant General Myint Aung, former regional commander, who still remained in the command structure as Adjutant General. But he had to accept the appointment of Colonel Kyaw Win, a protégé of Senior General Than Shwe, as his deputy director of DDSI. Nevertheless, a new "checks and balances" system was restored for the regional commanders in late 1992, as the SLORC and the cabinet were above their authority in the new line-up; new regional commanders appointed in late 1992 were not members of SLORC, and they were relatively junior.

After nearly five years in ministerial positions, the former regional commanders-turned-ministers had lost connection with their former command areas and power bases. In addition, some of them were notoriously corrupt. Senior General Than Shwe finally decided to take action. On 15 November 1997, the SLORC was transformed to the State Peace and Development Council (SPDC), bringing new blood to the leadership circle.[76] Former members of the SLORC, except the chairman, vice-chairman, secretary 1, secretary 2, and the two deputy prime ministers, were made members of the "Advisory Group" of the SPDC.[77] This body was abolished on 5 June 1998.[78] Moreover, all the members of the advisory group were forced to relinquish their commissions on 1 June 1998. An inquiry commission was formed under the National Intelligence Bureau to investigate bribery and corruption acts committed by some former SLORC members. To scrutinize the findings of the National Intelligence Bureau and submit a report with recommendations to the government, a committee was formed with a minister and two deputy ministers.[79] However, no further details have been released to the public.

Since 1992, with a few exceptions, there have been five waves of appointments for regional military commanders in the Tatmadaw. They were in October 1992, June 1995, November 1997, December 2001, and May 2006. Although some regional commanders had been in their command positions for about five or six years, there is little evidence that they built up power bases to challenge the central authority. Even the sacking of two regional commanders and the commander-in-chief of the air force in March 2002, in connection with the alleged coup attempt hatched by the family members of U Ne Win, was hardly based on any concrete evidence of a challenge to the Tatmadaw leadership.

With regard to inter-services rivalry among the senior commanders of the army, navy, and air force, this matter had been resolved by the mid-1960s as the commanders-in-chief of the navy and air force at the time more or less shared the same organizational background as their army counterparts. Brigadier General Thaung Dan, who became Chief of Staff (Air Force) in the mid-1960s, was one of the graduates from the wartime Military Academy sent to Japan for pilot training. Commodore Thaung Tin was, who became Chief of Staff (Navy) in the mid-1960s, was also a close comrade of army commanders. Moreover, the separate recruitment of officer cadets for the navy and air force stopped by the early 1970s. Since then almost all navy and air force officers came from the DSA where they studied together with army cadets.

Thus, building organizational unity within the Tatmadaw has been a continuous process and the present and future Tatmadaw leadership will take all necessary measures to prevent the Tatmadaw being subjected to open split and disintegration.

FORCE STRUCTURE

Commander-in-Chief Office

At the time of the independence, the War Office was the centre of all command for the army, navy, and air force. At the head of the War Office were Chief of Staff, Vice-Chief of Staff, Chief of Naval Staff, Chief of Air Staff, Adjutant General, and Quartermaster General. The Vice-Chief of Staff, [the position was vacant for nearly ten years until 9 April 1959], who was practically the chief of army staff and the head of the General Staff Office, was to oversee general staff matters and there were three branch offices: GS-1 Operation and Training; GS-2 Staff Duty and Planning; and GS-3 Intelligence. Moreover, Signal Corps and Field Engineering Corps were also within the domain of the General Staff Office. At the time of independence, according to the war establishment adopted on 14 April 1948, there was the Chief of Staff Office under the War Office. The Chief of Staff was a major general; it was subsequently upgraded to a lieutenant general. Vice-Chief of Staff was a Brigadier General. The Chief of Staff Office was staffed with one GSO-I with the rank of lieutenant colonel, three GSO-IIs with the rank of major, four G-IIIs with the rank of captain (for operation, training, planning, intelligence), and one Intelligence Officer (IO). The Chief of Staff Office also had one GSO-II and one GSO-III for field engineering, and the Chief Signal Officer and a GSO-II for signal. The Directorate of Signal and the Directorate of Field Engineering were under the General Staff Office. Under the Adjutant General Office were the Judge Advocate General, Military Secretary, and Vice-Adjutant General. The Adjutant General (AG) was a brigadier general whereas the Judge Advocate General (JAG), Military Secretary (MS), and Vice-Adjutant General (VAG) were colonels. The Vice-Adjutant General handled adjutant staff matters and there were also three branch offices: AG-1 planning, recruitment and transfer; AG-2 discipline, moral, welfare, and education; and AG-3 salary, pension, and other financial matters. The Medical Corps and the Provost Marshall Office were under the Adjutant General Office. The Quartermaster General Office also had three branch offices: QG-1 planning, procurement, and budget; QG-2 maintenance, construction, and cantonment; and QG-3 transportation. Under the QMG office were Garrison Engineering Corps, Electrical and Mechanical Engineering Corps, Military Ordnance Corps, and the Supply and Transport Corps. Both the AG Office and QMG Office had a similar structure to the General Staff Office, but they only had three Adjutant Staff Officers Grade-III (ASO-III) and three Quartermaster Staff Officers Grade-III (QSO-III) respectively. The navy and air force were separate services under the War Office, but under the Chief of Staff. However, the Directorate of Military Supplies was a separate department under the Permanent Secretary of the Ministry of Defence, not under the War Office. When the War Office was reorganized into the Ministry of Defence in 1952, the Commander-in-Chief was the chief over all three services: army, navy, and air force. Under the Ministry of Defence were the Commander-in-Chief Office, the Adjutant General Office, the Quartermaster General Office, the Military Secretary Office, the Judge Advocate General Office, the Permanent Secretary Office, and the Military Account Office. Under the Commander-in-Chief were three Deputy Commanders-in-Chief for the three services. This core structure remained relatively unchanged up to the present (see Figures 3.1 and 3.2). By the mid-1950s, the Commander-in-Chief position was upgraded to the rank of general. But the Deputy Commanders-in-Chief for all three services remained brigadier general or commodore. Directors of various corps were colonels. In the meantime, the Directorate of Defence Services Intelligence (DDSI) and the Directorate of Military Training (DMT) were formed in 1956 and they were placed under the General Staff Office.

When the Commander-in-Chief Office was reorganized in January 1963, there were two branches [Staff Duty and Operation] and four directorates [Intelligence, Signal, Training, and Field Engineering]. In October 1969 two more branches were added to the General Staff Office: Planning and Research. While the directors were colonels, heads of the branches were lieutenant colonels with GSO-I positions. The Colonel General Staff (Colonel GS) position was created within the Commander-in-Chief Office. In 1971, the Directorate of Ordnance was transferred from the QMG office to the General Staff Office. By 1972, the Commander-in-Chief and three Deputy Commanders-in-Chief positions were renamed Chief of Staff and Vice-Chiefs of Staff. The Vice-Chief of Staff positions were upgraded to the rank of major general in 1978. Vice-Chiefs of Staff for the navy and air force were also upgraded to rear admiral and major general. About the same time, on 27 December 1978, the Adjutant General was upgraded from brigadier general to major general, and the Military Appointment General and Judge Advocate General, from colonel to brigadier general. The next day, the Quartermaster General was upgraded from brigadier general to major general, and the Inspector General, from colonel to brigadier general.

At the top level, although the Chief of Staff post remained a general, the Vice-Chief of Staff (Army) was upgraded from major general to lieutenant general on 12 March 1981. By 1990, the Chief of Staff was upgraded to Commander-in-Chief of Defence Services with the rank of senior general and the position of Vice-Chief of Staff (Army) was upgraded to Deputy Commander-in-Chief of Defence Services cum Commander-in-Chief (Army) with the rank of general. Vice-Chief of Staff (Navy) and Vice-Chief of Staff (Air Force) became Commander-in-Chief (Navy) and Commander-in-Chief (Air Force). Chief of Staff positions were opened up for the three services with the rank of major general. AG and QMG were also upgraded to lieutenant general. Before 1988, the Light Infantry Divisions were directly answerable to the Colonel General Staff (Army); but since 1990 they under the Chief of Staff (Army). At the same time, the Colonel GS position was upgraded to Brigadier General Staff. Moreover, the Military Appointment General (MAG), the Military Inspector General (MIG), and the Judge Advocate General (JAG) were also raised to the rank of major general. Directors of corps, such as Signal, Supply and Transport, Ordnance, and so on, were upgraded to brigadier general, too, in 1990. (For details of command structure, see Figures 3.9 and 3.10.)

Meanwhile, for operational efficiency, two "Bureaus of Special Operations" (BSOs) were introduced under the General Staff Office on 28 April 1978 and 1 June 1979. In early 1978, U Ne Win visited the Northeast Command in Lashio to receive a briefing about the BCP military operations. He was accompanied by Brigadier General Tun Ye. At that time, Brigadier Tun Ye having been posted since November 1977 to the Ministry of Defence without given a proper command position. But he was the regional commander of Eastern Command for three years and, before that, he served in the Northeast

Command areas as commander of Strategic Operation Command and Light Infantry Division for nearly four years. As the BCP operated in three command areas (Northern, Eastern and Northeast), Brigadier General Tun Ye, at that time, was the most informed commander about the BCP (northeast region) in the Tatmadaw. At the briefing, U Ne Win was impressed by Brigadier General Tun Ye, and later realized that coordination among various regional commands was necessary; thus, he decided to form a bureau at the Ministry of Defence. Originally, the bureau was for "special operations", wherever they were, that needed coordination among various regional commands. Later, with an introduction of another bureau, there was a division of command areas. The BSO-1 was to oversee operations under the Northern Command, the Northeast Command, the Eastern Command, and the Northwest Command, and the BSO-2 was to oversee operations under the Southeast Command, the Southwest Command, the Western Command, and the Central Command. Initially, the chief of the BSO had the rank of brigadier general. Then, it was upgraded to the rank of a major general on 23 April 1979. In 1990, it was further upgraded to a lieutenant general. Between 1995 and 2002, Chief of Staff (Army) jointly held the position of BSO. However, in early 2002, two more BSOs were added to the General Staff Office; therefore, there were altogether four BSOs. Then the fifth bureau was established in 2005 and the sixth in 2007. Since 2002, chiefs of the BSOs were assigned to oversee the development projects and supervise ministerial coordination just like deputy prime ministers do. See Table 3.1.

With the expansion of armed forces and function, the Ministry of Defence was expanded accordingly. Thus, new functions were introduced and new directorates were opened. Some directorates were reorganized into separate directorates. Some were upgraded. New functions included cyber warfare

TABLE 3.1
Bureau of Special Operations, 2008

Sr.	*BSO*	*Commands*
1	BSO-1	Northern Command, Central Command, Northwest Command (– Magway Division)
2	BSO-2	Northeast Command, Eastern Command, Triangle Region Command
3	BSO-3	Southwest Command, Southern Command
4	BSO-4	Southeast Command, Coastal Region Command
5	BSO-5	Yangon Command
6	BSO-6	Western Command (+ Magway Division)

and organizational activities. The new Office of the Strategic Studies (OSS) was opened and it oversaw the DDSI. The chief of the OSS cum the DDSI was a lieutenant general. Then the OSS and the DDSI were integrated into the Defence Services Intelligence Bureau (DSIB) in 2002. The Directorate of Military Training (DMT) and Directorate of Defence Services Intelligence (DDSI) were reorganized and upgraded. The Directorate of Military Training became the Chief of Armed Forces Training Office (CAFTO) and its chief was a major general. A new command structure was introduced at the Ministry of Defence level in 2002. Several new positions were created to accommodate former regional commanders promoted to the rank of Lieutenant General. The most important position created is the Joint Chief of Staff (Army, Navy, Air Force) [(တပ်မတော်ညှိနှိုင်းကွပ်ကဲရေးမှူး - ကြည်း/ရေ/လေ) *Tatmadaw Hnyinaing Kutkaeyehmu (Kyi-Yay-Lay)*] that commands commanders-in-chief of the navy and air force. Another new position is the Chief of Bureau of Air Defence. While four Bureaus of Operations are reintroduced, the Chief of Bureau of Ordnance Production was created.[80] All these new positions are held by lieutenant generals. The Chief of Armed Forces Training was upgraded to a lieutenant general too. Under the Chief of Armed Force Training, three major generals for joint services training, military training schools, and strategic studies, are placed. Thus, the OSS was reorganized and placed under the CAFTO. In 2005 and 2007, two more BSOs were created; thus, there were six BSOs by 2008. In 2007, The Armed Forces Inspector and Controller General position, with the rank of lieutenant general, was created.

In term of directorate, the Directorate of Resettlement was established under the AG Office. On 1 April 1990, the Directorate of Public Relations and People's Militias was reorganized into two separate directorates: the Directorate of Public Relations and Psychological Warfare and the Directorate of People's Militias and Border Troops. In the early 2000s, the Directorate of Armour and Artillery was split into separate directorates: the Directorate of Artillery and the Directorate of Armour. Then in early 2004, under the AG Office, the Directorate of Recruitment, with the rank of major general, was created. Moreover, all the director positions were upgraded to the rank of major general. Therefore, at the Ministry of Defence level, the Tatmadaw has several directorates of support corps. Under the Adjutant General Office, there are three directorates: medical services, resettlement, and provost martial. Under the Quartermaster General Office are the directorates of military engineering (garrison section), supply and transport, ordnance services, and electrical and mechanical engineering. Under the General Staff Office, are directorates of signals, defence industries, security printing, public relations and psychological warfare, military engineering (field section), artillery, amour, and people's militias and frontier troops. In addition, the directorate of defence services historical museum and research institute and defence services computer center are also placed under the General Staff Office. Other independent departments within the Ministry of Defence are the directorate of procurement, record office, central military accounts, and camp commandant.

The Tatmadaw-Kyi (The Army)

At the time of Myanmar's independence, there were only fifteen infantry battalions under two regional commands,[81] an infantry division and an infantry brigade. In April 1948, soon after the communist insurgency began, the strength of the Tatmadaw battalions was reviewed in comparison with the communist troops and it was decided to form two new battalions. As a result, No. 1 Burma Regiment (BURGT) was formed with companies from No. 1 and 3 UMP Battalions, and No. 2 BURGT, with companies from the UMP (Yangon) and the UMP (Training). Meanwhile, as the law and order situation deteriorated elsewhere in the country, a conference on national security was held, and it was decided to organize an emergency levy. A total of eighteen levy battalions were formed under the Ministry of Internal Affairs in April 1948.[82]

These levies were formed under the Burma Police Act of 1945. They were regarded as "Special Police Reserves". As the purpose of the levies was to defend district cities and assist the Tatmadaw and police in operations, they were put under the Ministry of Internal Affairs. Later, for better coordination in "G,A,Q" matters, it was decided at the 32nd Cabinet meeting to bring the levies under the War Office from 1 October 1948. The levies were renamed "Sitwundan Tats" and put under the General Staff Office. The Sitwundan were transformed as "Burma Territorial Force" (BTF) and their headquarters was opened within the War Office. Major Aung Gyi was appointed Inspector General. Over thirty officers and 200 enlisted personnel from the Tatmadaw were attached to the Sitwundan for training and organization. In December 1948, the government asked Major General Ne Win and Major Aung Gyi to form fifty-two BTF battalions by 31 January 1949.[83] Three battalions of the Union Reserve Force were also formed in 1948. Therefore, by the end of 1948, a total of eighteen infantry battalions, three Union Reserve Force battalions, and eighteen BTF battalions were armed. Within a short span of time, Sitwundan expanded to thirty-two battalions.[84]

However, it became increasingly difficult to control the Sitwundan battlions, even for their sponsors. As the force was formed to cope with emergency situations, many of the Sitwundan members were not trained and were under the control of local politicians. By early 1952, only thirteen Sitwundan battalions remained under the War Office and the rest were disbanded. On 1 January 1955, the remaining 13 Sitwundan battalions were transformed into Burma Regiments (Burma Territorial Army), in short BURGT (BTA).[85]

In the early days of the insurgency, many new UMP battalions were formed to help the Tatmadaw in counter-insurgency operations. The UMP battalions were staffed by ex-PBF members and BSP supporters.[86] However, many UMPs were increasingly seen as a BSP army. By 1958, a rift appeared among the UMP battalions, along the lines of loyalty to Kyaw Nyein and Ba Swe on the one hand, and to U Nu, U Tin, and Bo Min Gaung on the other. The unity of the UMP became a problem for the Tatmadaw. Finally, on 1 October 1962, the UMPs were transformed into Tatmadaw battalions. Therefore, a total of twenty-seven new battalions were formed.[87] The Tatmadaw rapidly expanded and, by early 1968, twenty years after independence, it had ninety-nine infantry battalions with five regional commands, two infantry brigades and three LIDs. By 1988, it had a total of 168 infantry battalions with nine regional commands and eight LIDs (see Table 3.2). Since 1988, the number of infantry battalion has grown considerably. In 2000, it was estimated that the Tatmadaw-Kyi had 462 infantry battalions. In 2007, it was estimated that, in term of war establishment, the size of the Tatmadaw had reached 600,000 troops, and it had 504 infantry battalions.[88] However,

TABLE 3.2
Organizational Development of the Tatmadaw, 1948–89

Year	*Bn.*	*Year*	*Bn.*	*Year*	*Bn.*	*Year*	*Bn.*
January 1948	15	January 1959	57	January 1970	99	January 1981	145
January 1949	18	January 1960	57	January 1971	105	January 1982	146
January 1950	23	January 1961	57	January 1972	105	January 1983	146
January 1951	26	January 1962	57	January 1973	105	January 1984	147
January 1952	30	January 1963	84	January 1974	114	January 1985	157
January 1953	41	January 1964	84	January 1975	114	January 1986	157
January 1954	42	January 1965	98	January 1976	114	January 1987	158
January 1955	45	January 1966	98	January 1977	121	January 1988	168
January 1956	53	January 1967	99	January 1978	124	January 1989	178
January 1957	54	January 1968	99	January 1979	124		
January 1958	57	January 1969	99	January 1980	135		

Note: Bn. = Infantry Battalions.

this does not mean that the Tatmadaw has full strength; the implemented strength is much lower. In 1988, the war establishment for a battalion was 777 personnel; it was revised in mid-1990s to make it 814. But, according to some observers, the average manpower of the battalions has substantially declined: from 670 plus in 1988 to 350 plus in 1998, and 250 plus in 2008. Hence, the battalions are seriously under-strength. A leak document reported in the international media revealed that in late 2006, the Tatmadaw had 284 battalions with fewer than 200 personnel, and 220 battalions with between 200 and 300 personnel.[89]

For better command and communication, the Tatmadaw-Kyi formed regional military commands and infantry brigades. It occasionally reorganized its command structure in accordance with its impressive growth and the necessities of operations. Until 1961, there were only two regional commands (see Figure 3.5). They were supported by thirteen infantry brigades and an infantry division.[90] However, in October 1961, new regional military commands were opened, possibly borrowing the idea from Indonesia, leaving only two brigades (see Table 3.3). Now, there are five command HQs: Northwest, Eastern, Central, Southwest, and Southeast (see Figure 3.6).

Then, in June 1963, the Naypyidaw Command was temporarily formed in Yangon with the deputy commander and some staff officers from the Central Command. It was reorganized as a regional command, Yangon Command, on 1 June 1965.

A division of labour between garrison duty and mobile operation came when the Light Infantry Division (LID) system was introduced in 1966. Battalions under the regional commands engaged mostly in consolidation of the base areas, ensuring security of lines of communication, and training local militias. Battalions under LIDs were the strike forces in operations. Their training was somewhat different. The first LID was No. 77 LID founded on 6 June 1966. It was followed by No. 88 LID and No. 99 LID in the two subsequent years. In 1970, the Strategic Command HQ was established in Lashio because of alarming BCP advances in the northeast border region.[91] In 1972, three new regional commands, Northeast Command, Northern Command, and Western Command were opened in Lashio, Myitkyina, and Sittwe, giving the Tatmadaw-Kyi a total of nine regional commands (see Figure 3.7). Brigades were completely abolished in 1972. From 1976, more and more LIDs were formed, and by 1991 there were ten LIDs (see Table 3.4).

At the command level, new regional command HQs, Regional Operation Commands (ROCs), and Military Operation Commands (MOCs), were introduced in the 1990s as the Tatmadaw planned to increase its personnel.[92] The first military division to be formed after the SLORC takeover was the

TABLE 3.3
Reorganization of Command Structure, 1961

Name of the Regional Command	*Location*	*Former Commands and Brigades*
Northwest Command HQ	Mandalay	Northern Command No. 1 Infantry Division No. 1 Infantry Brigade No. 10 Infantry Brigade
Eastern Command HQ	Taungyi	No. 4 Infantry Brigade No. 6 Infantry Brigade No. 9 Infantry Brigade
Southeast Command HQ	Mawlamyaing	No. 3 Infantry Brigade No. 5 Infantry Brigade No. 13 Infantry Brigade
Southwest Command HQ	Pathein	Naypyidaw Command Hqs No. 8 Infantry Brigade No. 12 Infantry Brigade
Central Command HQ	Mingalardon	Southern Command No. 2 Infantry Brigade
No. 7 Infantry Brigade	Myitkyina	
No. 11 Infantry Brigade	Ba-an	

TABLE 3.4
Light Infantry Divisions

No.	*LID*	*Year*	*Location*	*Serial*	*First Commander*
1	LID-11	21-12-1988	Indine	BC 8809	Col. Win Myint
2	LID-22	23-06-1987	Pa-An	BC 8753	Col. Tin Hla
3	LID-33	09-10-1984	Sagaing	BC 7924	Col. Kyaw Ba
4	LID-44	04-04-1979	Thaton/Kyeikhto	BC 6605	Col. Myat Thin
5	LID-55	04-04-1980	Sagaing/Kalaw	BC 6662	Col. Phone Myint
6	LID-66	28-08-1976	Pyay/Innma	BC 5841	Col. Taung Zar Khaing
7	LID-77	06-06-1966	Hmawbi/Bago	BC 5367	Col. Tint Swe
8	LID-88	01-05-1967	Magway	BC 5603	Col. Than Tin
9	LID-99	12-08-1968	Meikhtila	BC 5332	Col. Kyaw Htin
10	LID-101	25-07-1991	Pakkoku	BC 9706	Col. Saw Tun

No. 11 LID in December 1988, in Indaing, near Yangon, with Colonel Win Myint as its commander. In March 1990, a new regional command was opened in Monywa with Brigadier Kyaw Min as commander and named Northwest Command, while the original Northwest Command in Mandalay was renamed Central Command, and the original Central Command in Taungoo was renamed Southern Command. A year later, No. 101 LID was opened in Pakokku with Colonel Saw Tun as commander. In 1992, in order to facilitate command and control, two regional operation commands (ROCs) were opened in Myeik and Loikaw. They were commanded respectively by Brigadier Soe Tint and Brigadier Maung Kyi. March 1995 was a watershed period for the Tatmadaw-Kyi as it established eleven military operation commands (MOCs) in that month. These MOCs are in Kyaukme, Loilin, Moe Kaung, Phugyi, Ahn, Pyinmana, Phekhon, Dawai, Kyauktaw, Kyigone, and Kaukayeik. MOC-4 was designated as the Airborne Division. Then in 1996 two new regional commands were opened. Coastal Region Command was opened in Myeik with Brigadier General Thiha Thura Thura Sit Maung as commander, by dissolving the ROC (Myeik), and Triangle Region Command in Kengtung was set up, with Brigadier General Thein Sein as commander (see Figure 3.8). Three new ROCs were opened in Kalay, Bamaw, and Mongsat, while the one in Loikaw was maintained. In late 1998, two new MOCs were opened in Bokepyin and Mongsat. Moreover, throughout the 1990s, the Tatmadaw created a number of tactical operation commands (Base HQs), in places such as Tatyan, Kawthaung, Tachileik, Kunlone, Hakha, Mongkhet, and Phapon, for territorial representation of the armed forces. Between 1999 and 2001, seven new MOCs were opened in Buthidaung, Hseinni, Mongpan, Mong Pyin, Ye, Kha Mauk Gyi, and Bamaw and four new ROCs were opened in Mong Phyet, Pyay, Laukai, and Sittwe. The ROC (Bamaw) became ROC (Tanaing). MOC-5 was moved to Taungoke as the Western Command was moved to Ahn. In December 2005, the Naypyitaw Command was established at Naypyitaw, the new capital of Myanmar. Hence, by early 2008, the Tatmadaw has thirteen Regional Commands, ten LIDs, twenty MOCs and six ROCs.

Regional commanders are major generals and LID or MOC commanders are brigadier generals. While the MOC is equivalent to the LID, as both command ten battalions, the ROC is much smaller in size, with merely four battalions; thus it is the regiment level with a brigadier general as commander. It is a position between LID/MOC commander [(တပ်မမှူး) *Tatma-hmu*] and Tactical Operation Command (TOC) commander [(ဗျူဟာမှူး) *Byuha-hmu*], who commands only three infantry battalions. Yet, the ROC commander enjoys financial, administrative, and judicial authority while the MOC commander does not have judicial authority. For more efficiency, new staff positions at the regional command were introduced. In the early 1990s, at the regional command level, there were only three grade one level staff: GSO-I, ASO-I, and QSO-I. Now, every regional command has one Colonel Regional Command General Staff, two GSO-Is, two ASO-Is, and two QSO-Is.

Since the corps are under the army, I would like to give some emphasis here on what is known as General Staff Corps. Special attention will be accorded to intelligence, signal and artillery, and armour corps. The origin of the military intelligence or the Directorate of Defence Services Intelligence (DDSI) can be traced to the immediate post-World War II period. Under the HQ Burma Command, Field Security Sections (FSS) were attached to Divisions for security and intelligence collection. Interrogation of war prisoners was done by Field Interrogation Units (FIU), which was within the FSS. When the HQ Burma Command was dissolved and the War Office was subsequently formed at the time of independence, the intelligence section was placed under the General Staff Office. Until 1956, there was only a G-II (Intelligence), along with G-II (Operations and Training) and G-II (Staff Duty and Planning), under the G-I (Army). The G-II (Intelligence) was assisted by two G-III officers and one IO (Intelligence Officer). These officers handled combat intelligence, security and counterintelligence, press and propaganda, administrative matters, and signal intelligence.

With the reorganization of the War Office in 1956, the Directorate of Defence Services Intelligence was born. The director at that time had the rank of lieutenant colonel. The directorate was staffed with two G-II officers and six G-III officers. Each G-III officer was assigned different duties and responsibilities: foreign intelligence, domestic intelligence, security and counterintelligence, censorship and liaison, administration, and training. In 1962, the DDSI was expanded to six G-II officers and fourteen G-III officer, and the director was upgraded to full colonel and a new deputy director post was created, with the incumbent given the rank of lieutenant colonel. Now six G-II officers are in charge of combat intelligence, political intelligence, security and counter-intelligence, foreign intelligence, liaison, and administration.

In 1948, there were three Military Intelligence Sections (MIS) in the Tatmadaw. No. 1 MIS was with the NBSD in Maymyo, No. 2 MIS with the War Office in Yangon, and No. 3 MIS with the SBSD in Mingalardon. Between 1949 and 1953, six more units were established in Lashio, Taunggyi, Pathein, Mandalay, Mawlamyaing, and Kengtung. The intelligence was further expanded and by the end of 1960, there were altogether twenty-one MIS units. New units were located in Chauk, Sagaing, Pakokku, Taungu, Ba-an, Maubin, and Thaton, and five more units in Yangon. In 1950, the Tatmadaw established the Military Intelligence Training Centre (MITC). It was reorganized in 1952 as the Military Intelligence Depot. Then in May

1958, it was again reorganized as the Defence Services Intelligence Centre [(ဗဟိုထောက်လှမ်းရေးတပ်) *Baho Htauk-Hlanye-Tat*]. About a year later, in March 1959, the DDSI established the Research and Information Unit [(စစ်ဖက်သုတေသနတပ်) *Sitphet-Thutaethana-Tat*] to support the operations of the various intelligence sections. In January 1963, the Research and Information Unit was reorganized as the Defence Services Intelligence Support Depot (DSISD) [(ထောက်လှမ်းရေးအကူတပ်) *Htauk-Hlanye-Aku-Tat*] with four internal departments: administration, operations, interrogation, and support.

The restructuring of DDSI in 1963 reduced the number of units to seven MIS units and two LMIS (Light Military Intelligence Section) units. These seven MIS units are placed under the DDSI and six regional commands: No. 1 MIS under Northeast Command (Mandalay), No. 2 MIS under Eastern Command (Taunggyi), No. 3 MIS under Central Command (Taunggu), No. 4 MIS under Southwest Command (Pathein), No. 5 MIS under Southeast Command (Mawlamyaing), No. 6 MIS under the DDSI (Yangon), and No. 7 MIS under Yangon Command (Yangon). No. 7 LMIS and No. 11 LMIS were at Myitkyina and Bamaw. In 1972, these two LMIS units were integrated to become No. 8 MIS under the Northern Command (Myitkyina). When two new regional commands were opened in Lashio and Sittwe, No. 9 MIS and No. 10 MIS were opened respectively. In 1983, No. 11 MIS was opened in Padaung. By the end of 1988, the DDSI had a total of fourteen MIS units in army, three naval intelligence — all of them in Yangon, three air force intelligence units — two in Mingalardon and one in Meikhtila — and the DSIC in Yekyiaing and the DSISD in Mingalardon.

The reorganization of the DDSI in 1985 upgraded the director to the rank of brigadier general, and deputy director, the rank of colonel. There were six G-I (lieutenant colonel) officers with different responsibilities: administration, combat intelligence, foreign intelligence, security and counterintelligence, navy, and air force. They were assisted by G-II and G-III officers. G-II officers were in charge of planning, training, administration, operations, special operations, foreign affairs, liaison, counter-intelligence, security, and political intelligence. The MIS units were further expanded all over the country, and by early 1991 there were twenty-three MIS units.[93]

In 1992, a new bureau, known as Office of Strategic Studies (OSS) was formed and staffed with DDSI personnel. According to a source, the OSS is divided into five departments: international affairs, narcotics, security, ethnic affairs, and science and environmental affairs. Some argued that the OSS was created as part of a rank-upgrading exercise for intelligence corps. The DDSI can accommodate only a brigadier as the director whereas the chief of OSS is a lieutenant general. Some intelligence units were upgraded and renamed. Thus, the DSIC was renamed the Defence Services Information Collection Training School, but the DSISD remained unchanged; commanding officers were raised to the rank of colonel. One more DSISD was established in the late 1990s. It appears that in late 2001, the DDSI was restructured as the DSIB, and upgraded. Twelve MI units were upgraded into battalions, commanded by a lieutenant colonel, at each regional command headquarters, while the rest remained unchanged. According to JIR (Jane's Intelligence Review), there are seven departments in the new structure. Five are for operational matters: internal security; border areas; counter-intelligence; foreign affairs; and computers. The remaining two handle internal affairs of the DSIB: administration and training.[94] Some observers, however, said that the departments are: operation, security, counter-intelligence, liaison, foreign affairs, administration, computers, navy, and air force. There were expectations that the DSIB would become a fourth branch of the Tatmadaw, co-equal with the army, navy, and air force.[95] With the benefit of hindsight, one can clearly see that the DSIB was under the General Staff Office. However, after the dismissal of General Khin Nyunt, chief of the DSIB, from power on 19 October 2004, the DSIB was completely overhauled and almost all the officers above the rank of major were either arrested or forced to retire. Many senior officers, including General Khin Nyunt, received long prison terms.[96] Some junior officers were transferred to infantry and sent to far, remote areas, but those who were in the inner circle of the senior MIS officers, or at the DSIB Headquarters, were arrested and received long prison terms. Major General Myint Swe, the then commander of the Yangon Command, was [temporarily] appointed as the new chief of intelligence.[97] Then by the end of the year 2005, the DSIB was reorganized as the Military Affairs Security (MAS). In May 2006, Major General Ye Myint, commander of Eastern Command, was appointed as chief of MAS; the MAS is still under the General Staff Office and the chief has the rank of lieutenant general. The appointment of a regional commander is an indication that the Tatmadaw leadership is trying to resolve the structural problem of the institutional divide between infantry and intelligence. It is likely that there will be some form of rotation between infantry and the intelligence service.

Just before the country's independence, the Burma Signals, also known as "X" Branch, was organized as HQ Burma Signals and three squadrons: No. 1 Signal Squadron, No. 2 Signal Squadron, and Burma Frontier Force Signal Squadron (BFFSS). Soon after independence, the HQ Burma Signals, which was formerly attached to the HQ Burma Command, was located within the War Office, and No. 1 Signal Squadron was reorganized as Burma Signals

Training Squadron (BSTS), and No. 2 Signal Squadron as Burma Signals Squadron (BSS) while BFFSS was transferred to the Ministry of Home Affairs. The BSTS, based in Maymyo, was formed with Operating and Cipher Training Troop, Dispatch Rider Training Troop, Lineman Training Troop, Radio Mechanic Training Troop, and Regimental Signals Training Troop. The BSS, based in Mingalardon, had nine sections: Administration Troop, Maintenance Troop, Operating Troop, Cipher Troop, Lineman and Dispatch Rider Troop, NBSD Signals Troop (formerly "J" Section), SBSD Signals Troop (formerly "K" Section), Mobile Brigade Signals Troop (formerly "L" Section), and Arakan Signals Troop. The Chief of Signal Officer (CSO), at the time of independence, was Lieutenant Colonel Saw Aung Din. The BSTS and BSS were later renamed No. 1 Signal Battalion and No. 1 Signal Training Battalion. In 1952, the Infantry Divisional Signals Regiment [(တပ်မအခြေပြုဆက်သွယ်ရေးတပ်ရင်း) *Tatma-Achekpya-Setthweye-Tatyin*] was formed. The Infantry Divisional Signals Regiment was later renamed No. 2 Signal Battalion. Meanwhile, the Burma Signals was reorganized, along with other corps, in 1956, and the HQ Burma Signals became the Directorate of Signal, and the director was elevated to the rank of colonel. In 1956, No. 1 Signal Security Battalion was formed with company strength. No. 3 Signal Battalion and No. 4 Signal Battalion were formed in November 1958 and October 1959 respectively.

In 1961, four signal battalions were reorganized into five signal battalions: No. 111 Signal Battalion under Northeast Command, No. 121 Signal Battalion under Eastern Command, No. 313 Signal Battalion under Central Command, No. 414 Signal Battalion under Southwest Command, and No. 515 Signal Battalion under Southeast Command. At the same time, No. 1 Signal Training Battalion was renamed Burma Signal Training Depot (BSTD), known in Myanmar as [(ဗဟိုဆက်သွယ်ရေးတပ်) *Baho-Setthweye-Tat*]. 1962 appeared to be a watershed year for the Directorate of Signal. No. 1 Signal Security Battalion was upgraded to full strength. In February, No. 1 Signal Battalion was formed and, in October, No. 2 Signal Battalion was formed by incorporating the signal battalion from BTF. Moreover, No. 1 Signal Store Depot [(ဆက်သွယ်ရေးပစ္စည်းတပ်ရင်း) *Setthweye-Pyitse-Tatyin*] was formed the same year. However, only in April 1979, did No. 3 Signal Battalion come into existence. In 1963, No. 1 and No. 2 Signal Workshops were formed in Yangon and Mandalay. Thus, by 1988, under the Directorate of Signals, there were one training depot, eight signal battalions, one signal security battalion, one signal store depot, and two signal workshops. With the expansion of the Tatmadaw since 1990, the signal corps was also expanded. Now, at least one signal battalion is under every regional command and LIDs and MOCs have signal companies.

At the time of independence the Tatmadaw had no artillery battalion as such. In 1947, No. 1 Field Artillery was transformed to No. 6 Burma Rifle. Only in 1952 did the Tatmadaw formally establish No. 1 Artillery Battalion with three artillery batteries [P, Q, and R], hastily formed in 1949. In 1952, the Tatmadaw formed three more artillery battalions. This formation remained relatively unchanged until 1988. Since the early 1990s, the Tatmadaw has been greatly expanding the artillery corps. According to some observers, there are about ninety artillery battalions, such as field artillery battalion, howitzer battalion, anti-aircraft battalion, target finding battalion, and missile battalion, under ten artillery divisions in the Tatmadaw.[98] Each artillery division, comprised of three tactical artillery operation commands, is designed to provide artillery support for three LIDs. However, many observers believe that the artillery battalions have a serious shortage of manpower, and some divisions are not in full division strength. Some even estimate that each battalion only has a manpower capacity of 20 to 25 per cent.

To further strengthen the existing No. 1 Armour Company, the Tatmadaw formed No. 2 Armour Company in July 1950. These two companies were merged on 1 November 1950 to become No. 1 Armour Battalion, based in Mingalardon. Then on 15 May 1952, No. 1 Tank Battalion, later renamed No. 2 Tank Battalion, was formed. The armour corps was perhaps the most neglected one for nearly thirty years since the Tatmadaw did not procure any new tanks or armour carriers since 1961. In the early 1990s, the Tatmadaw formed more armour and tank battalions. By 2000, the Tatmadaw had five armour battalions and five tank battalions under No. 71 Armour Division, based in Pyawbwe. In recent years, with the procurement of more armour carriers, some Myanmar observers believe that the Tatmadaw now has five armour divisions and these are mostly located in central Myanmar.[99]

The latest entrant to this field is the air defence battalions under air defence divisions. With the establishment of the Air Defence Office at the Ministry of Defence in 2002, the Tatmadaw began building up a separate corps for air defence. Until early 1990s, the Tatmadaw merely had one company strength of air defence battery within the armour and artillery corps, and it was mainly for point defence at the Mingalardon Airport and the Ministry of Defence. In the 1990s, a few more battalions within the artillery corps were designated as air defence battalions. Only in 2002 did the Tatmadaw form separate air defence battalions. According to some sources, the Tatmadaw now has three divisions of air defence battalions.[100]

In addition, the corps under the AG Office and QMG Office were also expanded in proportion to infantry and other corps. Under the AG Office, the most prominent corps is medical services. At the time of independence in 1948, the medical corps had two Base Military Hospitals (300 beds) in Mingalardon and Maymyo, a Medical Store Depot in Yangon, a Dental Unit, and six Camp Reception Stations in Myitkyina, Sittwe, Taungoo, Pyinmana, Bago, and Meikhtila. This core structure was further expanded and, by March 1953, five more Camp Reception Stations (Yangon, Mawlamyaing, Lashio, Loilin, and Chauk), a Staging Section, an Ambulance Unit, two Anti Malaria Units, one Field Ambulance, one Hygiene Section, one Mobile Surgical Unit, and the Medical Corps Centre were added. Between 1958 and 1962, the medical corps was restructured. All Camp Reception Stations were reorganized into Medical Battalions; thus, there were five medical battalions (Mandalay, Kalaw, Hmawbi, Pathein, and Mawlamyaing). Moreover, No. 1 Military Hospital (100 beds) in Meikhtila, No. 6 Cantonment Hospital in Bahtoo, No. 1 Advanced Medical Store Depot in Mandalay, and No. 1 X-ray Unit, the Nurses Training Wing, and No. 2 Convalescent Depot in Mingalardon, were added to the list. Between 1963 and 1988, a few more medical facilities were added and existing hospitals were reorganized and upgraded. Thus, in 1988, the Directorate of Medical Services had one 700-bed Defence Services General Hospital (Mingalardon), one 500-bed hospital (Maymyo), two 300-bed hospitals (Yangon and Meikhtila), six medical battalions (Mandalay, Taungyi, Taungoo, Pathein, Mawlamyaing, and Hmawbi), two 100-bed hospitals (Pyay and Lashio), one 75-bed hospital (Bahtoo), one 200-bed rehabilitation hospital (Yangon), one Medical Store Depot (Yangon), one Advanced Base Medical Store Depot (Mandalay), one Malaria and Hygiene Battalion (Hmawbi), and the Medical Corps Centre (Mingalardon). Since 1989, the Defence Services Medical Corps has been significantly expanded along with the infantry. By 2007, the Directorate of Medical Services has two 1,000-bed Defence Service General Hospital (Mingalardon and Naypyitaw), two 700-bed Military Hospitals (Pyin Oo Lwin and Aung Ban), two 500-bed Military Hospitals (Meikhtila and Yangon), one 500-bed Defence Services Orthopedic Hospital (Mingalardon), two 300-bed Defence Services Obstetric, Gynecological and Children Hospital (Mingalardon and Naypyitaw), three 300-bed Military Hospitals (Myitkyina, Ann, and Kengtung), eighteen 100-bed Military Hospitals (Mongphyet, Baan, Indaing, Bahtoo, Myeik, Pyay, Loikaw, Namsam, Lashio, Kalay, Mongsat, Dawai, Kawthaung, Laukai, Thandaung, Magway, Sittwe, and Hommalin), fourteen Medical Battalions (Mandalay, Taungyi, Taungoo, Pathein, Mawlamyaing, Hmawbi, Monywa, Sittwe, Myitkyina, Lashio, Bamaw, Keng Tung, Myeik, and Phugyi), one 500-bed Defence Services Liver Hospital (Mingalardon), one 300-bed Defence Services Rehabilitation Hospital (Mingalardon), one Hygiene Battalion (Mingalardon), one Medical Store Depot (Yangon), one Advanced Medical Store Depot (Mandalay), one Medical Workshop unit, one 25-bed

Military Hospital (Lanywa), one Artificial Kidney Unit (Mingalardon), and the Medical Corps Centre (Hmawbi). In a similar way, under the QMG Office, several new supply and transport battalions were formed throughout the 1990s. In the early 1950s, the Tatmadaw had two Supply battalions at Mandalay and Meikhtila, twenty-one Supply detachments, and two General Transport companies. In 1961, these units were reorganized into five Supply and Transport battalions and two Supply and Transport bases. Two new Animal Transport battalions were formed in the mid-1960s. While there were only six supply and transport battalions (Mandalay, Shwe Nyaung, Mingalardon, Pathein, Mawlamyaing, and Lashio) in 1988, by early 2002, a total of twelve new battalions were added to the list (Myitkyina, Sittwe, Monywa, Taungoo, Namsam, Keng Tung, Bamaw, Kalay, Baan, Laukai, Myeik, and Ahn). Moreover, two more Animal Transport Battalions were formed in the 1990s.

The Tatmadaw-Yay (The Navy)

The Tatmadaw-Yay was officially founded on 24 December 1947. In the early 1950s, the Tatmadaw-Yay had Yadanapon Naval Base (Yangon), Rakhine Naval Base (Sittwe), Mawlamyaing Naval Base, Pathein Naval Base, and Mandalay Naval Base, with a total of about 2,000 personnel. All these bases were commanded by naval lieutenant commanders (equivalent to major in army rank). The Mandalay Naval Base was founded in 1952 and abolished in 1956 when a new organizational set-up for the Tatmadaw-Yay was introduced. In 1956, Rakhine Naval Base, founded on 1 November 1948, was upgraded to Rakhine Naval Region Command HQ. Two new naval region commands were formed: Ayerwaddy Naval Region Command HQ and Thanintharyi Naval Region Command HQ were founded on 16 May and 16 September 1956 respectively. The commander of a naval region command HQ was a naval captain (equivalent to colonel in army rank). The Tatmadaw-Yay also had four naval bases (commanded by naval commanders) under the three naval region commands and the Tatmadaw-Yay HQ. They were Danyawaddy Naval Base (renamed Sittwe Naval Base in 1961) under the Rakhine Naval Region Command HQ; Mawyawaddy Naval Base (renamed Mawlamyaing Naval Base in 1961) under Thanintharyi Naval Region Command HQ; Pathein Naval Base under Ayerwaddy Naval Region Command HQ; and Yadanapon Naval Base under the Tatmadaw-Yay HQ in Yangon. This command structure continued to exist until the early 1990s. In December 1964, the Tatmadaw-Yay had a total of 306 officers and 7,595 other rank-and-file members.[101] No. 1 Naval Infantry (about 800 personnel) was formed in 1964 and dissolved in 1968, and No. 2 Naval Infantry was formed in 1967 and dissolved in 1968.[102]

In 1978, the Tatmadaw-Yay expanded its facilities under the present command structure. The Naval Training School was upgraded to the Naval Training Command HQ. The Naval Administrative Training School, the Naval Weaponry and Signal Training School, and the Naval Engineering Training School were established. The Tactical Naval Flotilla Operation Command [(ဗျူဟာစစ်ရေယာဉ်စု) *Byuha-Sit-Yay-Yin-Su*] was formed under the Tatmadaw-Yay HQ. Furthermore, the Tatmadaw-Yay HQ had the Central Naval Signal Unit, the Central Naval Ordnance Unit, the Central Naval Store Unit, the Central Naval Survey Unit, the Central Diving and Rescue Unit, the Naval Hospital, No. 1 and 2 Military Police Units (Navy), No. 1, 2, and 3 Naval Intelligence Units, and the Naval Radar Units. Under each naval region command HQ were: a naval signal unit, a naval store unit, a naval administrative unit, a naval ordnance unit, a naval engineering unit, a naval flotilla, a naval training unit, a naval base camp, and a naval forward camp.[103] By the early 1990s, the Tatmadaw-Yay had about 9,000 personnel.

In the early 1990s, the Tatmadaw-Yay upgraded its command structure. New naval region commands were introduced. Commanders of naval region command HQs became commodores. At present, the Tatmadaw-Yay has the Danyawaddy Naval Region Command HQ in Kyaukphyu, the Ayerwaddy Naval Region Command HQ in Yangon; the Mawyawaddy Naval Region Command HQ in Heinse; the Naval Training Command HQ in Seikgyi; the Pamawaddy Naval Region Command HQ in Heingyi; and the Thaninthayi Naval Region Command HQ in Kyunsu. Moreover, the Tatmadaw-Yay has two naval flotillas. Some observers believe that the Myanmar navy is in the process of forming a submarine flotilla. The Tatmadaw-Yay has upgraded its naval dockyard unit and engineering unit to the Naval Shipyard HQ, commanded by a commodore. It has also expanded its signal intelligence and radar facilities, strengthening its operational capabilities on the Indian Ocean. At present, in terms of war establishment, the Tatmadaw-Yay has about 22,000 personnel.

The Tatmadaw-Lay (The Air Force)

The Tatmadaw-Lay was also formed on 24 December 1947. In 1948, The Tatmadaw-Lay had forty Oxfords, sixteen Tigermoths, four Austers and three Spitfires with a few hundred personnel. The Tatmadaw-Lay decided to build an air base in Meiktila in 1948. However, the base was not operative until the early 1950s, as insurgents overran the area. On 2 June 1950, the Tatmadaw-Lay began building an air base in Hmawbi. The Mingalardon Air Base HQ was formed on 16 June 1950. No. 1

Squadron, Equipment Holding Unit and Air HQ — Burma Air Force, and the Flying Training School, were placed under the base. A few months later, on 18 December 1950, No. 2 Squadron was formed, with nine Dakotas, as a transport squadron. In April 1951, the Flying Training School under Mingalardon Air Base HQ was relocated to Hmawbi Air Base. In 1952, No. 1 Squadron was also relocated to Hmawbi Air Base. In 1953, the Flying Training School was again relocated, this time to Meiktila Air Base. At the same time, an Advanced Flying Unit (with Vampire Mark T55s) was formed under the Mingalardon Air Base. Therefore, in 1953, the Tatmadaw-Lay maintained Mingalardon Air Base HQ, Hmawbi Air Base, and Meiktila Air Base.[104]

In late 1955, the Tatmadaw-Lay formed a Maintenance Air Base in Mingalardon, No. 501 Squadron Group (Hmawbi Air Base), and No. 502 Squadron Group (Mingalardon Air Base HQ). Five years later, No. 503 Squadron Group was formed with No. 51 Squadron (Otters and Cessnas) and No. 53 Squadron (Bell 47Gs/Huskys and Alouettes) in Meiktila. In January 1960, the Tatmadaw-Lay relocated the Advanced Flying Unit, under Mingalardon Air Base HQ, to Myitkyinar, and built Myitkyinar Air Base. In 1962, the Tatmadaw-Lay opened a radar station in Mingalardon and a mobile radar station in Lwemwe (near Tachileik).[105]

The Tatmadaw-Lay continued to expand its operational capabilities by procuring more aircraft and recruiting personnel much faster than the Tatmadaw-Yay. In December 1964, the Tatmadaw-Lay had 323 officers and 5,877 personnel in other ranks.[106] In 1964, as it acquired T-33 jet trainers, the Tatmadaw-Lay upgraded its training facilities. The Flying Training School under Meiktila Air Base was transformed to No. 1 Flying Training School and the Advanced Flying Unit in Myitkyinar Airfield Base was transformed to No. 2 Flying Training School. The same year, a new radar station that could operate within a 120-mile radius was opened in Namsang. In 1966, new radar stations were opened and existing stations were upgraded. The Namsang Radar Station was upgraded to cover about a 200-mile radius. For security reasons, the Namsang Radar Station was renamed No. 71 Squadron. Three new radar stations were No. 72 Squadron in Lwemwe (70-mile radius), No. 73 Squadron in Kutkai (70-mile radius), and No. 74 Squadron in Hmawbi (200-mile radius). The same year, the Tatmadaw-Lay formed No. 1 Airborne Battalion with twenty-six officers and 750 other personnel of other ranks.[107]

On 1 January 1967, the Tatmadaw-Lay reorganized its command structure. No. 501 Squadron Group in Hmawbi became No. 501 Air Base HQ; No. 502 Squadron Group in Mingalardon became No. 502 Air Base

HQ; and No. 503 Squadron Group in Meiktila became No. 503 Air Base HQ in Meiktila/Shante. It also maintained airfield detachments in Lashio and Kengtung to cope with the insurgency of the Burma Communist Party in the northeast border region of Myanmar, and an air base in Myitkyinar. This command structure remained unchanged until the mid-1970s. Therefore, by 1974, the establishment included the Maintenance Air Base in Mingalardon; the Training Air Base in Meiktila (No. 1 Flying Training School, Administrative Training School, Technical Training School, Electronic Training School, Central Inspection Unit and No. 53 Squadron — attached to No. 503 Air Base HQ); No. 501 Air Base HQ in Hmawbi (No. 31 Squadron, No. 52 Squadron and No. 6 Squadron — attached to Training Air Base); No. 502 Air Base HQ in Mingalardon (No. 2 Squadron, No. 3 Squadron and No. 4 Squadron — attached to No. 501 Air Base HQ); No. 503 Air Base HQ in Meiktila/Shante (No. 53 Squadron — attached to Myitkyinar Air Base); No. 1 Squadron in Mingalardon (attached to No. 502 Air Base HQ); and No. 2 Flying Training School in Myitkyinar Air Base. The Tatmadaw-Lay also had several intelligence units and military police (air force) units.

On 13 May 1974, the Tatmadaw-Lay merged No. 6 Squadron, No. 1 Flying Training School, and No. 2 Training School into a Flying Training Base in Meiktila/Shante. No. 503 Air Base HQ (with No. 51 Squadron and No. 53 Squadron) was relocated from Meiktila/Shante to Myitkyinar. The Training Air Base (now with an Administrative Training School, Technical Training School, Electronic Training School, and Central Inspection Unit) was transformed to Ground Training Base in Meiktila. This command structure, with about 9,000 personnel, continued to exist until the early 1990s.[108] When the Tatmadaw-Lay upgraded its facilities and introduced two new air base HQs. Existing air base HQs were renamed. Therefore, since late 1990s, the Tatmadaw-Lay has maintained Hmawbi Air Base HQ (former 501 Air Base), Mingalardon Air Base HQ (former 502 Air Base), Myitkyinar Air Base HQ (former 503 Air Base), Namsang Air Base HQ (new base), Taungoo Air Base HQ (new base), Maintenance Air Base, Flying Training Base, and Ground Training Base. In the early 2000s, the Tatmadaw-Lay established new air bases in Myeik and Magway while it reorganized Maintenance Air Base to become Aircraft Production and Maintenance Air Base, to assemble training aircrafts locally. It also significantly upgraded its radar and electronic warfare facilities. Some reports indicate that new air bases were established in Homalin and Pathein.[109] If this information is correct, then the Tatmadaw-Lay may have nine air force bases. Then, in terms of war establishment, the Tatmadaw-Lay has about 23,000 personnel.

The expansion in size of the Tatmadaw-Yay and the Tatmadaw-Lay in Myanmar was not significant compared to that of the Tatmadaw-Kyi. Because of their relatively small sizes, both the Tatmadaw-Yay and the Tatmadaw-Lay are represented in the Tatmadaw command structure by commanders-in-chief of a lower rank than their counterpart in the Tatmadaw-Kyi. Moreover, since the early 1960s, officer recruitment (for non-engineering officers) for both services has been mainly from the DSA, where recruits for all services study together for four years, thus eliminating rivalry among different services. Besides this, throughout their careers, all officers (army, navy, and air force), study together at various training schools, such as the Defence Services Administration School and the Command and General Staff College, except for their specialized subjects.

CONCLUSION

In the fifty-year period from Myanmar's independence, the Tatmadaw has gone through various stages of institution building. A small, weak, and disunited Tatmadaw has emerged as a large, strong, and united one. Splits along the lines of racial background, organizational origins and political affiliation have been resolved. The gap between staff officers and field commanders has been bridged. Competition between intelligence officers and field commanders has been settled. There is no discrimination against one school of graduates over another in promotion. Rivalry between the three services of the Tatmadaw has been eliminated. The Tatmadaw has basically remained an army of infantry battalions, eliminating rivalries so prone to arise between services. In Myanmar, in 1988, out of a total of about 198,600 personnel in the Tatmadaw, the Tatmadaw-Yay had only 8,000 and the Tatmadaw-Lay force had about 15,000 each. This is, by any Southeast Asian comparison, the highest ratio of army to the total number of armed forces personnel. The present Tatmadaw leadership does not appear to think "downsizing" the Tatmadaw is an option in the foreseeable future as they believe the Tatmadaw is the most important state institution that holds the country together and that territorial representation of the armed forces is absolutely necessary. The territorial command structure will remain. At present, it is estimated that the Tatmadaw has a ratio of 2:1 between infantry battalions and support battalions, such as signal, supply and transport, medical, engineering, and ordnance and so on. It is most likely that the Tatmadaw will restructure its troops to a better ratio between infantry and support battalions, as the modernization of the armed forces is desirable.

FIGURE 3.5
The Command Structure of the Tatmadaw by Region (1948–61)

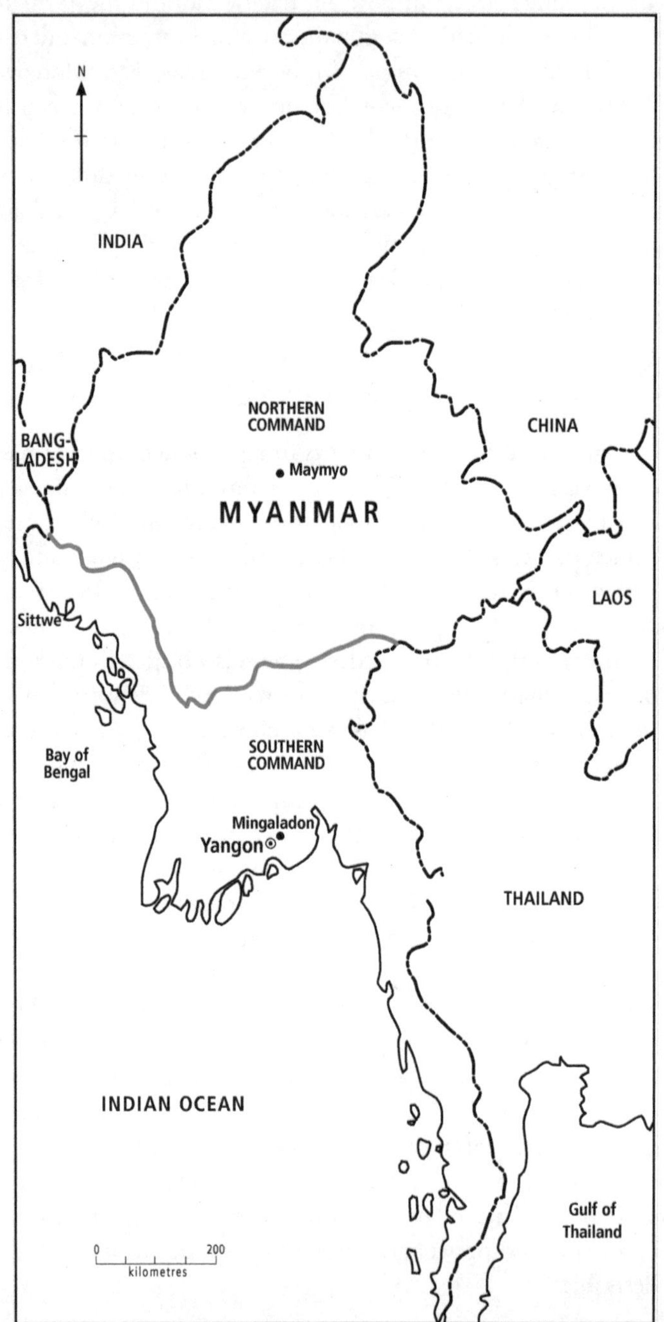

FIGURE 3.6
The Command Structure of the Tatmadaw by Region (1961–72)

FIGURE 3.7
The Command Structure of the Tatmadaw by Region (1972–89)

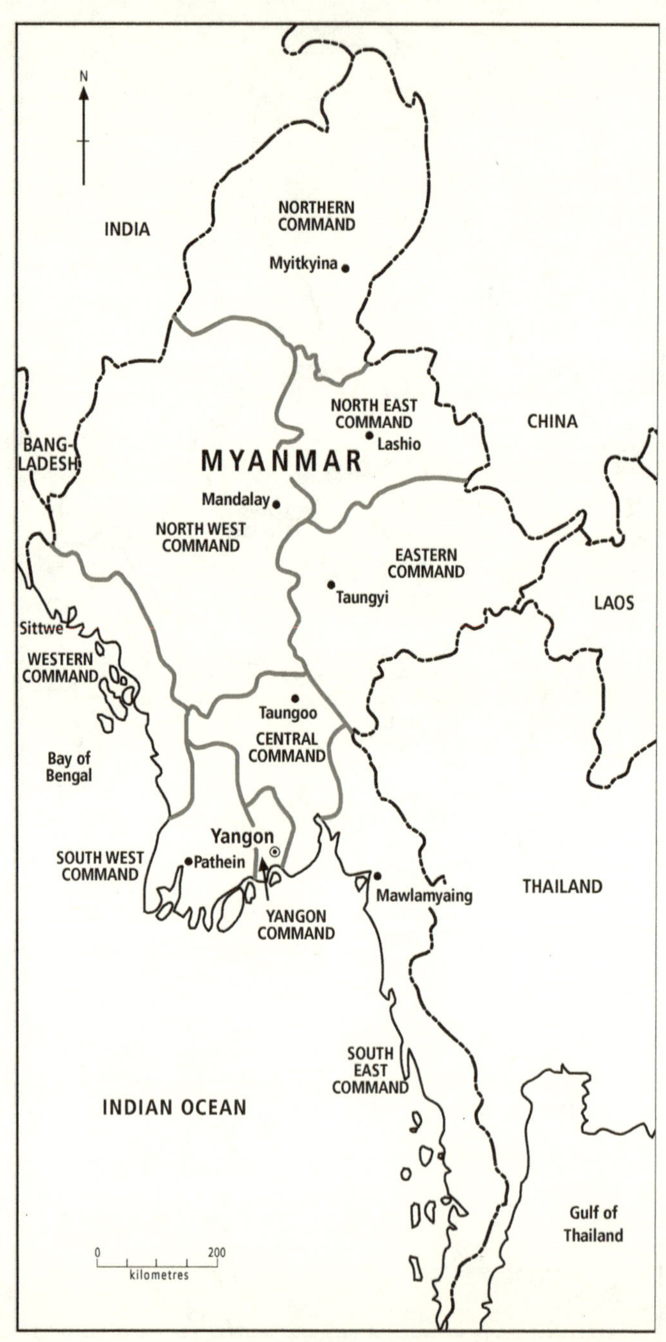

FIGURE 3.8
The Command Structure of the Tatmadaw by Region (1989–98)

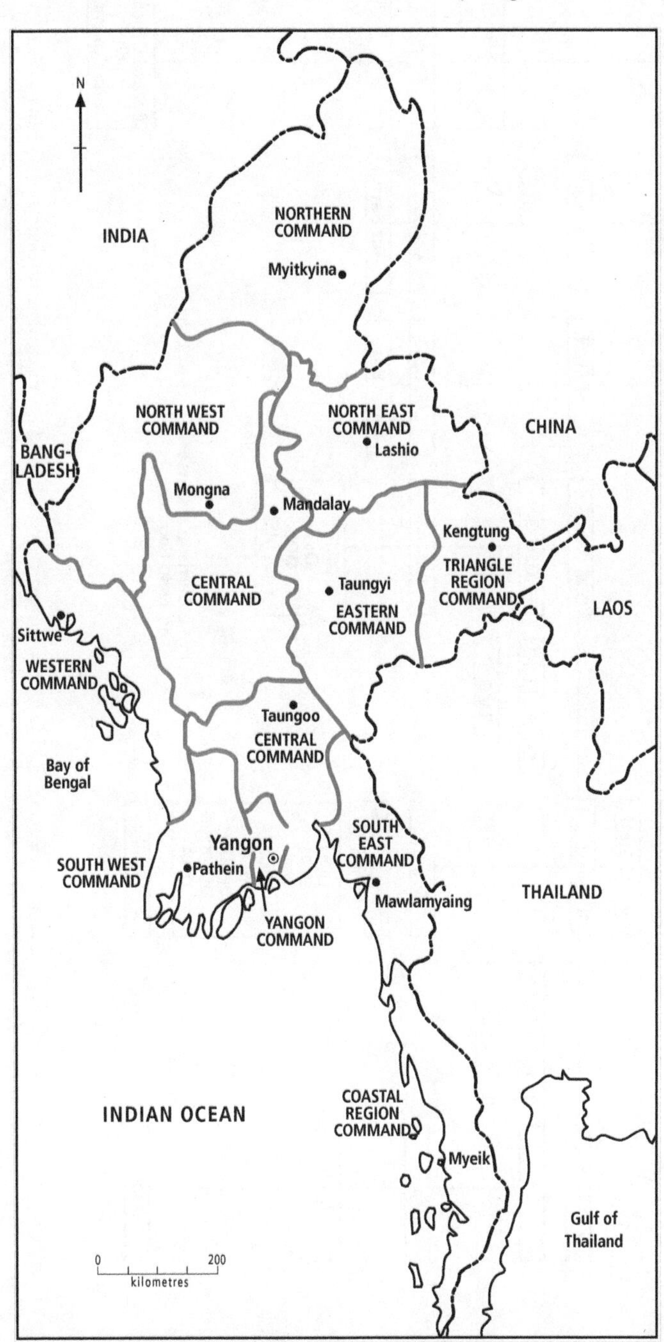

FIGURE 3.9
The Tatmadaw Command Structure, 1988

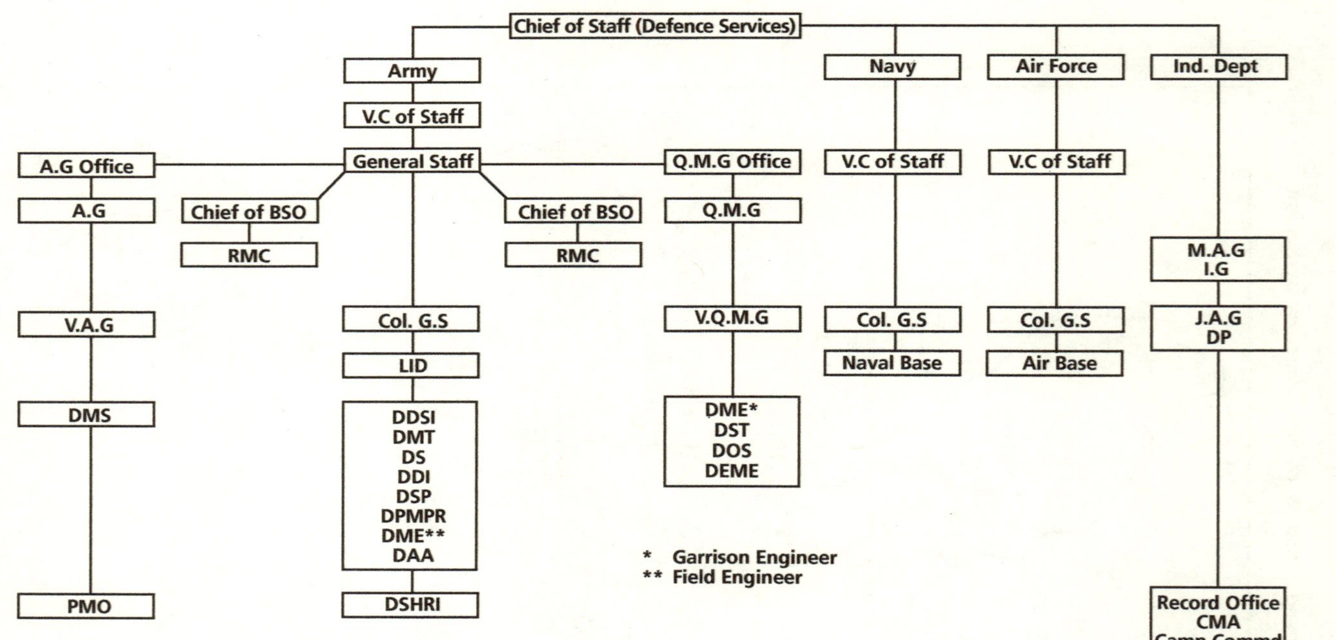

Notes:
V.C of Staff = Vice-Chief of Staff; A.G = Adjutant General; Q.M.G = Quartermaster General; V.A.G = Vice Adjutant General; V.Q.M.G = Vice Quartermaster General; BSO = Bureau of Special Operation; RMC = Regional Military Command; Col. G.S = Colonel General Staff; LID = Light Infantry Division; M.A.G = Military Appointment General; I.G = Inspector General; J.A.G = Judge Advocate General; DMS = Directorate of Medical Services; DDSI = Directorate of Defence Services Intelligence; DMT = Directorate of Military Training; DS = Directorate of Signal; DDI = Directorate of Defence Industries; DSP = Directorate of Security Printing; DPMPR = Directorate of People's Militias and Public Relations; DME = Directorate of Military Engineers; DAA = Directorate of Armours and Artillery; DST = Directorate of Supply and Transport; DOS = Directorate of Ordinance Services; DEME = Directorate of Electrical and Mechanical Engineers; DP = Directorate of Procurement; PMO = Provost Martial Office; DSHRI = Defence Services Historical Research Industries; CMA = Central Military Account; Camp Commd = Comp Commandant

FIGURE 3.10
The Tatmadaw Command Structure, 1998

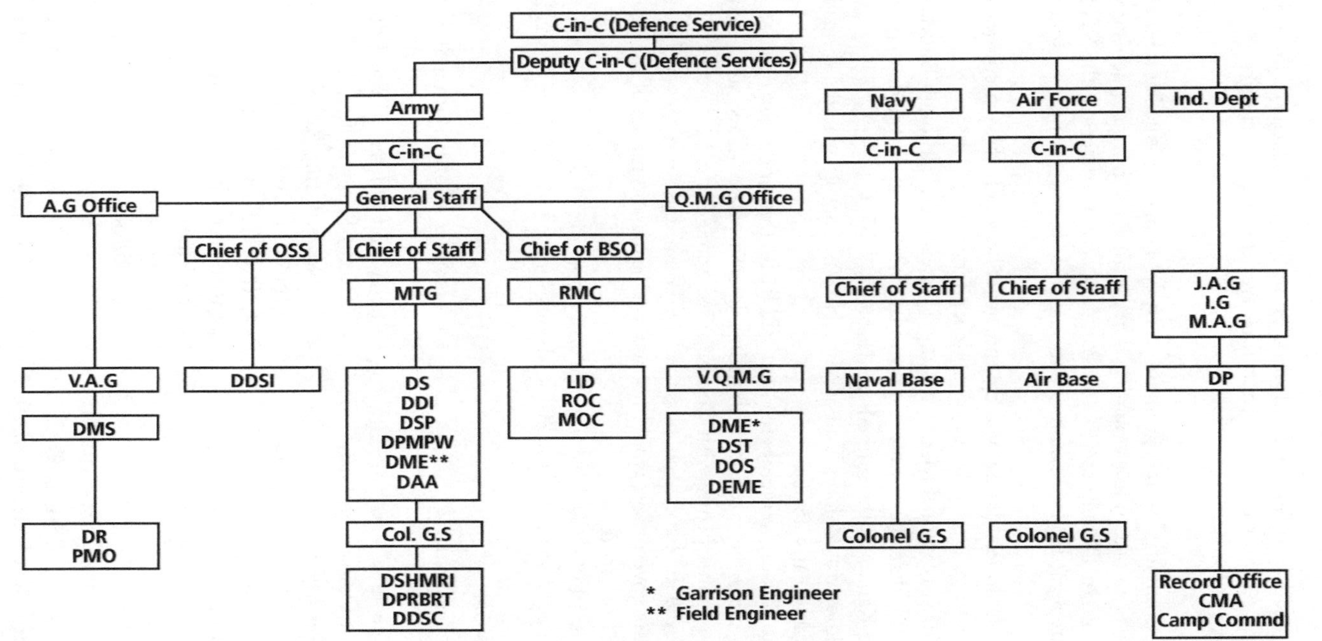

Notes:
C-in-C = Commander-in-Chief; OSS = Office of Strategic Studies; A.G = Adjutant General; Q.M.G = Quartermaster General; V.A.G = Vice Adjutant General; V.Q.M.G = Vice Quartermaster General; BSO = Bureau of Special Operation; RMC = Regional Military Command; G.S = General Staff; LID = Light Infantry Division; ROC = Regional Operation Command; MOC = Military Operation Command; M.A.G = Military Appointment General; I.G = Inspector General; J.A.G = Judge Advocate General; MTG = Military Training General; DMS = Directorate of Medical Services; DDSI = Directorate of Defence Services Intelligence; DS = Directorate of Signal; DDI = Directorate of Defence Industries; DSP = Directorate of Security Printing; DPMPW = Directorate of People's Militias and Psychological Warfare; DME = Directorate of Military Engineers; DAA = Directorate of Armours and Artillery; DST = Directorate of Supply and Transport; DOS = Directorate of Ordinance Services; DEME = Directorate of Electrical and Mechanical Engineers; DP = Directorate of Procurement; PMO = Provost Martial Office; DR = Directorate of Resettlement; DPRBRT = Directorate of Public Relations and Border Troops; DDSC = Department of Defence Services Computer; DSHMRI = Defence Services Historical Museum and Research Institute; CMA = Central Military Account; Camp Commd = Camp Commandant.

Notes

1 This problem is due to British discrimination in the recruitment to the British Burma Army, in favour of ethnic minorities over the Bamar majority.

2 See Appendix (1) for details.

3 Ibid.

4 The "Thirty Comrades" were a group of thirty Myanmar nationalists who went to Japan in 1941 to take military training. They formed the Burma Independence Army (BIA) on 26 December 1941 in Bangkok. The members of the "Thirty Comrades" are regarded by Myanmar nationalists as founders of the present day Tatmadaw.

5 For example, Colonel Maung Maung and his colleague had been considering organizing a reserve force even before independence.

6 CD. 875, Diary of Colonel Maung Maung. (For example, although Bo Maung Maung realized that there were Communists within the Tatmadaw, he saw Rightists and Karens as the immediate threat.)

7 He was later known as Colonel Chit Myaing. He was a key figure in the Tatmadaw in the 1950s and early 1960s.

8 Colonel Chit Myaing remembered that SITREPs (Situation Reports) at the time used to carry messages about burning down a whole village suspected of harbouring or sympathizing with Communists. Some of the captured weapons were not proved to have been possessed by communist insurgents. He also argued that the government would not win the hearts and minds of the people with this kind of tactics.

9 DR. 497, The 1948 COs' Meeting. See also Appendix (1).

10 DR. 9453, Interview with Colonel Chit Myaing for the History of the Tatmadaw, pp. 30–32.

11 Ibid., pp. 33–34.

(1) Brigadier Ne Win – Commander (North Burma Sub District)
(2) Colonel Ze Ya – General Staff Officer-1 (War Office)
(3) Lieutenant Colonel Ye Htut – CO (No. 3 Burma Rifles)
(4) Major Chit Myaing – 2-IC (No. 3 Burma Rifles)
(5) Lieutenant Colonel Tin Oo – CO (No. 6 Burma Rifles)
(6) Major Tin Maung – 2-IC (No. 6 Burma Rifles)
(7) Major Tun Sein – Company Commander (No. 5 Burma Rifles)
(8) Major Thaung Kyi – Company Commander (No. 3 Burma Rifles)
(9) Lieutenant Colonel Saw Tun Sein – CO (No. 1 Burma Regiment)

See also Mya Win, *Tatmadaw's Traditional Role in National Politics* (Yangon: News and Periodical Enterprises, 1992), p. 9; and Defence Services Historical

Museum and Research Institute (DSHMRI), "Myanmar Political History and the Role of the Tatmadaw", unpublished manuscript in Bamar (no date), p. 53.

12 For details on the Tatmadaw Committee and Leftist Unity Programme, see Maung Aung Myoe, Counterinsurgency in Myanmar: The Government's Response to the Burma Communist Party, unpublished Ph.D. dissertation (Australian National University, 1998).

13 DR. 9453, Interview with Colonel Chit Myaing for the History of the Tatmadaw, p. 50.

14 DR. 1535, Burma Army List 1952.

15 A Tatmadaw Researcher, *A Brief History of Myanmar in the Period between 1948 and 1988 and The Role of the Tatmadaw*, vol. 2, in Myanmar (Yangon: News and Periodical Enterprises, 1990), p. 187.

16 Mya Win, *A Brief History of Tatmadaw's Leaders*, in Myanmar (Yangon: News and Periodical Enterprises, 1991), pp. 11–12. The coup attempt would be seen as a move of the Communists or the Leftists by foreign countries.

17 DR. 9453, Interview with Colonel Chit Myaing for the History of the Tatmadaw.

18 Defence Services Historical Museum and Research Institute (DSHMRI), "An Administrative History of the Armed Forces in Burma", unpublished manuscript, vol. 2, p. 750.

19 Tonte on 14 August 1948, Mawchi on 20 August 1948, and Mawlamein on 1 September 1948.

20 Dr Maung Maung, *General Ne Win and Myanmar's Political Journey*, in Myanmar (Yangon: Bagan Publishing House, 1969), p. 313.

21 DR. 859, 1949 COs' Meeting.

22 Some of the Karen soldiers loyal to the Tatmadaw were reinstated after some time.

23 Dr Maung Maung, *General Ne Win and Myanmar's Political Journey*, p. 312.

24 CD. 350, Minutes of the COs' Conference held in January and February 1950. (The biggest headache of the time for the Military Secretary (MS), later renamed Military Appointment General, was U Nu's promotion of Lieutenant Colonel Lazum Tang to the rank of brigadier during his tour in upper Myanmar, without consulting the Tatmadaw leaders.)

25 Ibid.

26 DR. 9453, Interview with Colonel Chit Myaing for the History of the Tatmadaw.

27 Corps will include signal, medical, supply, ordinance, armour, and artillery and so on.

28 War Office, General Staff Office's letter No. -88/ E1/SD.

29 War Office, General Staff Office's letter No. -102/E1/SD, 28 August 1951.

30 War Office, General Staff Office's letter No. -103/E1/SD, 1 September 1951.

31 War Office, General Staff Office's letter No. -103/E1/SD, 29 October 1951.

32 War Office, Office of the Permanent Secretary's letter No. -1Ba(Lawa)52, 7 February 1952.

33 War Office, General Staff Office's letter No. -88/E1/SD, 23 September 1951.

34 Memorandum of the Fourth Meeting of the Defence Services Council, 19 September 1952, top secret.

35 Note that the Myanmar terms for Chief-of-Staff changed from *Sit Oo Si Choke* (စစ်ဦးစီးချုပ်) to *Kar Kwe Yae Oo Si Choke* (ကာကွယ်ရေးဦးစီးချုပ်). In the navy and air force also, Chief of Naval Staff and Chief of Air Staff changed to Vice-Chief of Staff (Navy) and Vice-Chief of Staff (Air Force). Their Myanmar equivalents are from *Yay Tat Oo Si Choke* (ရေတပ်ဦးစီးချုပ်) to *Du Ti Ya Kar Kwe Yae Oo Si Choke (Yay)* (ဒုတိယကာကွယ်ရေးဦးစီးချုပ်-ရေ) and *Lay Tat Oo Si Choke* (လေတပ်ဦးစီးချုပ်) *to Du Ti Ya Kar Kwe Yae Oo Si Choke (Lay)* (ဒုတိယကာကွယ်ရေးဦးစီးချုပ်-လေ).

36 CD. 350, Minutes of the COs' Conference held in January and February 1950.

37 CD. 349, Minutes of the Commanding Officers' Conference held at the War Office from 28 to 30 March 1951.

38 Ibid.

39 CD. 99, Documents distributed at the Tatmadaw Conference held in September 1954.

40 Colonel Aung Gyi was very suspicious of Brigadier Kyaw Zaw's motive for not authorizing a rescue mission for Lieutenant Colonel Maung Maung.

41 CD. 14, Matters relating to Brigadier General Kyaw Zaw.

42 Ibid.

43 Autobiography of Kyaw Zaw (unpublished).

44 Out of 148 AFPFL MPs, 97 were with the "Stable" faction.

45 The "Stable" faction was supported by one NUF MP and twenty Nationalities MPs.

46 The communist menace was discussed by U Sein Win in his book titled *The Split Story*. Sein Win argued that the Tatmadaw leaders realized that once the Communists came to power, they would be the first victims, and the army would go to pieces and the political split would pave the way for the Communists' ascension to power. He stated that the Tatmadaw's fear of the Communists was more out of physical necessity than because of ideology. See Sein Win, *The Split Story* (Rangoon: The Gurdian Press, 1959), p. 67.

47 Details of this coup plan were revealed by a journalist named Atauktaw Ohn Myint in the newspaper. Later he published a book titled (ခက်ဖွယ်ရယ်ကြုံ လက်နက်ကယ်စုံအညီနဲ့) *Khet Phwe Ye Kyone Laknat Kaw Sone Anyi Nae* [In the Face of an Armed Conflict]. It was claimed that thirteen senior commanders, including General Ne Win, Brigadier Aung Shwe, and Colonels Tun Sein, Kyi Win, Hla Maw, Maung Maung, Aung Gyi, Thein Toke, and Tin Pe, along with some leaders from the Burma Socialist Party, were on the assassination list.

48 Based on my observations, field commanders knew some of the moves undertaken by the Communists and the UMP battalions under the control of politicians. Some UMP troops and paramilitary forces were disarmed in several locations outside Yangon.

49 Although Brigadier Maung Maung was purged for alleged election bias in official publications, it was believed by some observers that his deep involvement with the CIA was the real reason. At that time, Brigadier Maung Maung had been authorized by General Ne Win to develop a counter-intelligence unit under the Directorate of Education and Psychological Warfare to cushion the poor performance of the existing Military Intelligence Services. But his over-personalization of the project had made General Ne Win angry at some stage. General Ne Win was somehow unaware of some of the activities of the unit. Besides, it is also possible that the Director of Intelligence, Colonel Maung Lwin, a close lieutenant of General Ne Win, was angry about such a rival organization. Therefore a clash naturally developed. Finally, when General Ne Win found out about an incident in 1960, possibly through Maung Lwin's intelligence, in which Brigadier Maung Maung allowed the CIA to interrogate a captured Chinese officer, without Ne Win's authorization, he dismissed Brigadier Maung Maung. Some observers said that Brigadier Maung Maung's strong anti-communist stance crossed the line between anti-BCP and anti-Chinese. It is necessary to note that General Ne Win was trying to settle border issues with the PRC and some kind of negotiations were going on for a coordinated military operation against the KMT. Clearly, General Ne Win did not want to upset the Chinese through CIA involvement in Myanmar affairs. Brigadier Maung Maung was finally assigned to Israel as ambassador.

50 Military attachés are usually sent for a term of not more than four years.

51 The BSPP was the only legal and ruling party in Myanmar in the period between March 1964 and September 1998.

52 All the senior commanders had to be members of the BSPP and they were elected as members of the Central Committee (discussed in more detail below).

53 This office was abolished on 27 June 1983 after the fall of Brigadier Tin Oo.

54 Alfred Stepan, "The New Professionalism of Internal Warfare and Military Role Expansion", in *Authoritarian Brazil: Origins, Policies, Future*, edited by Alfred Stepan (New Haven: Yale University Press, 1973).

55 CD 351, Minutes of the Commanding Officers' Conference held on 21 July 1951.

56 Interview with Colonel Saw Myint, Yangon, 4 May 1996.

57 For detail, see Maung Aung Myoe, Counter-insurgency in Myanmar: The Government's Response to the Burma Communist Party.

58 Defence Services Historical Museum and Research Institute (DSHMRI), "The National Ideology and the Role of the Defence Services"; and Director of Information (Government of the Union of Burma), *Is Trust Vindicated?* (Ministry of Information, Rangoon, 1960), p. 535.

59 At the 1962 Tatmadaw conference, the COs decided to transform the Tatmadaw into the People's Tatmadaw (People's Army); a national army protecting the socialist economic system. This was further discussed at the 1966 Tatmadaw conference, at which the COs recommended that the Tatmadaw should be transformed into a political, economic, and social force, in addition to maintaining its original defence role. The scope of the Tatmadaw was to cover not only protecting a socialist economic system, but also building one.

60 The atmosphere of the discussions was rather quiet and seldom argumentative. Attendance was more important than participation in the discussion.

61 In most communist countries, political commissars were attached to all levels of troops, but in Myanmar, the commanding officer was also the political commissar, in his role as chairman of the Battalion Party Organizing Committee.

62 Central Committee of the Burma Socialist Programme Party, *Organization and Duties of the Party Organizations within the Tatmadaw* (Yangon: BSPP Press, 1985).

63 Michael Voslensky, *Nomenklatura: Anatomy of the Soviet Ruling Class*, translated by Eric Mosbacher (London: Bodley Head, 1984).

64 Milovan Djilas, *The New Class* (New York: Federick & Praeger Inc., 1964).

65 Interestingly, the emergence of a "New Class" or "Privileged Class" was discussed in a book recently published by the government. See Sithu Aung and Maung Hmat (ရွှေပြည်တော်မျှော်မဝေးပြီမို့) *No Longer a Distance to the Golden Land*, in Myanmar (Yangon: News and Periodical Enterprises, 1995), p. 240.

66 Andrew Selth, "Can Burma's Military Regime Survive?", *Australian Quarterly*, vol. 68, no. 3, Spring 1996, p. 63.

67 See Appendix (2) for details.

68 See Appendix (3) for details.

69 In fact, Naval Captain Bo Shane (DSA-1) was known as a chosen Commander-in-Chief (Navy). But he died before such an appointment could be made. Another example was Major General Nyan Lin (DSA-1). He was also known as a chosen Commander-in-Chief (Army). Due to his poor health, he was transferred to the Ministry of Defence, without a portfolio.

70 See Appendix (4) for details.

71 After a major shake-up within the DDSI, in early 1984, Colonel Khin Nyunt was appointed the director of DDSI. It was he who rebuilt the DDSI from scratch to its present status. On 5 August 1985, the director of the DDSI was upgraded from colonel to colonel/brigadier. However, it was only in 1988 that the director was promoted to brigadier.

72 David I. Steinberg, "Burma/Myanmar: A Guide for the Perplex?", NBR Analysis, vol. 15, no. 1 (March 2004): 46.

73 Burma's Junta Banker Mentality (BBC, 29 September 2007, 13:45 GMT).

74 In September 2004, there was a clash between intelligence and infantry units in border town of Muse in the North East Command area, Shan State. When the regional commander received a complaint letter that there was a widespread corruption among intelligence officers in Muse checkpoint, he sent an infantry

unit headed by a colonel to conduct an investigation; the intelligence unit at the checkpoint refused to allow the colonel and his troops to come in. There was a brief intense confrontation and the regional commander authorized the colonel to use force if necessary; the infantry unit was quite prepared and happy to use force. Finally, the intelligence unit surrendered. The investigation found that there was a widespread corruption. The General Staff ordered to dismiss some officers and transfer others; but General Khin Nyunt refused to carry out and even overruled it. Moreover, General Khin Nyunt held a secret meeting among senior intelligence officers to investigate corruption among senior commanders to prove that intelligence officers were not the only corrupt people. The whole situation infuriated Senior General Than Shwe and Vice Senior General Maung Aye who concluded that they must take an immediate dramatic action rather than a gradual process.

75 For example, in the Southwest Command, the commander was authorized to repair and run the glass factory, which was virtually destroyed during the 1988 uprising, by his own means. This meant that the commander sold any product available to him, such as marine products, for foreign exchange to finance the renovation.

76 SPDC Declaration No. 1/97, 15 November 1997.

77 SPDC Declaration No. 3/97, 15 November 1997.

78 SPDC Declaration No. 1/98, 5 June 1998.

79 SPDC Order No. 1/98, 24 July 1998.

80 See Appendix (7) for details.

81 See Appendix (5) for details.

82 Bago, Insein, Pyapon, Myaung Mya, Maubin, Hanthawaddy, Tharawaddy, Prome, Thayet, Pakokku, Sagaing, Shwebo, Monywa, Tavoy, Hinthada, Minbu, Meiktila, Taungoo. See A Tatmadaw Researcher, *A Brief History of Myanmar*, vol. 2, p. 197.

83 Dr Maung Maung, *General Ne Win and Myanmar's Political Journey*, p. 312.

84 Beik, Kyikekami, Thaton, Pathein, Magway, Myin Gyan, Maw Like, Yamethin, Sittwe (North), Sittwe (South), Mandalay, Kyaukpyu, Than Dwe, and Yangon. See A Tatmadaw Researcher, *A Brief History of Myanmar*, vol. 2, pp. 197–98.

85 Ibid., pp. 203–04.

86 ရန်ကုန်ဘဆွေ၊ ရဲဘော်တို့နှင့်အတူ (ရန်ကုန်၊ တင်းကုတ်စာပေ၊ ၁၉၆၃) [Yangon Ba Swe, together with the Comrades, in Myanmar (Yangon: Tin Goak Sarpay, 1963)].

87 Defence Services Historical Museum and Research Institute (DSHMRI), *History of the Tatmadaw, in Bamar*, vol. 4 (Yangon: News and Periodical Enterprises, 1996), p. 131.

88 BBC (Burmese Service) 29 March 2007 (20:15 Myanmar Time); RFA (Burmese) 29 March 2007 (19:00 Myanmar Time).

89 Ibid.

90 See Appendix (6) for details.

91 Formerly, only No. 1 TOC of the Eastern Command was in Lashio.

92 In 1990, class battalions were transformed into Light Infantry Battalions (LIBs). For example, No. (2) Chin Rifles became No. 308 LIB.

93 Andrew Selth, Myanmar Revamps Its Military Intelligence Apparatus, *Asia-Pacific Defence Reporter*, June–July 1998, pp. 11–12.

94 *Janes Intelligent Review*, March 2002.

95 Ibid.

96 Deputy Chief of DSIB, Major General Kyaw Win, honourably retired and received no punishment. BG Kyaw Thein, BG Kyaw Han, BG Hla Aung also escaped prison terms, but BG Thein Swe, BG Than Tun, BG Khin Aung, and BG Myint Zaw received long prison terms. Among the colonels, only Colonel Ngwe Tun (Navy) and Colonel Sithu (Air) escaped from prison terms while Colonel Hla Min, Colonel Tin Oo, Colonel San Pwint, Colonel Than Aung, and Colonel Aung Ngwe received long prison terms.

97 *New Lights of Myanmar*, Special Supplement on Briefings given by General Thura Shwe Man and Lieutenant General Soe Win on 24 October 2004.

98 Please also see DVB Broadcast on 30 November 2002 (1430 GMT) and 2 August 2005 (1430 GMT). According to some sources, these divisions are located at Myeik, Thaton, Kyaukpadaung, Oaktwin, Mongkhun, Bago, Hsiphaw, Aungban, Bhamo, and Badan.

99 Some reports indicate that these divisions are in Pyawbwe, Taungoo, Ayerdaw, Indine, and Monywa.

100 See also DVB Broadcast on 30 November 2002 (1,430 GMT).

101 DR. 9692, History of the Directorate of Military Training.

102 DR. 8559, History of the Tatmadaw-Yay.

103 Each naval region command had its code number. For example, the Rakhine Naval Region Command HQ was No. 1, the Ayerwaddy Naval Region Command HQ was No. 2, and the Thanintharyi Naval Region Command HQ was No. 3. Units under the naval region command HQs also had code numbers. For example, signal unit was No. 1, naval ordnance was No. 6, and so on. Therefore, under the Thanintharyi Naval Region Command HQ, we could see No. 31 Naval Signal Unit (Mawlamyaing), No. 32 Naval Store Unit (Mawlamyaing), No. 33 Naval Administrative Unit (Mawlamyaing), No. 34 Naval Ordnance Unit (Mawlamyaing), No. 35 Naval Engineering Unit (Mawlamyaing), No. 36 Naval Flotilla (Mawlamyaing), No. 37 Naval Training Unit (Mawlamyaing), No. 38 Naval Base Camp (Myeik), and No. 39 Naval Forward Camp (Mali Island).

104 DR. 8556, History of the Tatmadaw-Lay.

105 Ibid.

106 DR. 9692, History of the Directorate of Military Training.

107 DR. 8556, History of the Tatmadaw-Lay.

108 Ibid.

109 Myanmar Air Force Annual Magazine 2006, p. 159.

4

ARMAMENT AND FORCE MODERNIZATION

Before 1988, the Tatmadaw had been poorly equipped and modestly maintained and its weapons were of World War II vantage. Most of the Tatmadaw's major arms procurements, including aircraft and surface ships, were made in the 1950s and early 1960s. Throughout the 1970s and 1980s, the Tatmadaw's order of battle had been a very modest one compared with most of its neighbours. In this regard, the force modernization in Myanmar has been one long overdue. With the coming of the SLORC in September 1988, the Tatmadaw began to pursue a force modernization programme. The Tatmadaw had injected a massive amount of resources to boost its order of battle.[1] Moreover, the Tatmadaw embarked on ambitious arm production and procurement programmes. The force modernization programme of the Tatmadaw since the early 1990s indicates that external security threats had significantly influenced the Tatmadaw's threat perception. In accordance with its modified military doctrine, the Tatmadaw has been building up conventional war fighting capabilities. While it procured most of its artillery, aircraft, and surface ships from oversea sources, the Tatmadaw relied more or less on its domestic defence industries for small arms production as it has long been pursuing a policy of self-sufficiency in small arms and ammunition production. Force modernization took place for all aspects of the Tatmadaw. Here I will discuss the modernization of three services of the Tatmadaw, mostly in terms of military capability and order of battle.

THE TATMADAW-KYI (THE ARMY)

In his analysis of the Myanmar Armed Forces, Andrew Selth remarked that:

> The army was essentially a lightly equipped infantry force organized and deployed for counterinsurgency operations. While it was experienced and battle-hardened, its heavier equipment was obsolete, its logistics and communications systems were very weak and operations were constantly hampered by shortages of transport, fuel and ammunition. The navy and air force were both very small services, largely relegated to roles in support of the army. The navy was only capable of coastal and river patrols, and the air force was structured almost exclusively for ground support. Both suffered from obsolescent weapons platforms, poor communications equipment, a lack of spare parts and a shortage of skilled manpower.[2]

In one way, the force modernization of the Tatmadaw-Kyi was closely related to the building of local defence industries. Since the day of Myanmar's independence, the Tatmadaw has been implementing a policy of self-sufficiency in small arms and ammunition production. To not only save its foreign exchange reserves, and depend less on foreign powers for arms and ammunition supply,[3] but also to maintain defence science and technological bases, the Tatmadaw-Kyi has built a number of ordnance facilities. In the early 1950s, the Tatmadaw began to build up its Defence Industries (DI), known as "Kapasa", under the General Staff Office. The first locally built small arm is known as BA-52 or "Ne Win Sten", a Myanmar copy of the Italian 9-mm TZ45 sub-machine gun. Although the design was rough, and the performance unreliable, it remained a standard sub-machine gun with the infantry until the mid-1980s, and with the support battalion until the early 1990s.[4] By the late 1950s, the DI expanded its arms and ammunition production facilities by entering into a contract with the Federal Republic of Germany state-owned Fritz Werner. Then, factories under the DI began to produce BA-63 Automatic Rifle (G-3A2) [*Maun-Pyan-Raiphae*], BA-72 Assault Rifle (G-3K) [*Che-Hmone-Ye-Raiphae*], BA-64 Light Machine Gun (G-4) [*Set-Lat*], BA-100 (G-3A3ZF) and 7.62-mm and 9-mm ammunition. The BA-63 Rifle has subsequently become the standard rifle of the Tatmadaw. Throughout the 1960s and 1970s, the Tatmadaw-Kyi built several DI factories on the western bank of Ayerwaddy River near Pyay. These factories also produced grenades (BA-80/BA-92 rifle grenade, BA-77 anti-personnel hand grenade, BA-88 offensive hand grenade, BA-91 defensive hand grenade, BA-101 general purpose grenade, and BA-109 hand grenade), anti-personnel mines (MM-1 and MM-2), and mortars (60-mm BA-100, 81-mm BA-90 and 120-mm

BA-97), as well as ammunition. In spite of the local production, the Tatmadaw-Kyi continued to buy small arms and heavy mortars from foreign sources. For example, it bought M-1 and M-2 carbine, M-79 grenade launcher, and 60-mm (M-19) and 81-mm (M-29) mortars from the United States. Moreover, the Tatmadaw-Kyi procured most of the rocket launchers, recoilless guns, towed artillery of various calibres, and signal/wireless machines from the United States, United Kingdom, the Federal Republic of Germany, Yugoslavia, and Israel.

Since the coming of the SLORC to power, the Tatmadaw decided to expand and strengthen its defence science and technology base. In the face of an arms embargo from the traditional suppliers and partners of arms and ammunition production, the Tatmadaw turned to the People's Republic of China (PRC) for help. In recent years, there have been some unconfirmed reports about new ammunition factories near Magway, built with the assistance of the PRC. It is believed that M-21 Automatic Rifle, M-22 Assault Rifle, and M-23 Light Machine Gun are now in production. They were displayed at the defence services museum in Yangon as MA-1, MA-2, and MA-3. Both MA-1 and MA-2 use 5.56-mm ammunition. The Tatmadaw equipped new infantry battalions with MA-1 and MA-2 as standard rifles.[5] To some observers, new defence facilities also produce of anti-personnel land mines. The PRC and Singapore were considered major sources of arms technology for Myanmar. In 2006, the Korean media reported that Daewoo was involved in building an arms factory in Myanmar, as a result of a contract worth US$133.8 million signed in 2002.[6] The Tatmadaw reportedly produced wireless communication equipment too.[7]

One of the most impressive areas of force modernization that took place since 1988 is in the field of armour and artillery. In the early 1950s, the Tatmadaw-Kyi procured a number of medium tanks, APCs, Scout Cars, and Bren Carriers from the United Kingdom and the United States. The army bought eighty Universal T-16 tracked Bren gun carriers in 1950, 1952, and 1959; forty Humber one-ton armoured personnel carriers in 1950; twenty-two Comet medium tanks (of WWII stock) in 1954; six Ferret scout cars in 1956; and fifty-one Daimler scout cars in 1961. However, no more procurement was made throughout the 1960s, 1970s, and 1980s. By early 1980s, it was estimated that fewer than 100 carriers were serviceable. Due to budgetary restraints, particularly the foreign exchange reserve, the Tatmadaw-Kyi has locally produced armoured carriers, known as Burma Army Armoured Cars (BAACs), based mainly on Mazda, Hino, and Nissan parts, since the early 1980s, including Armoured Personnel Carriers (APCs), Scout Cars (SCs), and Command and Control Carriers (CCCs). A total of forty-four carriers (BAAC-83 APC, BAAC-84 SC, BAAC-85 SC, BAAC-86 SC, BAAC-87 APC, and BAAC-87 CCC) were locally made between 1983 and 1991. The Tatmadaw-Kyi continued to produce a number of APCs in the 1990s. One of the latest productions was the tracked-armoured carrier equipped with 37-mm twin barrel Anti-Aircraft self-propelled guns for air defence batteries.[8] Up to the end of the 1980s, as it had never intended to build itself a fighting force for conventional regular war, the Tatmadaw-Kyi did not procure main battle tanks, light tanks, amphibious tanks, and armoured personnel carriers. It maintained a very modest armour wing under the Directorate of Armour and Artillery until the early 1990s. Beginning in 1990, the Tatmadaw-Kyi took a major step to boost its armour and artillery wing. It was reported that the Tatmadaw-Kyi bought about 100 Type 69 II Main Battle Tanks (MBT), about a dozen 59D MBT, over 100 Type 63 light (amphibious) tanks, about 250 Type 85 Armoured Personnel Carriers, and over fifty Type 90 APC from the PRC. A recent report, however, indicated that the Tatmadaw also has T-72 MBT and BTR-3U IFV (Infantry Fighting Vehicle) in its order of battle.[9] The *Wikipedia* on-line website provided the following order of battle for the Tatmadaw's armour corps.

139 T-72 MBT (PRC/Ukraine/Russia)
280+ Type 59D MBT (PRC)
190+ Type 69II MBT (PRC)
(xx) Type 80 MBT (PRC)
(xx) Type 85 MBT (PRC)
(xx) Type 55 MBT (India)
150+ Type 63 Light Tank (PRC)
1000 BTR-3U IFV (Ukraine)
250 Type 85 APC (PRC)
240 Type 90 APC (PRC)
140 EE-9 Cascavel AFV (Brazil)
(xx) AML 90 Armoured Cars (South Africa)
72 MAV-1 IFV (Local)[10]

Although some items are apparently in the Tatmadaw's order of battle, some models and the number of units appear to be purely a speculation.

In terms of infantry heavy weapons, the Tatmadaw-Kyi usually equipped its infantry battalions with 2-inch, 3-inch, 60-mm, 81-mm, and 82-mm mortars as light and medium mortars and 120-mm ones as heavy mortar. Most of these mortars were bought from the United Kingdom, the United States, and Yugoslavia. However, in the late 1980s, factories under the

Directorate of Defence Industries began to assemble 60-mm (BA-100), 81-mm (BA-90), and 120-mm (BA-97) mortars. In terms of towed artillery, the Tatmadaw-Kyi equips its artillery batteries with 6-pounder, 17-pounder, 25-pounder, 76-mm mountain gun, and 105-mm howitzer. It also operates 57-mm and 75-mm recoilless guns. In 1950s and 1960s the Tatmadaw-Kyi bought about a hundred 76-mm M48BI mountain guns from Yugoslavia, and about a hundred 105-mm M101 howitzers from the United States. In the early 1980s, the Tatmadaw-Kyi bought about 1,200 84-mm M2 Carl Gustaf anti-tank recoilless guns from Sweden. Since the early 1990s, although there is no way to confirm the number of artilleries, the Tatmadaw-Kyi did buy a number of 60-mm (Type-63) mortars, 82-mm (Type-53/67/76) mortars, 120-mm (Type-53) mortars, 122-mm (Type-55/56) mortars, 57-mm (Type-36) recoilless guns, 75-mm (Type-52/56) recoilless guns, 82-mm (Type-65/78) recoilless guns, 122-mm (Type-54) howitzers, 155-mm howitzers, and 107-mm (Type-63) and 130-mm (Type-63) multiple rocket launchers from the PRC. Moreover, there are some unconfirmed reports about artillery acquisition from various overseas sources, such as Israel (for 155-mm towed artillery and 120-mm mortars) and Russia (for 82-mm mortar and 122-mm multiple rocket launcher). It was also reported that Tatmadaw-Kyi took the delivery of 122-mm howitzers, a number of anti-tank weapons, and 107-mm Type 63 and 122-mm Type 90 Multiple Launch Rocket System (MLRS) from the PRC. Some reports stated that the Tatmadaw bought thirty units of 240-mm truck mounted MLRS from North Korea.[11]

There are some reports about the Tatmadaw procuring surface-to-surface missiles (SSMs). Since there are some missile battalions under the artillery corps, there are reports about the Tatmadaw's procurement of SSMs from China and North Korea. Andrew Selth reported that the Tatmadaw was interested in buying short-range ballistic missiles (SRBMs) from China and North Korea. He further stated that China agreed to sell some M-11 SRBMs for the Myanmar military. Besides, the Tatmadaw held discussions with a North Korean agency to buy Hwasong (Scub-type) SRBMs in 2003.[12] In March 2004, before the House International Relations Committee, Matthew Daley, deputy assistant secretary in the bureau of East Asian and Pacific Affairs in the U.S. State Department, stated that North Korea offered Myanmar surface-to-surface missiles. Some defence analysts speculated that the Tatmadaw might have procured SSMs from Ukraine. In December 2006, a South Korea press reported that Daewoo signed a deal with the Myanmar government in May 2002 to build an arms factory near Pyi, Bago Division, worth US$133.8 million.[13] Some analysts believed that this deal included the supply of some parts for missile development in

Myanmar. There is some speculation that the Tatmadaw has undertaken a guided missile development programme with the help of some firms from Singapore. To some observers, the Tatmadaw became serious about buying SSMs after its confrontation with Thai forces in early 2002. Besides, the Tatmadaw's military doctrine of "People's War under Modern Conditions" required deployment of such SSMs for firepower at the defence line at the border. The Tatmadaw could buy Chinese SSMs since it was a customer of China Precision Machinery Import-Export Corporation (CPMIEC); it bought HN-5 shoulder-launch missiles for air defence and C-801 and C-802 anti-ship cruise missile for warships. The CPMIEC could provide the Tatmadaw with M-9 (DF-15) and M-11 (DF-11) SSMs. Both M-11 (DF-11) and M-9 (DF-15) are road-mobile single-stage, solid-propellant SRBMs. The basic variant DF-11 has a range of 280–350 km and delivers a single-warhead of 500 kg. The improved DF-11A has an extended range of over 500–700 km. DF-11 can carry both high-explosive (HE) warhead and fuel-air explosive (FAE). DF-15 can carry a 500 kg single warhead and has a maximum range of 600 km. Both missiles are launched from transporter-erector-launcher (TEL) vehicles, to provide full road and cross-country mobility. The TEL vehicle carries the missile to the launch site with pre-calculated coordinate data, or to an unprepared new location by using GPS to obtain coordinate data.

Another area of force modernization within the armour and artillery field is air defence. Until 1988, the Tatmadaw had just an anti-aircraft battery, located near Mingalardon airport. Myanmar's air defence system was very modest since it maintained a small number of U.S.-made Bofors 40-mm anti-aircraft guns, U.S.-made 3.7-inch Mk 3A towed anti-aircraft guns, and Yugoslavia-made 20-mm M38 anti-aircraft gun. With these weapons, the Myanmar air defence system was primarily a point defence and very-low-altitude-air-defence-system (VLAADS). Since 1989, the armed forces has expanded to over a dozen of air defence battalions. It is now reported that the Tatmadaw has about thirty air defence battalions grouped into three air defence divisions under the air defence command. There has been some unconfirmed report that the Tatmadaw bought the BAe Dynamics Bloodhound Mk.II surface-to-air-missiles from Singapore. However, it appeared that the Tatmadaw is more interested in the Man-Portable Air-Defence System (MANPADS). This is indicated by the procurement of a number of Chinese-made Honying (HN-5A) shoulder-launch missiles, a variant of the Russian SA-7 Grail. The passive infrared homing HN-5 is normally operated in visible weather conditions. The missile can attack jet aircraft from the tail aspect or attack helicopters from all aspects.

Modifications on the HN-5A include all-aspect attacking ability and improved infrared seeker with greater detecting range and anti-background noise capability, and a larger warhead.[14] The HN-5A has a maximum range of 3,000 metres and a maximum altitude of 3,000 metres. It is speculated that the Tatmadaw is in possession of a number of SAM-7.[15] Moreover, the Tatmadaw bought several 37-mm twin barrel towed anti-aircraft gun systems, 57-mm single barrelled towed anti-aircraft systems and 57-mm twin barrel self-propelled anti-aircraft gun systems from China.

In 2001, *The Jane's Defence Weekly* reported that the Tatmadaw bought at least 100 Igla-1E [SA-16 "Gimlet"] low altitude, surface-to-air missile systems from Bulgaria. The SA-16 Gimlet (Igla-1 9K310) is a Russian-made MANPADS with a solid propellant guided missile. It is an improved version of SA-18 GROUSE (Igla 9M38) MANPADS.[16] The system is designed for destroying low flying aircraft and helicopters. The missile can be launched to follow or meet enemy aircraft. The Igla-1E is a passive infrared-seeking missile that can engage targets to a maximum range of 5,200 metres and an altitude of 3,500 metres or minimum range of 500 metres and an altitude of 10 metres.[17] The Igla-1E, like U.S.-made Raytheon Stinger, is considered a deadly dangerous air defence weapon as its conical-scan seeker head enables it to filter out many types of simple flares deployed as infrared countermeasures (IRCM). It appears that the Tatmadaw considered MANPADS the most cost effective air-defence weapon that posed a serious threat to air superiority or supremacy of opponents.

Since the early 2000s, the Tatmadaw has shown more interest in procuring air defence weapons, mostly from Russia and Eastern European countries. Other unconfirmed reports indicate the possible procurement of the TUNGUSKA Gun/Missile system. In April 2006, during his state visit to Russia, Vice-Senior General Maung Aye, reportedly discussed the purchase of Russian air defence systems, Tor-M1 [SA-15], and BUK M1-2 [SA-17].[18] The *Wikipedia* gave the following inventory list for Myanmar air defence.[19]

48 × TOR M1 [SA-15] Gauntlet SAMs
24 × BUK M1-2 [SA-17] Grizzly SAMs
24 × Tunguska [SA-19] Grisom Gun/SAMs
24 × SA-6 Gainful SAMs
24 × Pechora-2M SAMs
48 × SA-2 Guideline SAMs
2 × BAe Dynamics Bloodhound Mk.II SAMs
400 × SA-18 Grouse MANPADS
200 × HN-5 MANPADS

100 × Igla-1E [SA-16] Gimlet MANPADS
200 × 14.5 mm KPV [quadruple] AAA
200 × 37 mm/40 mm/57 mm AAA

However, there is no way to verify the information and we must be cautious in using the data. If the information has some element of truth, we can then safely assume that the Tatmadaw has considerably strengthened its air defence capability. If indeed the Tatmadaw acquired SA-15, SA-17, SA-6, SA-2, Pechora 2M, and SA-19 for its air defence, regardless of the quantity, then it must now have both SHORAD [Short Range Air Defence] and HIMAD [High to Medium Altitude Air Defence]. See Table 4.1.

TABLE 4.1
Air Defence Systems and Ranges

Sr.	*Missile*	*Range (M)*	*Altitude (M)*	*Remark*
1	SA-19	10,000	3,500	SHORAD
2	SA-15	12,000	6,000	SHORAD
3	SA-6	24,000	12,000	HIMAD
4	SA-17	30,000	15,000	HIMAD
5	Pechora 2M	32,000	20,000	HIMAD
6	SA-2	55,000	40,000	HIMAD

The SA-19 or Tunguska Gun/Missile system is a SHORAD commonly deployed in Russia and Eastern European countries. India also has this air defence system. It is designed to provide day and night protection for infantry and tank regiments against low-flying aircraft and helicopters in any weather condition. The Tunguska-M1 gun/missile system, mounted on a 34t tracked vehicle with multi-fuel engine, is a popular choice for low-level air defence. The system can engage targets while stationary and on the move, using missiles for long-range targets and guns for close-in defence. It is designed for defence against both fixed-wing aircraft and helicopters, and can also fire on ground targets.[20] The Tunguska-M1 vehicle carries eight 9M311-M1 SAM (NATO designation SA-19 Grison), and two twin-barrel 30-mm anti-aircraft guns.[21] In terms of fire control, the system has target acquisition radar and target tracking radar, optical sight, digital computing system, tilt angle measuring system, and navigation equipment. Radar detection range is 18 km and tracking range is 16 km.

The principal advantages of SA-15 [Tor-M1] is reportedly its ability to destroy two targets simultaneously in any weather condition, or at any time of the day or night; the use of both the powerful and jamming-resistant radar with electronic beam control and vertically launched missiles enables it to maintain high speed and manoeuvrability inside an entire engagement envelope; it has a high degree of automation of combat operation provided by the electronic equipment suite. Tor detects targets at a distance of 25 km and kills them at a distance of 12 km. The SA-6 is a two-stage, solid-fuel, low-altitude SAM. It has radio command guidance with semi-active radar terminal homing. It is a medium-level air defence system designed to protect ground forces from air attack. SA-17 is a new mobile SAM system from the Russian arms industries. It claims to be able to hit six targets flying simultaneously from different directions and at different altitudes. The Pechora-2M is an effective air defence weapon system against all aerodynamic means of attack. Although it is a HIMAD, this missile system is also effective in shooting down low-flying and small-size targets. It is also claimed to be capable of destroying ground-based targets. The SA-2 missile system is designed for the defence of both fixed targets and field forces. It is to cope with the threat posed by small groups of aircraft rather than massed raids. The SA-2 missile system has a known history of shooting down high-altitude reconnaissance aircraft such as the U-2. If the Tatmadaw is interested in ballistic missile defence systems, it can choose from among the Russian made S-300PMU series air defence systems.[22] China's PLA operated S-300PMU-1 and S-300PMU-2 SAM systems. In 2003, Vietnam bought S-300PMU-1 systems from Russia.[23]

Along with missile systems, the air defence system must include a series of air defence radar. The radar operation in Myanmar is usually undertaken by the air force. Until 1960, the Tatmadaw had no radar in its order of battle. The KMT aggression in the 1950s was the primary factor driving the Tatmadaw to procure radar. In 1960 some officers and those from other ranks from the army and air force were sent to the United States for training, and on their return, brought back TPS-ID type radars that were installed in Lwe-Mwe and Lwe-Taw-Khan. The Tatmadaw then bought four radars from the United Kingdom in the early 1960s. The British made DASR-I Radar (Decca Air Surveillance Radar – 1) was installed in No. 71 Squadron in Namsam in 1963, and became operational the next year. The radar had coverage of a 250-mile radius. In 1967, it was replaced by the DASR-II. For No. 72 Squadron in Lwe-Mwe, the AR-1 (medium range radar) was installed in 1965 and became operational the next year. The radar had a coverage of a 100-mile radius. It was relocated to Mingalardon Airport in 1998 as an airfield radar. Another AR-1 Radar was installed in No. 73 Squadron in Kutkai in 1966. Again it was relocated to Shante in 1990 as an airfield radar. No. 74 Squadron in Hmawbi received DASR-III (two-channel search radar) in 1966, which had an effective range of a 250-mile radius. Only this radar facility can do somewhat basic interception.

Despite the radar facilities, the Tatmadaw had neither the interceptors nor an air defence force, as the Vice-Chief of Staff (Air Force) correctly pointed out at the COs conferences in 1968 and 1969. According to the report, between 1 October 1966 and 31 March 1969, radars detected 100 unknown aircraft in Myanmar air space.[24] The Tatmadaw maintained a small battery of anti-aircraft artillery, comprised mostly of guns, in Mingalardon, for airfield defence. Only in the early 1990s, by procuring HN-5 from China, did the Tatmadaw begin to give serious attention to air defence. Although there are some reports about the procurement of radar and electronic warfare equipment from China in the 1990s, no detail is known to the public. What is more apparent is the fact that after its confrontation with Thai forces in 2001 and 2002 along the Myanmar-Thai border, the Tatmadaw took a serious interest in establishing an elaborate network of air defence systems in Myanmar.

In late 2002, the Myanmar Armed Forces appeared to acquire some 36D6 mobile radars from Ukraine.[25] The 36D6 [NATO designated TIN SHIELD] is a highly mobile radar system; due to its fast changeover from travel position to fire position and vice versa, it is designed to detect air targets at low, medium, and high altitudes, and to perform friend-or-foe identification. The radar system is able to provide targeting and bearing of active jamming, integrated computer-aided systems of control, and guidance of anti-aircraft guided missile complexes. Myanmar will be interested in procuring more air defence radar and air defence systems from either Russia or Ukraine. As the radars in Myanmar are very old and the Tatmadaw has procured air defence missiles, it is reasonable to expect the Tatmadaw to buy new and more advanced radars for Myanmar, since it needs more radars to cover the whole air space. Myanmar needs at least six fixed radar stations to cover its air space. Some observers even claimed to have seen the Tatmadaw operating Russian-made either P-37 or 1L-117 radars; but we cannot confirm this. The Tatmadaw certainly can choose from a variety of Russian-made air defence radars.

However, some of the weaponry may have problems with maintenance. For example, the HN-5 MANPADS has been with the Tatmadaw for more than fifteen years and the hot and humid weather in Myanmar would make the sensors vulnerable to a high rate of wear and tear. Moreover, the identification system might be another major problem in Myanmar's air defence. The IFF (identification of friend or foe), which is the primary means of identification, has several drawbacks which account for the high rate of friendly fire incidents in the history of air war. In addition, air defence systems require a highly capable and responsive C^3I (Command, Control, Communication, and Intelligence) infrastructure which serves as a force multiplier. The survivability and efficiency of the C^3I infrastructure for effective execution of air defence missions has become extremely important and any degradation of its performance has an immediate and direct impact on air defence systems. The C^3I infrastructure is vulnerable to ECMs (electronic counter measures).

All new developments suggest that the air defence in Myanmar has transformed from point defence to area wise defence. The Tatmadaw used to maintain just a company-size battery of anti-aircraft artillery, armed with 37-mm twin-barrel guns, for the protection of the Mingalardon airfield and the command headquarters in Yangon. With the procurement of MANPADS and SAMs for high and medium range air defence, the Tatmadaw is now capable of "area wise defence". The Tatmadaw also appears to have introduced a multi-layered air defence system: outer ring, medium ring, and inner ring. Jet fighters are assigned to air defence missions in the outer ring. Both aircraft and SAMs will be deployed in the medium ring, and anti-aircraft guns and MANPADS in the inner ring. Yet it is not clear whether the Tatmadaw's air defence system has transformed from passive to active defence. In an era of modern high-technology warfare, passive defence is no longer an attractive option. Air defence nowadays includes pre-emptive strikes, long-range interception, and electronic warfare against the enemy's air defence facilities and air bases or aircraft carriers.

The Tatmadaw appears to focus on two different types of air defence missions in Myanmar. One is the air defence for key political and military installations and the other is battlefield air defence. The former involves the construction of communication and radar networks and SAMs batteries for area wise defence, creating a form of ground based air defence environment. The latter involves the deployment of MANPADS against hostile aircraft and attack helicopters for protection of ground forces, including tanks and artilleries.

Signal Intelligence is also another important area of force modernization. The Defence Services Museum displayed the signal and telecommunication systems used by the Tatmadaw in the period between 1948 and 1988.

Most of them were from the United Kingdom and the United States. These included Redifon No. 53 and Redifon G251, Pye FM-8702, WS-62, HF-15B, TRA 309 and TRA 906 HF radio receivers, and AN/PRC-6, AN/PRC-9, and AN/PRC-10 transceivers. Some transceivers came from Yugoslavia, the Soviet Union, West Germany, and Japan. The TRA 906 Squadcal HF SSB transceiver has been in service since the 1960s and it is the company-level radio communication equipment. The Tatmadaw began to use PRM 4051 Squadcal 2HF manpack transceivers, together with LA-97 scrambler, since the late 1980s, mostly for regional command, infantry division, and tactical operation command levels.

According to Desmond Ball, the Tatmadaw acquired XD-D6M and XD-D6M1 HF transceivers from China in the early 1990s. The first use of the instrument was reportedly at the Marnepalaw battle in December 1994. The machine is now widely used at all levels of command, together with LA-97 scrambler. Desmond Ball also reported that the Tatmadaw bought SC-120 and SC-130 models HF transceivers from Israel in 1997. They are used for scrambled communications between the Ministry of Defence and the regional commands and infantry divisions. Various models of VHF FM transceivers are widely used at all levels of commands in the Tatmadaw since these instruments are readily available in the market. Desmond Ball claimed that each Tatmadaw company and column has at least one ICOM 2GXAT set. Some units use ICOM IC-2100 mobile VHF FM radio transceivers. The LA-97 scrambler, locally produced by the Tatmadaw since 1997–98, is modelled on South African made LA-54 scramblers acquired in 1992–93, with nearly half the parts coming from Singapore. Desmond Ball stated: "They [LA-97 scramblers] reportedly cost about 200,000 kyats each to produce in 2000. An Army-controlled purchasing company is used to buy both the domestically-produced components and the parts acquired from Singapore. The sets are tested by the No. 2 Communications factory in Mingalardon; this includes quality control checks on the circuit boards. They are then transferred into service through the No. 1 Communications Maintenance Company in Indaing."[26] He further stated that the Tatmadaw plans to acquire about 2,200 units of LA-97 but could produce only 273 units between 1997 and 2002. "According to the plans", Desmond Ball claimed, "the Ministry of defence is to have 15 sets, including five for communications with forward and front-line units; the 12 Regional Commands are to have 925 sets; the TOC and MOC HQs are each to have six sets; the Battalion and Company 'on patrol' is to have one set; the LIDs are to have at least 461 sets (with 922 reckoned to be needed); and the Reserve forces are to have 199 sets."[27]

Although it is difficult to get reliable information about the type of new signal equipment that the Tatmadaw procured, we know it certainly increased its signal intelligence and security capability, which in turn has enhanced its command, control, communication, and intelligence capabilities. Desmond Ball argued that newly acquired equipment, which included an extensive array of signal interceptions and DF systems; maritime surveillance systems and Electronic Warfare (EW) systems, had provided the Tatmadaw with "a comprehensive ability to intercept the radio traffic of ethnic groups in the border area as well as monitor telecommunications in Yangon". Moreover, he continued to remark that the Tatmadaw, for the first time, has obtained the ability to collect significant foreign signal intelligence, jam foreign signals, and conduct limited EW operations.

Desmond Ball also argued that maritime surveillance capabilities, including various sorts of Signal Intelligence (SIGINT) systems as well as other technical collection systems (such as coastal radars), have been a major feature of Myanmar's defence modernization since 1988–89. To him, in addition to the shore-based facilities and stations along the coastline,[28] "important electronic surveillance capabilities have also been acquired as part of the modernization of the navy's surface combatant force and some of the navy's new EW systems can collect ELINT over considerable ranges". It is reported that newly acquired coastal patrol boats from PRC are equipped with the BM/HZ-8610 ELINT/ESM system, which is a high-sensitivity and high accuracy DF system that covers the 2-18 GHz frequency band. The BM/HZ-8610 system is a sophisticated radar signal processing system that can provide warning, DF, and analysis of hostile radar system. The air force has also reportedly acquired a number of EW facilities. Some observers on the Myanmar Armed Forces believe that the air force has been in the process of installing new radars (from 170 to 210-mile radius) in several locations, such as Myitkyina, Hmawbi, Nansam, Myeik, Ann, Coco Island, Lwemwe, Kutkai, and Shante.

Another closely-related area to ELINT is the Information Warfare capability of the Tatmadaw. There are some reports that the Tatmadaw received technical assistance from some Singaporean farms in developing information warfare capability. Several computer technicians were sent to Singapore for training. Recently, a number of Tatmadaw officers were sent to India, under the Indian Armed Forces Scholarship programme, for training in computer science and information warfare. Moreover, the Myanmar government has also reportedly sought Malaysia's assistance in information technology. Some defence analysts indicate that Myanmar has the potential for information warfare capabilities.

THE TATMADAW-YAY (THE NAVY)

The Tatmadaw-Yay was the least known service of the Myanmar Armed Forces, due primarily to the nature of warfare the Tatmadaw had been fighting in the recent past. This does not mean that the Tatmadaw-Yay was not involved in counter-insurgency warfare. Until the mid-1970s, the navy did engage in such fighting. However, as air power proved more decisive in the campaigns, the Tatmadaw-Yay's role was more or less overlooked. The primary role of the Tatmadaw-Yay had been restricted to patrolling rivers and inshore waters and supporting the army in counter-insurgency operations. Due primarily to this nature of its missions and its financial limitations, the Tatmadaw-Yay maintained a very modest fleet of mostly small and lightly armed boats. Yet the Tatmadaw-Yay never lost sight of coastal surveillance and territorial water protection duties as is reflected by its procuring a small number of corvettes and costal patrol crafts.

At the time of independence, the Tatmadaw-Yay had a fleet consisting mostly of a small number of ships transferred from the British Navy, which included a *River*-class frigate named Mayu (Ex. HMS FAL), two Motor Minesweepers (MMS 197 and 201) and 12 Harbour Defence Motor Launches (HDML).[29] See Figure 4.1 for the Tatmadaw-Yay's procurement of warships over the years. As the insurgency situation was getting worse,

FIGURE 4.1
Tatmadaw-Yay's Procurement of Warships

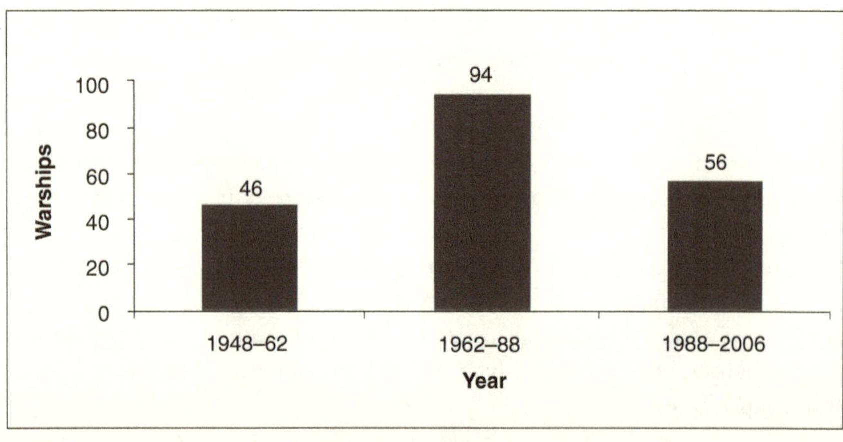

the Tatmadaw-Yay transformed some UB-type and S-type boats into river gunboats.[30] Only in 1951, did the Tatmadaw-Yay buy four Landing Crafts-Gun (LCG — Indaw, Inlay, Inma and Inya),[31] ten CGC Motor Gun Boats (MGBs), and four Patrol vessels.[32] Five years later, the Tatmadaw-Yay bought five *Dark*-class Motor Torpedo Boats (MTBs).[33] In 1958, the Tatmadaw-Yay took delivery of ten Y class river gunboats (Y-301 to Y-310) from Yugoslavia, armed with a two-pounder gun and a 40-mm anti-aircraft gun. The same year, the Tatmadaw-Yay bought six PGM-class coastal patrol crafts (PGM 401–406) from the United States. Moreover, the Tatmadaw-Yay bought an Ocean Minesweeper (Yan Myo Aung).[34] In July 1962, the Tatmadaw-Yay commissioned two Japanese built Tugs (603 and 604), powered by Dorman Engine 178-264 SHP, and two Bangladeshi built Tugs (605 and 606), powered by Caterpillar D 343 Marine Engines. Then, two years later, the Tatmadaw-Yay bought two more Japanese built Tugs (163 and 164), powered by Mitsubishi DM 24 MK engines.

Between 1963 and 1968, the Tatmadaw-Yay made major procurements from overseas. It took delivery of eight Landing Craft Medium (LCM), seven CGC Gunboats, one PCE-827-type corvette (Yan Taing Aung), one *Admirable*-class corvette (Yan Gyi Aung), and one Landing Craft Utility (LCU-603) from the United States, one Light Force Support Ship (Yan Lone Aung) from Japan, and twenty-five *Michao*-class River Patrol Boats (001-025) from Yugoslavia. Meanwhile, beginning in 1960, the Tatmadaw-Yay began to build up its own naval dockyard facilities. Moreover, it made use of the facilities of state-owned shipyards. In October 1960 and March 1961, the Tatmadaw-Yay commissioned two N-class corvettes (Nawarat 501 and Nagakyay 502), powered by Paxman Ricardo Turbo Charge Diesel Engine, built by Dawbon Government Dockyard.[35] It was followed by the production of a number of small river patrol boats. In 1960 The Burma Naval Dockyard built ten River Patrol Crafts (RPC 1 to 10) modelled on THORNY Craft R-Z6 and powered by Diesel Marine Engine 125. In December 1967, the Tatmadaw-Yay commissioned two Landing Craft Mechanized ships (LCM — 709 and 710) built by Naval Engineering Depot. Then in 1969, the Tatmadaw-Yay also commissioned two Y-class river gunboats (Y-311 and Y-312) built by Simalike Government Dockyard. These 122-feet long gunboats, which have a displacement of 140 tons and cruise at nine knots, were armed with two 40-mm Bofor guns and four 20-mm Oerlikon guns. Moreover, the Tatmadaw-Yay turned some captured Motor Fishing Vessels (MFVs) into gunboats armed with machine guns for inshore and offshore patrol. In 1970, in the Tanintharyi Naval region, a programme known as "Doone-Hlay" was launched to transform ten MFV into gunboats (Yan Naing 501 to 510).[36]

Between 1978 and 1982, the Tatmadaw-Yay procured six River Patrol Craft (PBR 211–216) from the United States, three *Swift*-class Coastal Patrol Boats (PGM 421–423) from Singapore, six *Carpentaria*-class River Patrol Craft (PBR 111–113, 117, 119–120) from Australia, and three *Osprey*-class Offshore Patrol Craft (FV 55, 56, and 57, Indaw, Inma, and Inya) from Denmark. Indaw (FV-55) has the helicopter deck with hanger.[37] In 1983, the Tatmadaw-Yay bought a transport vessel from an overseas supplier. Moreover, the Naval Dockyard built two Coastal Patrol Craft (PGM 411–412) in 1982 and one Coastal Land Craft Utility (LCU-605) in 1984. In 1986, the Tatmadaw-Yay commissioned two locally-built Coastal Patrol Craft (PGM 413–414). The following year, the Tatmadaw-Yay took a delivery of a transport vessel from the Myanmar Shipyard. In the same year, it transformed two captured motor-boats into gunboats for coastal patrol. Major naval procurements from overseas suppliers stopped altogether by the early 1980s.[38]

Throughout the 1990s, the Tatmadaw-Yay took delivery of a number of naval craft from the PRC and Yugoslavia. In 1990, it commissioned three PB-90-class coastal patrol boats (UMS 424, 425, and 426), armed with eight 20-mm Hispano guns, which can cruise at a maximum speed of 30 knots. A year later, the Tatmadaw-Yay placed an order of ten 59-metre long *Hainan*-class Type 037 Sub-chasers from the PRC. The first batch of six craft arrived in Yangon in January 1991 and the second batch of four in May 1993 (UMS 441–450).[39] These Sub-chasers are armed with four twin 57-mm guns, four twin 25-mm guns, both fore and aft, and are equipped with anti-submarine mortars, rocket depth charges, and radars. They can cruise at a maximum speed of 30 knots, and have an effective range of 1,300 miles at 15 knots.

In March 1994, the Tatmadaw-Yay signed a procurement contract with the PRC for a delivery of six 63-metre long *Houxin*-class (1G Missile Escort) Fast Attack Crafts-Missile (UMS 471–476).[40] The first two units were delivered in November 1995 and the rest in 1996 and 1997. These missile escorts were armed with four YJ-1 (C-801) surface-to-surface missiles, capable of active radar homing to 40 km at a speed of 0.9 mach, as well as four twin 37-mm and four twin 14.5-mm guns. The Missile Escort is capable of 28 knots at its maximum speed and has an effective range of 1,300 miles at 15 knots. For the first time, the Tatmadaw-Yay acquired anti-ship cruise missile capability and (somewhat) significant firepower.

There had been some speculation that the Tatmadaw-Yay was interested in buying two or three *Jiangnan* Type 65 frigates. However, it is most likely that the Tatmadaw-Yay is interested in *Jianghu* I Type 53 guided missile frigate. The *Jianghu*-class frigate is usually armed with four HY-2 SSM and 100-mm guns. While the Tatmadaw-Yay would be interested in procuring frigates from overseas sources, it is keen to build corvettes, coastal patrol craft, and river gunboats or river patrol craft. The Naval Dockyard and the Myanmar Shipyard built a number of Fast Attack Craft, Coastal Patrol Craft, and River Patrol Craft. With technical assistance and weaponry from the PRC, the Tatmadaw-Yay also locally built six 50-metre long Fast Patrol Craft — Gun (UMS 551–556) — between 1995 and 2006.[41] They are armed with two twin 57-mm guns, two twin 40-mm (Bofor) guns, and four twin 25-mm guns both fore and aft, two mine sweeping rails, and three rocket depth charges (five each). These warships have a displacement of 212 tons and cruise at the maximum speed of 24 knots. There are some unconfirmed reports that the navy has built four Fast Attack Craft — Missile (UMS 557–560) at its naval dockyard. The Naval Dockyard also built four River Patrol Craft in 1990s. River Patrol Craft are lightly armed with 20-mm guns. In the same period, the Myanmar Shipyard built two Burma PGM-type coastal patrol crafts, presumably to be taken over by the Tatmadaw-Yay. The Tatmadaw-Yay also built a total of fourteen 27-feet long assault boats (Ngaman-001 to 014) armed with two BA-64 LMGs and one 12.7-mm gun.[42]

The Tatmadaw-Yay built two corvettes with the assistance of the PRC (corvette halls, weapons, and electronic equipment) in its own Naval Dockyard.[43] According to *Strategic Affairs* (16 November 2000 issue), the Tatmadaw-Yay has bought two Chinese hulls for conversion into corvettes (75 metres long and 1,200 DWT). The corvettes will be equipped for anti-submarine warfare and with OtoMelara 76-mm Compact guns. Although it is not yet clear what surface-to-surface missiles it will carry, it is most likely that the corvettes will carry C801 sea-skimming missiles. It is believed that Israel is supplying the electronics and radar for navigation, fire-control, and surveillance. However, it appears that the Tatmadaw-Yay launched a major ship building programmes in 2000. The Tatmadaw-Yay commissioned a locally built 77-metre long corvette (UMS 771), known as Anwarahta, on 7 September 2000. The warship was equipped with Chinese weapons and radar system. The second corvette (UMS 772) was launched in 2001. However, some observers state that the navy launched its third corvette (UMS 773) in 2005. It is now building a frigate (F-108) to add to its order of battle.

The Tatmadaw-Yay did not leave out the other services in its order of battle. It paid much attention to the shipbuilding facilities at the Naval Dockyard. It is believed that the Tatmadaw-Yay has been in the process of developing its technical know-how to build and repair most of its surface ships. Moreover, the Tatmadaw-Yay did not overlook its transport wing either. In the early 1990s, it commissioned two LCUs (608 and 609) by transforming captured Dolphin-9 and M.T Dacca. Moreover, it also absorbed M.V Aung Zeya from the state-owned Five-Star Line for the purpose of general transport.

For the first time, the Tatmadaw-Yay acquired brown water capability. It is believed that the Tatmadaw-Yay is building up blue-water capability and it can realize such a capability in the near future. Within next ten to fifteen years, according to some knowledgeable experts, the Tatmadaw-Yay would need to build up its naval forces to comprise at least half a dozen frigates, a dozen each of Corvettes, Offshore Patrol Vessels, Fast Attack Craft (missile) and Coastal Patrol Craft (Sub-chaser), and a couple of dozen of Fast Attack Craft (gun) and Coastal Patrol Craft, plus a number of Mine Sweepers, transport ships, river gunboats or river patrol craft, LCMs, and LCUs.

THE TATMADAW-LAY (THE AIR FORCE)

The relatively small and ill-equipped Tatmadaw-Lay before 1990 had virtually no aircraft that could be classified as combat aircraft. Although most of the aircraft in the Tatmadaw-Lay inventory were trainers, they were used for multiple purposes.[44] The primary mission of the Tatmadaw-Lay since its inception has been to provide transport, logistical, and close air support to the Tatmadaw-Kyi in counter-insurgency operations. In its entire history, the Tatmadaw-Lay had never been in an air battle. Since the early 1990s, the Tatmadaw-Lay has been undergoing a major expansion and modernization programme. It has procured supersonic fighters and air-to-air missiles — the first time, it has acquired air superiority fighters and power projection capability.

The *Tigermouth* and *Oxford* aircraft received by the Tatmadaw-Lay from the Royal Air Force at the time of independence in 1948 remained in service for a few more years: only a few aircraft were air worthy. Soon after the country's independence, the Tatmadaw-Lay bought three *Spitfire* and four *Auster* aircraft. At the height of insurgency the Tatmadaw-Lay even lost some airfields and some aircraft to insurgent forces.[45] The Tatmadaw-Lay pooled all available resources to combat the insurgents' increasingly powerful challenges. In fact, in 1950, it was reported that there were only two *Spitfire* aircraft that could be equipped with rockets.[46] In order to meet operational requirements, some *Oxford* aircraft were fitted with rocket packs and bomb racks.[47] The Tatmadaw-Lay, however, was in process of procuring more aircraft.

Indeed, in 1949, the Tatmadaw-Lay introduced five *Consul* aircraft that stayed in service for eight years. The following year, the Tatmadaw-Lay bought ten *Chipmunk* aircraft for training and nine *Douglas DC-3 Dakota* planes for transport. With these new aircraft, the Tatmadaw-Lay, for the first time, formed two squadrons in June and December 1950. In the meantime, owing to heavy fighting with insurgents, the Myanmar government decided to procure more aircraft. In 1951, the Tatmadaw-Lay decided it should acquire

Provost aircraft that are more suitable for Myanmar weather. The *Provost* aircraft were put into service in 1954 and they remained in service until the mid-1980s. In the meantime, the Tatmadaw-Lay also procured two *Bristol Freighter Mark 21* in 1953 for light transport.[48]

It is fair to say that 1953 and 1954 were watershed years for the Tatmadaw-Lay since it bought thirty *Supermarine Spitfire* from Israel and twenty *Supermarine Seafire* from the United Kingdom in 1953, and forty *Hunting Provost T-53* and eight *DH Vampire T-55* also from the United Kingdom in 1954. In 1956, the Myanmar Air Force (MAF) bought ten *Cessna 180* from the United States. The same year, the Tatmadaw-Lay for the first time introduced six *Kawasaki Bell 47G* as its helicopter fleet. The following year, the Tatmadaw-Lay procured twenty-one *Seafury* from the United Kingdom, six *Beachcraft* from the United States, and nine *Otter* from Canada. In 1958, it procured seven more *Kawasaki Bell 47G* from Japan and twelve *Vertol H-21* from the United States.[49]

By 1960, all *Oxford, Spitfire, Tigermouth, Auster, Counsel*, and *Seafire* aircraft were no longer in the Tatmadaw-Lay inventory. Only eight *Chipmunk*, six *Dakota*, two *Bristol*, thirty-seven *Provost*, eight *Vampire*, eight *Cessna*, fourteen *Seafury*, six *Beachcraft*, nine *Otter*, seven *Bell 47G*, and twelve *Vertol* aircraft remained in the Tatmadaw-Lay service (see Table 4.2). Yet not all the aircraft were air worthy. In 1963, the Tatmadaw-Lay bought eight *Lockheed T-33* aircraft. Within the next five years, it had acquired twenty-four more *Lockheed T-33* aircraft. In the same period, the Tatmadaw-Lay bought a total of thirteen *Aerospatial SA-316B Alouette IIIs* helicopters from France and seventeen *Kaman HH-43 Huskie* light transport helicopters, for search and rescue, from the United States. It then procured no more aircraft until the mid-1970s. These helicopters formed the core of the Tatmadaw-Lay's helicopter squadron.[50]

In the meantime, since January 1968, the Burma Communist Party (BCP), one of the strongest insurgent organizations in Myanmar, had been launching a new military front in the northeast border region of Myanmar. With the benefit of hindsight, apparently with strong material and moral support from the Chinese Communist Party, the BCP grew fast and built military strongholds on the eastern side of the Thanlwin River. This situation required the Tatmadaw to fight a different type of counter-insurgency warfare, which is more a conventional, than an anti-guerrilla one. Although the counter-insurgency warfare in lower and central Myanmar did not require close air support and aerial bombing to ensure victory, the new form of fighting proved that air power was increasingly important. The Tatmadaw-Lay played a vital role in counter-insurgency operations throughout the 1970s and 1980s, particularly in the northeast border areas.

TABLE 4.2
Procurement of Aircraft (1948–62)

Aircraft	*Unit*	*Service*	*Country/Source*	*Remark*
Tigermoth	6	1947–55	United Kingdom	
Oxford	6	1947–56	UK	
Auster	4	1948–56	UK	
Spitfire	33	1948–57	UK/Israel	3 (1948): 30 (1953)
Consul	5	1949–56	UK	
Dakota	9	1950–78	Air Burma/India	1 (gift from Indonesia)
Chipmunk	10	1950–81	UK	
Vampire Mk T55	8	1951–76	UK	
Seafire	20	1953–58	UK	
Bristol F. Mk 21	2	1953–67	UK	
Provost T-53	38	1954–76	UK	
Bell 47G	13	1955–74	Japan	1 (from Kayah State)
Vertol	6	1955–74	United States	
Cessna M180	10	1956–	US	
Beechcraft	6	1956–	US	
Otter	9	1957–80	Canada	
Seafury	20	1958–60	UK	
Alouette	13	1960–	France	
Mikoyan MI-4	1	1961–66	Soviet Union	Gift (October 1961)
Total	219			

In order to contain the further expansion of the BCP in the northeast border area, the Tatmadaw pooled all available resources for counter-insurgency operations. The Tatmadaw-Lay opened air detachments in Lashio and Kengtung. However, there were several limitations that prevented the full utilization of air power. The operational limitations of T-33 were — apart from the fact that the aircraft were getting old and there were few or no spare parts available — partly due to the lack of airfields good enough for these aircraft to operate. In Myanmar, there were only ten airfields that had runways more than 1,800 metres long, of which only Mingalardon, Mandalay, and Myitkyina have over 2,500-metres long runways. The T-33s' combat radius was relatively small. In Myanmar, only Mingalardon, Shante, and Myitkyina had airfields good and long enough for the T-33s to operate. As a result, its combat effectiveness was very limited. Though an air detachment was opened in Lashio, two T-33 aircraft were located in Meikhtila. With a full tank, the T-33 can fly for about two hours. Just flying to Lashio from Meikhtila took forty-five minutes and it was another ten minutes to Kunlone or the battlefront. Therefore, the T-33 could stay on the target for no more than ten minutes. As a result, when the Tatmadaw-Lay planned to procure some new aircraft, the combat radius and STOL (Short-Take-Off-and-Landing) feature became major points for consideration.

Until 1975, the Tatmadaw-Lay made no major procurement. In 1975, the MAF acquired several new aircraft. It also benefited from the International Narcotic Control Programme (INCP). Under the INCP, the Tatmadaw-Lay negotiated with the U.S. military attaché in Yangon to take delivery of eighteen *Bell 205A* (between 1975 and 1978) and seven *Bell 206B* (in 1978) from the United States.[51] Moreover, in 1976, under the same programme, the Tatmadaw-Lay was able to procure one *F-27 Mark-100* for the police, but which remained with the Tatmadaw-Lay up to the present. At about the same time, in March 1975, the Tatmadaw-Lay signed a contract with Sisai Marchetti in Italy to buy *Aermacchi SF-260* aircraft. In April the first batch of ten *SF-260* aircraft arrived in Yangon. The second batch of another ten *SF-260* aircraft arrived four years later. Although these Italian-made two-seat trainers could be used as light attack aircraft, they were rarely put into combat action, but were used mostly for training. However, these aircraft seemed to have some problems for the Tatmadaw-Lay as the fuel was imported from Italy. In order to strengthen its transport liaison, the Tatmadaw-Lay also bought one FH-227B and four FH-227E in 1978.[52]

As it appeared that the *Lockheed T-33* and *Vampire T-55* were no longer operational and effective, the Tatmadaw-Lay began to search for a new aircraft. By 1975, almost all the T-33 aircraft were out of service. The last Vampire T-55 was put in operation in 1977, against the BCP positions in Chu-Shwe front. In its search for new suitable aircraft to make Myanmar's environment secure, the Tatmadaw-Lay found the Swiss-made *Pilatus PC-6* an effective aircraft for multi-purpose operations.[53] The PC-6 is a STOL utility transport aircraft that could be fitted with machine guns, rockets, and bombs. Because of its STOL features, these aircraft could be deployed in most airfields. In the late 1970s and throughout the 1980s, some PC-6 aircraft were deployed in Lashio for effective close air support for counter-insurgency operations. The first batch of two PC-6 aircraft arrived in Yangon on 14 November 1976 and the second batch of another two PC-6 arrived on 12 February 1977. Three more PC-6 were bought in 1978. In 1979, the Tatmadaw-Lay procured eight Pilatus PC-7 aircraft from Switzerland. PC-7 is a light trainer that can be transformed to a light attack aircraft for counter-insurgency warfare. Another eight PC-7 aircraft were bought the following year. In the early 1980s, the Tatmadaw-Lay also absorbed one F-27 Mark 500 (1981), one Cessana Citation-2 (in 1982 — for the forest department) and one FH-227J (1982 — under INCP). During the 1986–87 budget year, the Tatmadaw-Lay bought ten PC-9 from Switzerland.[54] (See Table 4.3 for Tatmadaw-Lay's aircraft procurements between 1962 and 1988.)

Since 1990, according to some observers, the Tatmadaw-Lay has bought more than 100 aircraft from China, which included F-7 IIK interceptors, FT-7K trainers, A-5 ground attack aircraft, FT-6M trainers, K-8 trainers, and Y-8 transport aircraft. In December 1990, the Tatmadaw-Lay took first delivery of ten *Chengdu* F-7IIK fighters and two GAIC FT-7 twin-seat trainers. In May 1993, the Tatmadaw-Lay received another batch of twelve F-7IIK fighters. According to some sources, further deliveries of F-7IIK squadrons were made in 1995, 1998, and 1999. If this source of information is correct, then, between 1990 and 2000, the Tatmadaw-Lay received about sixty-two F-7IIK fighters from the PRC. The F-7IIK, the Chinese copy of Mikoyan MiG-21 "Fishbird" interceptor, can be fitted with rocket pods, and

TABLE 4.3
Procurement of Aircraft (1962–88)

Aircraft	*Unit*	*Service*	*Country/Source*	*Remark*
Huskie	16	1962–78	United States	
Lockheed T-33	22	1962–88	US	
Beech (Queen Air)	1	1965–87	US	
Beagle	3	1966–92	UK	
Bell-205	20	1975–	US	DEA anti-drug programme
SF-260	20	1976–89	Italy	
PC-6	7	1976–	Switzerland	
Fokker F-27	2	1976–	Holland	1 (F-27 MK 500) in 1981
FH-227 VIP/B/J	3	1978–	US	VIP & B (1978): J (1982)
Bell-206	7	1978–	US	DEA anti-drug programme
PC-7	16	1979–	Switzerland	
Cessna Citation II	1	1982–	US	For Forest Department
Turbo Trush	5	1984–	US	DEA anti-drug programme
Bell-212	1	1986–	US	DEA anti-drug programme
PC-9	7	1986–	Switzerland	
Total	131			

carry infrared seeking PL-2 AAMs (Air-to-Air Missiles). Four underwing hardpoints, two inner hardpoints, and outer pylons can carry rockets and bombs in addition to AAMs and two type 30-1 30-mm cannons. F-7IIK can be used for ground attacks though it is primarily an interceptor. The Tatmadaw-Lay also benefited from the procurement of A-5C aircraft from China. Equipped with two Norinco Type 23 23-mm cannons and ten hardpoints that carry bombs, rockets, ASM, and AAM, the A-5C, an export version of NAMC Q-5 "Fantan", is a ground attack aircraft suitable for counter-insurgency warfare. Between 1992 and 2000, it was estimated that the Tatmadaw-Lay received thirty-six A-5C aircraft from the PRC. In addition to Chinese-made fighter aircraft, the Tatmadaw-Lay also bought a squadron of *SOKO G-4 Super Galab* from Yugoslavia in 1991. The G-4 Super Galebs, powered by VIPER MK 632-46 Turbo Jet Engine, can be armed with (32) 57-mm rockets and (8) 128-mm rockets and are suitable for counter-insurgency operations. In addition to these aircraft, the Tatmadaw-Lay has bought a number of air-to-air missiles from China. The AAM is reported to be PL-5. Yet there are many technical problems and operational limitations.

In terms of trainers, the Tatmadaw-Lay initially received several FT-7 twin seat aircraft, which is the export version of GAIC JJ-7 (Chinese copy of MiG-21 "Mongol-B"). The Tatmadaw-Lay also procured two FT-6 trainers (Chinese copy of MiG-19 known to NATO as "Farmer") from the PRC. According to some sources, the Tatmadaw-Lay also received about thirty PT-6 trainers from the PRC throughout the 1990s. Both aircraft can be used as interceptor or ground attack fighter, provided that they are fitted with air-to-air missiles, rockets, and bombs. However, it appeared that the Tatmadaw-Lay was interested in more advanced trainers. As a result, in 1998 and 1999, it bought twelve K-8 Karakorum jet trainers from the PRC.[55] The K-8 is a joint venture between Chinese HAIG (Hongdu Aviation Industry Group) and Pakistani PAC (Pakistan Aeronautical Complex). With five hardpoints, one centreline, and four under the wings, the K-8 trainers can be easily transformed to light ground attack aircraft, carrying rockets and bombs, and suitable for counter-insurgency warfare.

For transport, it was reported that the Tatmadaw-Lay bought four SAC Y-8 from the PRC to strengthen the existing fleet of *Fokker* aircraft. Moreover, several newly procured helicopters could be also used as light transport aircraft. The Tatmadaw-Lay procured a range of helicopters from Russia and Poland. It was reported that it bought thirteen PZL W-3 Sokol multi-purpose helicopters and twenty Mil Mi-2 helicopters from Poland and thirteen Mil Mi-17 helicopters from Russia. Mil Mi-2, known as "Hoplite", is an effective gunship for the Tatmadaw-Lay. Soon after the first batch of Mil Mi-2 arrived in mid-1991, some of these helicopters were put into counter-insurgency operations against the infiltrating KNU troops in Ayerwaddy Delta. Four Mil Mi-2, four Sokol, and two Bell-205 helicopters were grouped as an air detachment stationed in Bogalay for "Operation Mondaing" in October 1991. During the operation, Mil Mi-2s were fitted with a range of weapons to provide ground attack and air cover for the heliborne operations. It was reported that four Mil Mi-2 helicopters made a total of eighty sorties over seventeen targets with nearly eighty-two flying hours. Four Sokol helicopters, though they were purely light transport aircraft with no weapon, carrying twenty commandos, each flew 443 missions within 197 flying hours.[56] Primary missions of the Bell-205 helicopters were for VIP transport and for search and rescue. They flew 263 missions with over 114 flying hours.[57]

In 2001, it was reported that the Tatmadaw-Lay bought twelve MiG-29/29UB from Russia. The Tatmadaw had been negotiating a deal with Russian for some time — from as early as 1997. However, due to economic reasons, the deal had been delayed. There seems to have been renewed interest when Bangladesh acquired a squadron of MiG-29 in 1999. Finally, the deal was struck in mid-2001 (see Table 4.4). It appears that the Tatmadaw-Lay has been seriously considering air superiority aircraft. Moreover, for effective air operation, the Myanmar government has been building new airfields

TABLE 4.4
Procurement of Aircraft (1988–2003)

Aircraft	*Unit*	*Service*	*Country/Source*	*Remark*
F-7 IIK	58	1990–	China	
FT-7	4	1991–	China	
G-4	6	1991–	Yugoslavia	
MI-2	20	1991–	Poland	
Sokol	13	1991–	Poland	
A-5	36	1992–	China	
FT-6	2	1992–	China	
Y-8	4	1992–	China	
MI-17	13	1995–	Russia	
PT-6	30	1996–	China	
K-8	12	1998–	China	
MiG-29B/UB	12	2001–	Russia	2 (MiG-29UB)
Total	210			

and upgrading existing ones. For example, a new airfield 4,000 metres long and seventy metres wide, is in the process of being constructed in Magway, while airfields in Kawthaung, Myeik, Dawei, and Mawlamyaing are being upgraded.[58]

In the late 1990s, some experts on Myanmar Armed Forces indicated that the Tatmadaw-Lay was also interested in either the J-10 or F-8 IIM. This was mainly due to the fact that the PLA Air Force had introduced these aircraft to a visiting Myanmar military delegation in October 1996. Chengdu J-10 is a multi-role fighter and Shenyang F-8 IIM is an export version of PLA-AF's Shengyang J-8 IIM interceptor. But the Tatmadaw-Lay decided to buy Russian-made MiG-29s instead. During the visit of Vice-Senior General Maung Aye to Russia in April 2006, it was reported that the Tatmadaw planned to procure more MiG-29 aircraft from Moscow. See Figure 4.2.

Moreover, the Tatmadaw-Lay planned to assemble PT-6 trainers in Myanmar. In recent years, it assembled one Aviawin light aircraft in 2002, one Experimental-2 (Ex-2) light aircraft in 2005, and one STOL CH-701 light aircraft in 2006.[59] It appears that more STOL CH-701 aircraft will be assembled in Myanmar.

FIGURE 4.2
Procurement of Aircraft between 1948–2006

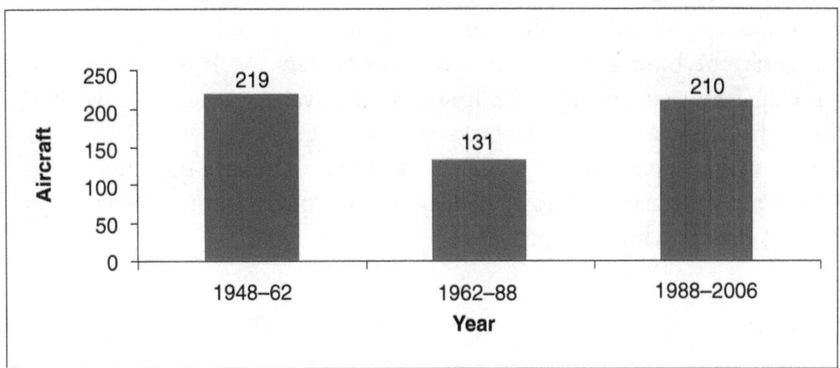

CONCLUSION

Despite the current force modernization programme, the Tatmadaw-Kyi, particularly the infantry, is still armed with technologically less sophisticated weapons. But it never lost sight of technological advancements and new forms of warfare as it has been in the process of developing electronic warfare and information warfare capability. However, it can be argued that, to a certain extent, the Myanmar Armed Forces has acquired a certain level of technological sophistication. The acquisition of main battle tanks, light tanks, armoured personnel carriers, and various calibres of artillery has certainly enhanced the Tatmadaw-Kyi's firepower and mobility. For the first time in its history, the Tatmadaw is now capable of amphibious warfare. It has become more capable of fighting a limited conventional warfare. Moreover, the Tatmadaw, for the first time, has built up a more or less elaborate system of air defence system, although the focus is very much on low-altitude-air-defence-system (LAADS). The newly procured signal intelligence equipment have also greatly enhanced the C^3I capabilities of the Tatmadaw. While the Tatmadaw continues to pursue a policy of self-sufficiency in small arms production, it procures most of its heavy artillery from overseas suppliers.

At this point in time, the Tatmadaw-Yay is capable of effective patrol over Myanmar's territorial waters. It is no doubt in the process of building blue water capability. Since it plans to move from brown water to blue water capability (as its motto goes — (ရေညိုမှသည်ရေပြာသို့ချီ) *Yay Nyo Hma Thi Yay Pyar Tho Chi* — meaning from brown water to blue water capability), more surface ship, such as frigates and corvettes, are being acquired. The Tatmadaw-Yay is also developing its shipbuilding facilities and technological base. Meanwhile the Tatmadaw-Lay is still very much limited in its power projection. For example, both F-7IIK and A-5C have relatively small combat radius. Compared with the air forces of neighbouring countries, particularly Thailand's, the Tatmadaw-Lay's air power is relatively low. It is in the process of procuring air superiority aircraft and more advanced multi-role fighters. Although it has acquired advanced aircraft such as the MiG-29, it has problems with operational capability, in addition to lacking qualified pilots. So far, only Mingalardon and Mandalay International Airport have runways long enough for MiGs to operate.

Notes

1. For some information about defence budget, please see Chapter 5.
2. Andrew Selth, *Burma's Arms Procurement Programme* (Canberra: SDSC, WP. 289, 1998).
3. In the early stage of insurgency, the Tatmadaw learned that it could not rely on foreign power for help. In fact, it was Pakistan, India, and Yugoslavia that helped the Tatmadaw with weapons and ammunitions to fight against the insurgents. When the Tatmadaw requested the British, through British Service Mission,

to help the latter set some preconditions, such as new battalions having to be formed with ethnic minority (class battalions), rather than with the Burmese people.

4 Some Police Stations are issued with these BA-52 sub-machine guns.

5 The showroom at the Defence Services Museum has displayed several models of assault rifles, sub-machine guns, and light machine guns.

6 *Irrawaddy Magazine* [online edition], 7 December 2006.

7 Desmond Ball, *How The Tatmadaw Talks: The Burmese Army's Radio Systems*, SDSC Working Paper No. 388 (May 2004): 14.

8 This model can be seen at the Defence Services museum.

9 Clifford McCoy, "Myanmar's Losing Military Strategy", *Asia Times* [online edition], 7 October 2006 <www.atimes.com> (accessed 5 January 2007).

10 *Wikipedia* (accessed 25 January 2007).

11 *Wikipedia* (accessed 28 January 2007).

12 Andrew Selth, *Burma's North Korean Gambit: A Challenge to Regional Security?* (Canberra: SDSC, 2004).

13 Daewoo — A Serial Suitor of the Burmese Regime, *Irrawaddy Magazine* [online edition], 7 December 2006.

14 China also produced HN-5B, with improved performance, and HN-5C, which is the truck-mounted version of the HN-5A. The HN-5C carries eight missiles stored in two 4-cell launcher-containers, each holding four missiles. The launcher is mounted on a 6 × 6 lightweight truck. Additional detecting and tracking equipment include TV and infrared cameras.

15 Some of these SAM-7s are from Khun Sa's Mong Thai Army stock.

16 The SA-16 features a new seeker and modified launcher nose cover. Whereas the SA-18 9M39 missile is fitted with an aerodynamic spike on the nose, the 9M310 missile of the SA-16, has the spike replaced with an aerodynamic cone held in place with a wire tripod. On the SA-18 the protective cover of the seeker is conical; on the SA-16, it is tubular with a prominent lip at the forward edge. The 9M313 missile of the SA-16 employs an IR guidance system using proportional convergence logic, and an improved two-colour seeker, presumably IR and UV. The seeker is sensitive enough to home in on airframe radiation, and the two-colour sensitivity is designed to minimize vulnerability to flares.

17 *Jane's Defence Weekly*, 17 January 2001.

18 *Russia to Supply Wide Range of Arms to Myanmar* (PTI, 4 April 2006); *Air-to-Minerals Missile* (Kommersant, 4 April 2006).

19 Accessed 7 January 2007.

20 Tunguska entered service with the Russian army in 1988 and has been exported to Germany, India, Peru, and Ukraine. Recently, India displayed its Tunguska Gun/Missile system at a military parade.

21 The missile has semi-automatic radar command to line-of-sight guidance, with a maximum speed of 900 m/s and can engage targets travelling at speeds of up to 500 m/s. Its range is from 15 to 6,000 m for ground targets and 15 to

10,000 m for air targets. The guns have a maximum firing rate of 5,000 rounds per minute and a range of 3,000 m against air targets. This extends to 4,000 m against ground targets.

22 The S-300PMU *Grumble* [SA-10 land-based, SA-N-6 naval version] surface-to-air missile system is able to engage a number of targets simultaneously, countering intensive aircraft raids at low-to-high altitude. The SA-10 offers significant advantages over older strategic surface-to-air missile systems, including multi-target handling and engagement characteristics, a capability against low-altitude targets with small radar cross-sections, such as cruise missiles, a capability against tactical ballistic missiles, and possibly a potential to intercept some types of strategic ballistic missiles. The S-300PMU1 is an extended range version of S-300PMU with a limited anti-ballistic missile capability. The system has an effective range of 150 km and a maximum altitude of 40,000 metres. It can engage six targets simultaneously with twelve missiles in flight, two per target. The S-300 PMU1 mobile multi-channel air defence missile system can defeat modem and future aircraft, strategic cruise missiles, tactical battlefield ballistic missiles, and other targets with a reflection surface up to 0.02 square metre, flying at speeds of up to 2.800 m/s in massive enemy air raids and heavy clutter and severe ECM environments. This system was developed from S-300 PMU and differs from it through improved technical and operational characteristics. The S-300PMU2 *Favorit* variant is a new missile with a larger warhead and better guidance with a range of 200 km. The S-300 PMU2 *Favorit* air defence missile system is designed for the defence of vital facilities of the state and its armed forces against mass strikes by modem and future aircraft, strategic cruise missiles, tactical and theatre ballistic missiles, and other air attack weapons over a full range of altitudes and speeds, in heavy ECM environments. It can engage targets flying from ten metre to twenty-seven kilometre above the surface at a speed of up to 10,000 km/h. It is claimed that it has a kill ratio ranging from 0.8 to 0.93 against aircraft and from 0.8 to 0.98 against Tomahawk-class cruise missiles. S-300PMU3, also known as S-400 SA-20 *Triumf*, is a new generation of air defence and theatre anti-missile weapon. It is intended to detect and destroy airborne targets at a distance of up to 400 km. The *Triumf* system includes radars capable of detecting low-signature targets. It can intercept targets with velocities of up to 4.8 km/sec, corresponding to a ballistic missile range of 3,500 km.

23 *Jane's Defence Weekly*, vol. 40, no. 9 (3 September 2003): 14.

24 CD. 884-4, The 1968 CO Conference, p. 3; CD. 883-4, The 1969 CO Conference, p. 3.

25 William Ashton, "The Arms Keep Coming: But Who Pays?", *Irrawaddy Magazine*, vol. 14, no. 4 (April 2004); National Defence College, *Annual Magazine of No. 5 Course* (Yangon: NDC, 2004), photographs on page 118.

26 Desmond Ball, *How The Tatmadaw Talks*, SDSC WP-388, p. 14.

27 Ibid.

28 For example, in February, the JDW reported that the radar station on Zadetkale

Island is just completed (*Jane's Defence Weekly*, 21 February 2001). Other reported radar stations are on Ramree Island, Coco Island, Haigyi Island, Thanhlet Point (Yangon), and Zadetgyi Island. See Desmond Ball, "SIGINT Strengths Form A Vital Part of Burma's Military Muscle", *Jane's Intelligent Review* (March 1998).

29 DSHMRI, *Tatmadaw Thamaing, 1948–1962*, vol. 4 (Yangon: DSHMRI, 1996), p. 183.

30 Some of these S-type boats are Sagu, Seinda, Shwethida, Sinmin, Shwe Puzun, Setkya, Setyahat, and etc.

31 All ships were decommissioned in early 1970s while Indaw was transferred to the People's Pearl and Fishery in December 1970.

32 DSHMRI, *Tatmadaw Thamaing, 1948–1962*, vol. 4, pp. 183–84.

33 All five MTBs (201, 202, 204, 205, and 206) were decommissioned in 1975.

34 Yan Myo Aung was decommissioned in January 1982.

35 These corvettes were decommissioned in 1995.

36 DSHMRI, *History of the Tatmadaw, 1962–1974*, vol. 5 (Yangon: DSHMRI, 1997), pp. 260–80, Yan Naing 510 was the boat that clashed with a Thai Naval vessel in December 1998, off Ranong. Yan Naing 504 was recently on the list of auction in the newspaper (Kyemon Newspaper, 14 February 2002).

37 FV 56 — Inma was sunk in 1986.

38 DSHMRI, *History of the Tatmadaw, 1974–1988*, vol. 6 (Yangon: DSHMRI, 1998), p. 308.

39 These coastal patrol craft (Sub-chasers) were numbered and named: 441-Yan Sit Aung, 442-Yan Myat Aung, 443-Yan Nyein Aung, 444-Yan Khwin Aung, 445-Yan Min Aung, 446-Yan Ye Aung, 447-Yan Paing Aung, 448-Yan Win Aung, 449-Yan Aye Aung, and 450-Yan Zwe Aung.

40 These Fast Attack Craft are named after astrological stars (Seik-hta, Mar-ga, Han-tha, Ze-Hta, Ban-Na, and Du-wa).

41 UMS-551 was commissioned on 2 January 1996.

42 The first one was commissioned on 6 May 1996. These shallow-water amphibious gunboats were primarily for the army in security operations.

43 In recent years, the Myanmar Shipyard and the Naval Dockyard bought new and advanced ship building equipment. The Myanmar Shipyard succeeded in winning overseas contracts.

44 For example, PC-7 trainers were fitted with bomb racks and machine guns and used as light attack aircraft. PC-6s were used as light transport aircraft as well as bombers. Dakota aircraft were used not only for transport and airdrop, but were also put into action for aerial bombing or surgical air strikes.

45 The MAF lost two aircraft in Maymyo and airfields in many parts of the country.

46 DSHMRI, *Tatmadaw Thamaing, 1948–1962*, vol. 4, p. 195.

47 In fact during the test, the Chief of Air Staff Lieutenant Colonel S. Khin was killed.

48 DR. 8556, History of Tatmadaw-Lay.

[49] Ibid.

[50] DSHMRI, *History of Tatmadaw, 1962–1974*, vol. 5, pp. 287–88.

[51] DR. 8556, History of Tatmadaw-Lay.

[52] DSHMRI, *History of the Tatmadaw, 1974–1988*, vol. 6, p. 311.

[53] Secret war in Laos revealed that PC-6 could effectively be used for multi-purposes.

[54] DSHMRI, *History of the Tatmadaw 1974–1988*, vol. 6, p. 311.

[55] It was also reported that the Pakistani air force would also replace its JJ-7s and CJ-6s trainers with K-8s.

[56] The Sokol Helicopter can be armed with 23-mm twin GSz canon, sixteen 57-mm MAR-2 Missiles, ZR-8 Ball-Type Bomb Dispenser, ASO-2W anti-Missile system, and 7.62-mm Assault Rifle. Moreover, it can also carry the PLATAN Mine Laying System or S-8 Non-Guided Missile Launcher or GAD air-to-air infrared missile launcher or MALUTKA wire-guided anti-tank missile system or SZTURM Radio Wave-guided Anti-Tank Missile System.

[57] Lieutenant Colonel Tin Win, "The Role of Helicopters in the 'Operation Mondaing'", *Myanmar Air Force Annual Magazine 1999*, pp. 46–49.

[58] As a result of the upgrade, some air squadrons were deployed.

[59] *Myanmar Air Force Annual Magazine 2006*, pp. 118–22.

5

MILITARY TRAINING AND OFFICER EDUCATION

Military training in Myanmar is the second task of the Tatmadaw, the first being combat duty and the third being public works. Training is the most important business of the Tatmadaw in peacetime and can take many forms. Military training is the key to achieving combat readiness. The Tatmadaw has been developing a training regime to provide officer education and leadership training for its officers. In this context, a wide range of skills needs to be developed and a variety of people need to be trained. This chapter discusses the development of military training in Myanmar from 1948 to the present. In the mid-1990s, in accordance with its modified military doctrine, the Tatmadaw introduced a new training regime to train its officers and men to be capable of fighting conventional warfare.

MILITARY TRAINING PROGRAMME

At the time of Myanmar's independence in 1948, in accordance with the War Establishment, a major was appointed as G-II (general staff officer — grade II) for military training and operations at the insufficiently staffed war office. He was assisted by two G-IIIs captains, one of whom was responsible for military training. The G-II was under the G-I (staff duty), a lieutenant colonel, of the General Staff Office. Then in September 1950, the War Office introduced a new set-up in which a new G-I (training) was appointed under the Vice-Chief of General Staff while the G-I (staff duty) was placed under the Deputy Chief of General Staff. The G-I (training) oversaw the Burma Regimental Centre, Burma Army Training Depot, Burma Army Central

School, Burma Army Officers' Training School, Burma Army School of Education, and Burma Army Staff College.[1]

Until 1953 there was neither a directorate of military training nor a proper training policy. Most of the officers were sent overseas for training. Although the Tatmadaw could send several officers to foreign training schools to take junior officer courses, mostly in the United Kingdom, India, and Pakistan, it was incapable of securing places in such training facilities as the staff college and the artillery school. At the 1953 Tatmadaw conference, held on 24 August, the then Commander-in-Chief of the Armed Forces, General Ne Win, pointed out the weaknesses of the military training programme in Myanmar. In his words:

> the most serious weakness of the General Staff Office is the training area. Because of the weakness in training programmes, operational drawbacks become more and more common in battles. Difficulties in training programmes are lack of time and shortage of training materials — both manuals and equipment ... Because of the lack of skills in battlecraft and operation of weapons, fire power does not match enemy casualties. The war office has been trying hard to get materials for training. As we do not think the existing training facilities and schools are sufficient or of international standard, we plan to establish a Combat Forces School and a Military Academy in the near future. The training programmes of these schools will determine the future course of the Tatmadaw. In order to run these training schools on our own, we have sent out trainees not only to England, India and Pakistan, as happened in the past, but also to the United States, Australia and Yugoslavia.[2]

In his speech at the conference, Lieutenant Colonel Aung Gyi (BC 3509), a G-I in the War Office, said that training programmes must consist of basic, operational, and advanced training in both military studies and academic studies. These training programmes must be conducted at five different levels: battalion, brigade, regional command, training schools, and overseas training facilities. He further stated: "we must accept that the quality of the Tatmadaw is very low as it is comprised of officers, the majority of whom neither understand military science and military thoughts nor have any knowledge of military history and have no military experience beyond guerrilla warfare".[3] Lieutenant Colonel Maung Maung (BC 3507),[4] G-I (training), mentioned that a training directorate would be organized in the near future and that this directorate would issue training directives. While military and academic studies would be provided by training schools, field training must be provided by battalions, brigades, and regional commands. He also said that he would like to appoint only those officers who had attended foreign staff colleges as commandants, chief instructors, and instructors at the training schools.[5]

Starting in 1952, the Tatmadaw sent a number of military delegations abroad to study military training programmes and training policies. Delegations went to India, Pakistan, Israel, Yugoslavia, East Germany, the United Kingdom, the United States, the Soviet Union, and some European countries. Their reports helped shape the training policies and programmes of the Tatmadaw. In order to strengthen the training wing of the Tatmadaw, another post of colonel in late 1955 was created at the General Staff Office, in addition to the existing colonel (general staff), as director of military training and combat forces, responsible for strategic planning, training programmes, and weaponry. Moreover, new training facilities for both officers and those of other ranks, such as the Burma Army Non-Commissioned Officers School, the Burma Army Combat Forces School, the Defence Services Academy, and the National Defence College, were opened in the mid and late 1950s.

In May 1953, the General Staff Department of the South Burma Sub-District (SBSD) published Training Directive No. 1 for the army. Then, in 1955, Directive No. 2 was published. At this stage, training was provided mostly at the regional command level. At about the same time, the training branch of the War Office published several training manuals, almost all of which were translations of the British Army manuals, from English into Myanmar. About the same time, the War Office began to publish a journal entitled *Sit Hnalone* (စစ်နှလုံး), the predecessor of the *Sitpyinyar* (စစ်ပညာ) [Military Affairs] Journal, the first volume of which came out in 1956.

Since 1953, discussions on the military training programmes of the Tatmadaw had been an important part of annual Tatmadaw conferences. At the 1953 Tatmadaw conference, for a better training regime and education for Tatmadaw personnel, the Tatmadaw formed a twenty-seven-member Training Committee on 28 August 1953. This committee was to draw up charters and curricula for training schools. By the time the Directorate of Military Training (DMT) was formally established in January 1956, the Tatmadaw was well into the process of developing a training regime of its own. Many officers and other ranks had returned from foreign training schools. Between 1948 and 1954, 907 officers and 344 of those of other ranks were sent abroad for various training programmes.[6] Defence cooperation between the Tatmadaw and other armed forces facilitated the process. Beginning in 1952, more Myanmar cadets were sent to the Royal Military Academy at Sandhurst. By 1956, about sixty-five cadets had attended Sandhurst.[7] By the mid-1950s, the Tatmadaw had begun to send its senior officers to other foreign staff colleges, such as the U.K. Staff

College at Kimberley, the Australian Army Staff College at Fort Queenscliff, and the U.S. Staff College at Fort Leavenworth.[8] Between 1953 and 1963, altogether eighteen senior officers were sent to Fort Leavenworth.[9] By the early 1960s, the DMT emerged as an influential branch of the General Staff Office. It also became the most important source of officer education as it was responsible not only for running training programmes and publishing a quarterly journal on military science, training manuals, and books on military affairs, but also developing a military doctrine.

When the DMT was reorganized in January 1963, it comprised four major branches: Training and Infantry Branch — MT-1; Tactical Planning Branch — MT-2; Strategic Planning and Doctrine Branch — MT-3; and Administration and Coordination Branch — MT-4.[10] By the late 1960s, the DMT had developed the "people's war" doctrine and the "four-cut" strategy. The success of counter-insurgency operations in the late 1960s and throughout the 1970s reflected the DMT's capability in developing a military doctrine and a training regime suitable for the Tatmadaw in Myanmar.[11]

In spite of the fact that many officers were sent to foreign training schools in the 1950s, until the mid-1970s — contrary to the wishes of Colonel Maung Maung (BC 3507) — almost all the directors of the DMT and commandants of the Tatmadaw's training schools were officers trained during the Second World War by the Japanese. In his writing about the graduation ceremony of the 13th Intake of the Defence Services Academy (DSA) in March 1971, Dr Maung Maung wrote:

> Colonel Tun Tin (director of military training) attended the third intake of the wartime military academy. His company commander (at the academy) was no other than Colonel Tun Aung Kyaw, the commandant of the Defence Services Academy. Colonel Tin Thein, the commandant of the Command and General Staff College, was a platoon commander when I was in the fourth intake of the academy.[12]

Although the DSA is modelled on West Point of the U.S. Army, its social interaction is that of the Japanese style Senpai-Kohai [senior-junior] relations; the DSA cadets established a strong Akogyi-Nyilay [elder-younger] bound. Thus, in a way, the training regime makes the Tatmadaw remain more or less an institution of "British structure with Japanese heart".

After 1963, the number of officers and other ranks sent abroad for training decreased dramatically. The programme of sending Myanmar cadets to Sandhurst stopped. Between 1948 and 1962, a total of 1,070 officers and those of 782 other ranks were sent abroad. However, between 1963 and 1989, only 415 officers and eighty-three of those of other ranks were sent.[13] After 1971, trainees were sent to only four countries: the United Kingdom, the United States (1980 to 1988), the Federal Republic of Germany (FRG), and Australia (1984 and 1987).[14] Most of the training programmes in the United States were for air force personnel while some army officers went on training in Fort Benning and Fort Leavenworth. Seven senior officers attended the American Staff College at Fort Leavenworth between 1980 and 1985. Engineering officers from the Defence Industries branch took courses in the FRG.

In the mid-1980s, when Colonel Sein Ya, a graduate of Sandhurst, became the director of DMT, he planned to send more officers to foreign training schools. He led several delegations, including one to Australia in 1987, to explore the possibility of sending more Tatmadaw officers to foreign training schools. After the military takeover of the state in September 1988, the places in the military training schools of the United States, the United Kingdom and Australia were lost due to political developments in Myanmar and the subsequent termination of defence cooperation programmes. But the Tatmadaw was able to secure some places in military training schools in Malaysia, Singapore, India, Pakistan, and the People's Republic of China (PRC). Between 1990 and 1999, 389 army personnel, 98 navy personnel and 455 air force personnel were sent abroad for training.[15] Out of a total of 942 persons, 615 went to the PRC, 53 to India, and 34 to Pakistan. Among 455 air force personnel, 330 went to the PRC, 7 each to India, Pakistan, and Singapore, 37 to Russia, and 12 to Yugoslavia. Out of 98 naval personnel, 79 were sent to the PRC and 8 to India while the remaining 11 went to Pakistan. 206 army personnel went to the PRC for training, in facilities such as the Staff College, armour and artillery schools.[16] Another set of data shows that between 1990 and 2005, the Tatmadaw sent 665 officers and 249 others of other ranks to China for 163 different courses. Some army officers were sent to India for armour and artillery training. The Indian armed forces also offered places at National Defence College and Staff College.[17] Malaysia also brought Tatmadaw officers to study at its staff colleges.[18] Since early 2000, the Tatmadaw began to send more and more trainees to Russia. According to a Russian news agency, over 1,500 Tatmadaw officers went there to study nuclear physics, aviation and other military related subjects.[19]

In the late 1980s, as mentioned earlier, the Tatmadaw decided to modernize and expand its forces. All the directorates of the armed forces were upgraded, including the DMT. Therefore, in 1990, the director of military training was upgraded to brigadier. Throughout the 1990s, existing training schools were also upgraded and new training schools were opened.[20] The Chief of Armed Forces Training was appointed in the General

Staff Office, with the rank of major general, in June 1995. Major General Saw Lwin became the first chief. The commandant of the National Defence College was also upgraded to major general, while all the commandants of other training schools for officers were made brigadier general. In 2001, the Chief of Armed Forces Training was further upgraded to a Lieutenant General post and three positions with the rank of major generals were created as Vice-Chief of Armed Forces Training (Joint Services Exercises), Vice-Chief of Armed Forces Training (Armed Forces Training), and Vice-Chief of Armed Forces Training (Strategic Studies). The creation of the post for the joint services exercises indicated the fact that the Tatmadaw is serious in developing conventional warfighting capability.

Under the force modernization and expansion programme, the Tatmadaw introduced a number of new training schools. At present, the Chief of Armed Forces Training Office runs ten Defence Services (Army) Basic Training Depots, three Defence Services (Army) Non-Commissioned Officers Schools, the Infantry Support Heavy Mortar Training School, the Land/Air Warfare School, two Defence Services (Army) Combat Forces Schools [Bahtoo; Bayint Naung], the Defence Services Academy [Pyin Oo Lwin], the Defence Services (Army) Officers Training School [Bahtoo], the Defence Services Administration School [Pyin Oo Lwin], the National Defence College [Yangon], the Command and General Staff College [Kalaw], the Defence Services Medical Academy [Yangon], the Defence Services Technological Academy [Pyin Oo Lwin], the Defence Services Institute of Nursing and Paramedical Science [Yangon], the Defence Services Technological College [Hopone], and twelve Advanced Command Training Centres.

In order to prove that it is serious about military training, the Tatmadaw leadership appears to have taken a number of measures. First, those with the rank of commander of light infantry and military operation command and above, must have a Master's degree in defence studies offered by the National Defence College. As a result, almost all the LID and MOC commanders at present have Master's degrees. Second, for further promotion to higher command positions, it now appears that senior commanders should have experience in serving at various training schools; thus the commanders will have staff, command, and instructional experience. (Of course, the commandant must have served as either LID or MOC commander in the previous post.) Third, the commanders of Command Training Centres were upgraded to the rank of brigadier general. The command training centre is the place for training both officers and rank and file together for platoon, company, battalion, tactical operation command, and light infantry division level exercises.[21] The Tatmadaw also initiated joint service training exercise programmes. It appears that the prospective regional commander must have served as commandant of the training institutes; the promotion order in August 2006 indicated that trend.

In order to strengthen its three capabilities — military, organizational, and administrative — it was decided that the Tatmadaw must be built through four means: training, administration, welfare, and morale. It appears that training involves both physical training and psychological training and is also in support of both the administrative and morale means. In fact, its military training is probably the most important factor that enhances the capabilities of the Tatmadaw. It is claimed that the entire training regime is to transform the Tatmadaw "from quantity to quality".[22] In terms of physical training, it is stated that fitness, endurance, skilfulness, know-how, and self-confidence must be imparted. With regard to psychological training, it is to train troops to accept the three Main National Causes, the national ideology, and national policy with conviction. In this context, Senior General Than Shwe reminded its troops that:

> Lessons can be drawn from some wars in the world where, [no matter] how modernize[d] the weapons and how well equipped the troops were, advanced weapons were abandoned and [they] suffered the [sic] defeat in the face of difficulty due primarily to the lack of strong will to fight. Moreover, psychological warfare as a special operation is placed [as] top priority in military principles. Being able to demoralize and destroy the enemy without actually fighting them rather than becoming victorious after fighting them in battle is the merit of psychological warfare. In the world today, unscrupulous psychological warfare is being massively waged with extensive utilization of information technology. Therefore, for all the member[s] of the Tatmadaw to be imbued with the spirit to fight, to understand the psychological warfare machinations of the opposing groups and to be able to shield off the enemy's thrust of false propaganda, in-service information and educational projects must be carried out.[23]

As for the importance of military training, in September 2001, General Maung Aye explained that "the Tatmadaw had been striving to uplift its training sector and it should be not only a constant learning".[24] On 5 April 2002, at the passing out ceremony of No. 44 Intake of the DSA, Senior General Than Shwe explained the aims and objectives of Tatmadaw's training in his speech. He said: "The objective of training is to fight and win the modern war. At present, it is important to understand that, instead of single service warfare by army, navy and air force, combined arms or joint warfare has become a feature of warfighting. Thus, it is necessary to understand the characteristics of individual services. One needs to know [the] effectiveness of electronic measures and weapon systems." The editorial in the May 2004 issue of the *Sitpyinyar* [Military Affairs] Journal stated: "For the warfare of [the] future, it is important to lay [the] objective to produce military genius and highly qualified personnel. In this way, by implementing this well developed objective in [sic] decade by decade, we will be able to produce commanders well versed in command and control at strategic, operational and tactical levels, as well as in staff duties... It is a main duty of the institutes and academies under the Tatmadaw to train and produce military genius."[25]

As a result, the training programme was also expanded and upgraded to catch up with developments in military affairs. It appears that the directorate of military training has been undertaking major research work on military science and technology. As mentioned earlier, the first issue of *Sitpyinnyar* Journal was published in June 1956. Under the leadership of Colonel Maung Maung (who later became Brigadier), the DMT initiated a series of publications on field manuals and manuals for standard weapons in the Tatmadaw.[26] The Directorate of Military Training stopped the publication of the *Sitpyinnyar* Journal in January 1992; the last issue was out in January 1992 (31:1). The directorate resumed the publication only in January 1998 (32:1), and it was temporarily suspended for a year — after the distribution of the January 1999 (33:1) issue — from May 1999, until the May 2000 (34:2) issue was out. Moreover, it is noteworthy that the publication was changed from a quarterly to a four-monthly. Between 1998 and 2004, the directorate, later renamed the Chief of Armed Forces Training Office (CAFTO), published altogether eighteen issues of *Sitpyinnyar* Journal; a total of 178 articles appeared, of which twenty-seven were on warfare, doctrine, and strategy, twenty-three on leadership and training, thirty-five on weapon systems and technology, fourteen on tactics and warfighting, fourteen on campaigns, operations, and battles, fifty-one on country or regional forces, and fourteen on other issues.[27] Although the DMT stopped publishing the *Sitpyinnyar* Journal in 1992, it nevertheless published a few books on warfare: *The Art of War by Sun Tzu* (1992); *The Art of War in Myanmar* (1994); *A Brief History of Myanmar Armed Forces, Traditions of the Tatmadaw, Insurgency in Myanmar*, and the *Role of the Tatmadaw in Myanmar* (1994); *Military Thoughts of Clausewitz* (1994); and *Military Thoughts of Liddell Hart* (1994). Several instruction manuals were also published.[28] However, between 1994 and 1998, the DMT practically stopped all publication.

The Directorate of Military Training also produced several field manuals for the Tatmadaw. It appears that the DMT became active again only after the appointment of Brigadier General Aung Kyi, a former trainee at Ford Benning, in 1998. A series of field manuals — based mostly on the Western strategic literature and U.S. Army or Marine field manuals — was published: *Manual for Infantry Battalion: Guerrilla Operations* (2000); *Defensive Campaign in Border Areas* (2000); *Light Infantry Division Operations* (2000); *Manual for Application of People's War Strategy* (2000); *The Manual for Military Operations on Urbanized Terrain* (2000); *Infantry Reconnaissance Platoon* (2000); *Technique and Tactics for Tunnel Warfare* (2000); *Tactics for Urban Warfare* (2000); *Nuclear, Biological and Chemical Warfare* (2000); *Mountain Terrain Operations* (2000); *The Infantry Platoon* (2001); *The Tactical Operation Command* (2001); *Urban People's Air Defence* (2001); and *Manual for Infantry Sergeant* (2003). It is known that manuals for "Infantry Company" and "Combined Arms Warfare" are underway for publication. Moreover, some books on military history were also published: *Campaigns in the World War II* (2000); *History of War* (2001); *Theories of War* (2001); *Military Campaigns in the History of Warfare* (2003). Other instruction manuals were also published.[29] In 2003, the CAFTO began publishing a new four-monthly journal named *Sittheikpan-Hnit-Nipyinnyar* (စစ်သိပ္ပံနှင့်နည်းပညာ) [Military Science and Technology] Journal; the publication was delayed for years and so far only four issues have come out.

There are some changes in the training regime too. While guerrilla and counter-guerrilla warfare continue to occupy a large portion of the training regime, joint services and combined arms exercises have increasingly become important. In this context, joint services and combined arms exercises of "Bayintnaung", "Sinbyushin", and "Kyansittha", at the division level, were conducted in 1995 and 1997. However, due to the cost, no more exercise has been conducted since. In addition, since 2002, at the tactical level, the training regime at the tactical level gives more emphasis to the penetration form of manoeuvre with breaching attack than on the usual frontal and envelopment attacks; accordingly, it applied Liddell Hart's idea of expanding torrent with suppressing element, assault element, and exploitation element.[30] But there appears to be no major changes in terms of defence and retrograde operations.[31] Moreover, editorials in the *Sitpyinnyar* Journal urged Tatmadaw personnel to catch up with the latest developments in theories of war, principles of war, military doctrine, strategies and tactics, and new weapons and technologies, as well as to digest the lessons from the history of warfare. In the September 2003 issue of *Sitpyinnyar* Journal, the CAFTO explained the importance of military training in the following terms:

> The most important essential for building a modern Tatmadaw with high military capability is the [sic] training and education. The [sic] training and education is [sic] a strategic level [and] necessary task for the Tatmadaw.... In modern warfare, due to developments in technology there are changes in strategies and tactics. Instead of single service warfare by army or navy or air force, it has [become] increasingly common to witness the combined arms warfare with corps and services. In this light, modern armed forces give special emphasis on [sic] joint or combined armed warfare in military training. The strategic objective of the Tatmadaw training regime is to upgrade the quality of all the Tatmadaw personnel, including [their] capability to take care of the [sic] command and control and the [sic] logistic[s] matter[s] in modern warfighting, and to instill the spirit of maintaining good traditions, morale, and discipline of the Tatmadaw.[32]

Before I proceed with the training programmes for officers, I would like to discuss training programmes for Non-Commissioned Officers (NCOs) and those of other ranks. The Military Computer and Technological Institute (MCTI) and ten Defence Services Army Training Depots (DSATD) are for new recruits. The MCTI is designed to produce technicians for the Tatmadaw after three-year training programmes. Although the MCTI offers Bachelor of Technology (B. Tech) degrees, the graduates are not commissioned, but appointed only as non-commissioned officers, such as warrant officers in the engineering corps. Established on 26 December 2000 in Pyin Oo Lwin, the MCTI was known as the Military Technological College. The college was renamed as Military Technological Institute on 1 July 2002. The college recruited two intakes of students before being moved to Hopone on 22 October 2002 due to serious fights between its students and cadets from the Defence Services Technological Academy (DSTA). All students were sent back home and the institute was closed down for a year. Meanwhile the institute was reorganized on 28 November 2002 for a fresh start. A new batch of 500 students was recruited and classes began on 3 February 2003. Then on 8 May 2003, the institute was renamed Military Computer and Technological Institute (MCTI). The MCTI offered diplomas in mechanical engineering, civil engineering, electronic engineering, electrical power engineering, mechatronic engineering, metallurgy, and computer engineering. So far four batches of 1,257 students in all have completed the diploma courses.

Three Defence Services Non-Commissioned Officers Schools (DSNCOS), Infantry Support Heavy Mortar Training School (ISHMTS), Land/Air Warfare School (LAWS), and twelve Advanced Command Training Centres (ACTC) offered a number of courses for NCOs and those of other ranks. Most of the courses are at the tactical level. Courses at the DSNCOS and ACTC include ambush and counter-ambush, counter-insurgency weapons and tactics, individual battle initiative for tactical independence, commando tactics, and scouting. The ISHMTS offers courses on 81-mm mortar, 60-mm mortar, the 75-mm recoilless rifle gun, BA 103 rocket launcher, 106-mm mortar, .5-calibre heavy machine gun and 84-mm recoilless (anti-tank) rifle. Special to corps training programmes, such as courses for signal operators, mechanic and artillery fire control operators, were available in various support corps centres. The NCOs and those of other ranks in the Tatmadaw-Yay and the Tatmadaw-Lay also have to undergo their special-to-corps courses at respective training centres.

PRE-COMMISSION TRAINING

The pre-commission training programmes, designed to produce junior officers with background knowledge in the operation of weapons, battlecraft, and fieldcraft skills, operational staff procedures, military history, military science and technology, military instruction and drill, military ethos, physical fitness, and military leadership, are run by the Defence Services (Army) Officers' Training School (commonly known as OTS) and the Defence Services Academy (DSA), under the DMT. These two schools have been central to officer training in Myanmar since they produce most of the officers for the three services of the Tatmadaw. It is important, however, to note that the officer corps of the Tatmadaw, particularly in the army, has three different kinds of officers from recruitment. They are OTS officers, DSA officers, and Teza officers. Whichever background they may have, one thing in common among these officers is that all of them are trained to take orders without questions, to accept collective responsibility and collective leadership, and to carry out missions promptly with whatever means that are necessary. Since the training programmes for the first two types of officers will be discussed later, I will provide only background information about Teza officers here.

The first intake of Teza or Alot-Thin-Bo (apprentice officer/under-officer) was introduced in 1971 with 115 cadets. Cadets were high-school leavers within the age range of sixteen to nineteen years. The cadets studied intermediate college-level courses and basic military training at the DSA during the first six months. They then underwent a year-and-a-half period of training at the OTS. At the OTS, they studied military science and courses designed for the junior level of command. Then the cadets were sent out to battalions for a year of fieldwork before they were commissioned into the army. It took, therefore, three years to be commissioned by this route. Later, Teza cadets were sent to the Burma Army Training Depot (BATD) for the first twelve months, instead of the DSA, and then to the Defence Services (Army) Non-Commissioned Officers' School (DSNCOS) to study section commander-level courses before they underwent a six-month training period at the OTS for military science. After that, they were posted to infantry battalions for nine months, before going to the Defence Service (Army) Combat Forces School for the last three months to study platoon commander-level courses. Then cadets were commissioned, mostly into the army. In 2000, the Tatmadaw stopped recruiting Teza officers. Altogether 4,958 Teza officers were commissioned into the Tatmadaw through thirty intakes by 2002. The last intake of 141 Teza cadets held their passing out parade at the Officers' Training School on 10 May 2002, attended by Vice-Senior General Maung Aye.

The Officers' Training School (OTS), the predecessor of the present day Defence Services (Army) Officers' Training School, was established on 1 January 1946, before the country's independence in 1948, in Maymyo. It was moved to Bahtoo in June 1957, then to Hmawbi in 1964, and back again to Bahtoo in 1991. Until around 1970, commandants of the OTS were Japanese-trained officers. The OTS is the place for fresh university graduates and non-commissioned officers (NCOs) from the Tatmadaw to undergo military training to become commissioned officers. Up to the No. 28th Intake in 1961, most of the cadets were NCOs from the Tatmadaw. Only a very small percentage of cadets had high school or higher-level education. A total of 2,541 officers were commissioned through twenty-eight intakes (1st to 28th) from the OTS before 1960. Beginning with the No. 29th Intake, after a four-year break from the preceding one, most of the cadets have had university education. Some NCOs with a lower level of education are also placed in the programme. Engineers and veterinary surgeons are recruited through this programme. Between March 1962 and August 1988, the OTS commissioned 5,981 officers through forty-six batches (29th to 75th).

In the 1990s, the Tatmadaw introduced a special programme of officer recruitment for NCOs with post-high school education or university degrees at the OTS. The OTS cadets have three different types of background. The first is fresh university graduates within the age range of twenty-one to twenty-three. The second is NCOs with a university degree or high school certificate. Recently, this pattern has become more common. Many young people with a high school certificate join the army as privates, later pursuing university education through correspondence courses. After four or five years, they become graduates as well as sergeants with five years of military service. They are then entitled to sit for the OTS entrance examinations. Even without a university degree, if they have more than seven years of service and become sergeants, they are entitled to sit for the entrance examinations. The third group is NCOs with only primary or secondary education. The candidate must be a corporal with over ten years of service and within the prescribed age range, and be recommended by his CO. Officers commissioned from the OTS are usually posted to the army. The training period usually lasts for about nine months and courses are designed to provide basic military training and military strategy and tactics for junior levels of command. Between May 1949 and September 1988, seventy-five intakes of officers were trained at the OTS.[33] Some of the cadets in the earlier years were commissioned as police officers.[34] Within a forty-two-year period, a total of 9,828 cadets were trained at this school. In 1997 alone, the OTS produced 698 commissioned officers through the No. 97th and No. 98th Intakes. Between September 1988 and December 1999, 5,914 officers were commissioned from the OTS in twenty-six intakes.[35] The OTS stopped recruiting fresh university graduates since the early 2000s. Nevertheless, in the period between September 1988 and December 2007, the OTS produced a total of 7,888 officers through thirty-five batches (76th to 110th). A total of 161 cadets from the 110th batch completed their course on 26 April 2007. Thus, so far, through 110 batches, the OTS produced a total of 16,251 officers for the Tatmadaw.

The Defence Services Academy (DSA) was opened in Bahtoo on 14 February 1955. It recruits high school leavers within the age range of sixteen to nineteen years for a four-year training programme at the academy. The graduating cadets are awarded either BA or BSc degrees and are commissioned into the three services of the Tatmadaw. Now the DSA has also introduced a degree course in computer science. However, a major portion of the course is devoted to military science. The first intake of fifty-four cadets began its course on 4 July 1955. Only forty cadets graduated on 1 June 1959. Meanwhile, the DSA was relocated to Pyin Oo Lwin on 20 June 1957. In the 1990s, the academy recruited about 250 cadets each year. In 1996, however, an additional 240 cadets were recruited exclusively for the air force. They were for the No. 63 flying course.[36] Between 1959 and 1999, a total of 4,449 officers (3,411 in the army, 590 in the navy, and 448 in the air force) were commissioned through forty intakes.[37] From the time the State Law and Order Restoration Council (SLORC) came to power in September 1988 until December 1999, 1,760 officers were commissioned from the DSA.[38] Now the academy has a capacity to train 3,000 cadets per batch each year for its three-year training programme. At one stage, one intake had 3,289 cadets.[39] Because of this large number, the cadets are organized into three battalions rather than the usual companies. In terms of course structure, since 2000, the DSA has introduced a computer science degree; thus the academy has produced hundreds of officers with background in computer science. The 49th Intake of the DSA graduated on 15 December 2006.[40] The 50th Intake of the DSA had 2,122 cadets at the time of entrance.[41] Moreover, the DSA has begun to run Ph.D. programmes of its own. The DSA, so far, has produced 19,749 officers through fifty intakes, of which 17,367 are for army, 1,014 for the navy, and 1,368 for the air force.

Before the opening of the Defence Services Institute of Medicine (DSIM) in November 1993, medical and dental officers were recruited through a month-long basic military training programme at the Medical Corps Centre.[42] The medical corps of the Tatmadaw has always been short of doctors. The Tatmadaw has been implementing a national service scheme for medical school leavers since the early 1950s. Recruitment became more difficult in the 1990s and this situation resulted in the opening of the DSIM. The DSIM offers courses for both basic and advanced degrees in medicine and surgery. The first batch of forty-seven cadets from the DSIM were commissioned as lieutenants on 17 December 1999, after six years of study and a year as house-surgeons. The DSIM, now renamed Defence Services Medical Academy (DSMA), has become the most important and only source of medical officers for the DMS. So far, a total of 1,525 medical officers were commissioned through nine intakes. See Table 5.1.

The DSMA also runs twenty graduate programmes in medical sciences. So far, the DSMA has produced seven Doctor of Medical Science Degree holders. In terms of Master of Medical Science, by early 2008, the DSMA has produced 335 specialists, of which fifty-eight are physicians and forty-one are surgeons. At present, another 242 medical officers are taking Master's courses in eighteen different specializations.

Established on 1 February 1994, the Defence Services Institute of Technology (DSIT) produces engineering officers for the Tatmadaw.[43] It offers degrees in mechanical engineering, civil engineering, electrical power engineering, electronic engineering, defence industrial engineering, chemical engineering, marine engineering, aeronautical engineering, and metallurgical engineering.[44] At the opening ceremony of the first intake of the DSIT, General Maung Aye, deputy commander-in-chief of the defence services and commander-in-chief of the army, explained that "the DSIT was established with a view to providing reliable and efficient engineer officers of high character

TABLE 5.1
Defence Services Medical Academy

Sr.	*Intake*	*Commencement*	*Date of Commission*	*Graduates*
1	1st Intake	3 May 1993	17 December 1999	47
2	2nd Intake	9 February 1995	23 April 2001	66
3	3rd Intake	23 February 1996	29 April 2002	93
4	4th Intake	7 March 1997	30 January 2003	55
5	5th Intake	9 March 1998	1 January 2004	117
6	6th Intake	3 March 1999	31 December 2004	133
7	7th Intake	14 February 2000	28 December 2005	212
8	8th Intake	16 March 2001	28 December 2006	467
9	9th Intake	25 March 2002	28 December 2007	335
	TOTAL			1,525

Source: Government Gazettes; pamphlets distributed at the passing-out parades; interviews.

for service to the nation".[45] After five years of study, cadets are commissioned as lieutenants.[46] There were 100 cadets in the first intake; soon, four withdrew from their courses and another twelve were dismissed in their second year as they bullied their juniors. Therefore, only eighty-four from the first batch of cadets graduated from the DSIT in April 1999 (see Table 5.2). Seven are in the navy and six are in the air force. Some engineers from the Directorate of Military Engineering are also taking their Master's course at the DSIT. The DSIT was renamed Defence Services Technological Academy (DSTA) in November 1999. Now the DSTA recruits over 500 cadets each year. So far, the DSTA has produced a total of 2,538 engineering officers, of which 165 are civil engineers, 798 mechanical engineers, 312 electrical power engineers, and 477 electronic engineers.

The DSTA has added new specializations meanwhile. In 2006, five more categories were added: naval architecture, marine electrical systems and electronics, aerospace-avionics, aerospace-propulsion and flight vehicles, and mechatronic. The DSTA also offers graduate courses for military officers. In the 1999–2000 academic year, the DSTA introduced a Master's degree programme in civil, mechanical, and electrical power. The first batch of fifteen Master's candidates, five each in the above mentioned three subjects, began their courses on 10 May 1999. However, the programme was temporarily suspended and resumed only in 2007. In the meantime, military engineers were sent to Russia or universities under the Ministry of Science and Technology

TABLE 5.2
Defence Services Technological Academy

Sr.	*Intake*	*Commencement*	*Date of Commission*	*Graduates*
1	1st Intake	4 July 1994	11 April 1999	84
2	2nd Intake	29 April 1995	10 April 2000	102
3	3rd Intake	10 May 1996	9 April 2001	111
4	4th Intake	12 May 1997	12 April 2002	131
5	5th Intake	13 May 1998	9 April 2003	218
6	6th Intake	10 May 1999	9 April 2004	214
7	7th Intake	5 January 2000	24 December 2004	213
8	8th Intake	19 March 2001	24 December 2005	382
9	9th Intake	18 March 2002	21 December 2006	543
10	10th Intake	14 November 2002	21 December 2007	540
	TOTAL			2,538

Source: Government Gazettes; pamphlets distributed at the passing-out parades; interviews.

for graduate studies. The second batch of five Master's candidates began their courses on 25 June 2007. Then, on 15 January 2007, the DSTA opened its doctoral programme; twenty-one candidates registered in mechanical, electrical power, electronic, and chemical engineering.

The Defence Services Institute of Nursing (DSIN) opened on 24 February 2000, is the newest nursing officer training centre for the Tatmadaw. Before the birth of the DSIN, nursing officers, all female, were trained at the Medical Corps Centre in Mingalardon. The Nurses Training Wing was set up on 1 June 1959, as part of the Medical Corps Centre, to recruit women for military hospitals.[47] The training programme included three years of course work and a two-year apprenticeship for commission. Through this programme, a total of 761 nursing officers were commissioned in sixteen batches. On 15 May 1996, a BSc (Nursing) programme was commenced in the Defence Services Institute of Medicine. After four years of course work and a year of apprentice-ship, cadets are awarded a degree in nursing and commissioned as second lieutenants. On 20 November 2002, the DSIN was renamed Defence Services Institute of Nursing and Paramedical Sciences (DSINPS). Moreover, since 2000, a new training regime has been introduced and the graduates are no longer commissioned into the Tatmadaw; they are appointed to official level positions, equivalent to second lieutenant and up to the rank of lieutenant colonel, in the course of their time in service. Since then, the DSINPS has been recruiting only male candidate for four-year degree programmes in nursing or paramedical sciences, such as pharmacy, radiography, physiotherapy, and medical technology. So far the DSINPS has produced 1,034 graduates in five intakes, of which 858 are nurses. See Table 5.3.

TABLE 5.3
Defence Services Institute for Nursing and Paramedical Science

Sr.	*Intake*	*Commencement*	*Date of Commission*	*Graduates*
1	1st Intake	24 February 2000	5 December 2004	58
2	2nd Intake	25 January 2001	7 January 2005	237
3	3rd Intake	25 March 2002	6 January 2006	433
4	4th Intake	6 January 2003	5 January 2007	214
5	5th Intake	24 February 2004	7 January 2008	92
	TOTAL			1,034

Source: Government Gazettes; pamphlets distributed at the passing-out parades; interviews.

The DSINPS also offers a Master's degree programme. The first batch of sixteen candidates for the Master of Nursing Science (M. NSc) degree began their studies on 7 March 2005 and graduated on 9 March 2007. The second batch of twenty-six M. NSc candidates was accepted on 5 March 2007. The DSINPS also offered B. NSc (bridging) for in-service nurses and two batches of forty-three nursing officers have completed their courses.

POST-COMMISSION TRAINING

The post-commission training in the Tatmadaw is designed to give its officers both training and education. This includes a number of special-to-corps courses. Political education is also provided. However, the DMT plays its most significant role in officer education and leadership training. It runs the Defence Services (Army) Combat Forces School, the Defence Services Administration School, the Land/Air Warfare and Paratroop School, the Command and General Staff College, and the National Defence College. Most officers attend all-corps courses at each rank, from lieutenant to lieutenant colonel, while some officers go to special-to-corps courses conducted at the relevant corps schools. The special-to-corps courses provide the specialist knowledge officers need to develop for their corps' operational requirements.

Post-commission training programmes are coordinated to the extent that special-to-corps and all-corps training are complementary. For example, an infantry officer has to take courses in signals and intelligence, which are offered by their respective corps. While the Directorate of Defence Services Intelligence, the Directorate of Armour and Artillery, and the Directorate of Signal provide some training programmes for infantry officers, the Directorate of Engineering and the Directorate of Mechanical and Electrical Engineering offer courses exclusively for their own officers. The navy and the air force also have their training centres. The Directorate of People's Militias and Public Relations operates several training centres for the political education of the officer corps. The post-commission training is also centred on the effective management of personnel and resources, command and leadership, and efficient performance of staff duties.

A few years after their commission, army officers have to undergo training at the Defence Services (Army) Combat Forces School (DSCFS). Established in January 1955 in Bahtoo, the DSCFS provides training for junior officers holding ranks between lieutenant and major. Courses offered are the platoon commander course for lieutenants, company commander course for captains, and battalion commander course for majors. Courses usually last about three to five months, and include military leadership, staff duties, military strategy and tactics, military laws, military history, principles of war, counter-insurgency warfare, and so on. The first platoon commander course was opened in May 1955. About 150 junior officers per batch are trained for fifteen weeks. The first company commander course was opened in April 1952 at the Burma Army Central School (BACS), the predecessor of the DSCFS. The BACS trained up to nine batches of company commanders. Then the DSCFS took over from the tenth batch in July 1954. From the 61st batch in October 1973, the DSCFS accepted trainees from the police force. In the 1980s and 1990s, about a hundred captains per batch were given training for twelve weeks. From the 130th batch in September 1995, the DSCFS received officers from the fire brigade and prison department for the company commander course.[48] In May 1982, the battalion commander course was introduced at the DSCFS with forty majors from the army as trainees.[49] The course, which lasts twenty-one weeks, is designed to produce officers capable of leading a battalion in battle and of understanding basic tactics at division-level manoeuvre. Until the opening of the Armoured and Artillery Training School in 1990, officers in the armoured and artillery corps had to undergo their specialized training at the DSCFS for platoon and company level.[50] Those officers who passed these courses were considered for promotion to lieutenant colonels and battalion commanders. In order to accommodate the expansion of the armed forces, a new DSCFS was established in Bayint Naung in March 2000.

In May 1958, the Land/Air Warfare School was opened to meet the operational requirements of the Tatmadaw. Three months later, the Paratroops School was also opened. This was the time the Tatmadaw was fighting the Kuomintang (KMT) in the border region. Many troops were airlifted to the front. In April 1963, the two schools were merged to become the Land/Air Warfare and Paratroops School (LAWPS). At the LAWPS, courses were offered for both officers and those of other ranks.[51] Most of the instructors (officers) were sent abroad, for example to the United Kingdom and the United States, for training. Some military officers went to the LAWPS for training. Many of the officers who attended the school are now in top positions at the Tatmadaw. They include General Maung Aye, deputy commander-in-chief of the armed forces and commander-in-chief of the army, and many senior commanders of the present day. Despite some heliborne operations, in the past the paratroopers and airborne operations were of little use to the Tatmadaw in counter-insurgency warfare. However, as the Tatmadaw is in the process of developing an airborne division, in accordance with its modified military doctrine and strategy, the LAWPS is becoming increasingly important.

The Burma Army Administrative Support Training School (BAASTS), renamed Defence Services Administration School (DSAS) in January 1997, was opened on 1 March 1964 in Pyin Oo Lwin. Courses are offered for both officers and those of other ranks. Officer courses are designed to produce good adjutant officers and quarter-master officers as well as judicial officers. Almost all junior officers are required to attend courses at the DSAS. The school also offers a diploma course in military law.[52]

Established in June 1990, the Armour and Artillery School (AAS) offers special-to-corps courses for officers and those of other ranks serving in artillery, armour, and air defence battalions. However many junior officers, mainly in their immediate commission period, go to the AAS for artillery training. This is to provide them with a basic knowledge of mechanized warfare. Between 1990 and 1999, 750 officers were trained for artillery warfare and 315 officers were trained for armoured warfare.[53] In early 2000s, as the Directorate of Armour and Artillery was split up, the new Directorate of Armour established its own Armour Training School in Maingmaw.

In 1950, the Directorate of Defence Services Intelligence established the Military Intelligence Training Centre. Courses were opened for intelligence officers at the battalion and brigade levels. Although the Myanmar term for the school remained unchanged "*Sit Htauk Hlanye Atatthin Kyaung*"

(စစ်ထောက်လှမ်းရေးအတတ်သင်ကျောင်း), it was renamed in English as the Military Intelligence Depot. Then, in May 1958, the Military Intelligence Training Centre was renamed the Defence Services Intelligence Centre (DSIC). The DSIC offers courses for both officers and those of other ranks. For infantry officers, the combat intelligence (officer) course and the counter-intelligence (officer) course are offered. Some of the officers who have attended these courses are chosen to serve in the intelligence corps. They are further trained in interrogation, intelligence gathering and analysis, special security operations, and other specialized subjects.

Established in October 1951 as the Burma Signals Training Regiment, the Defence Services Signals and Electronic School (DSSES) has gone through a number of changes in structure and training regime. Being the Signal Corps Centre, until its transformation to the DSSES on 23 January 1997, it offered a number of courses for both officers and those of other ranks. Infantry officers take the infantry signals officer course to gain basic knowledge of combat-level signals operations. Officers in the signals corps have to take courses designed for signals platoon, signals company, and signals (electronic) engineering. These courses include radio operation, signals intelligence, interception, cipher making and decoding, electronic warfare, and so on.[54] In order to catch up with the developments in electronic and information technology, a number of new courses are offered for infantry officers. According to some sources, this includes a basic course on the C^4I (Command, Control, Communication, Computer, and Intelligence) warfare.[55]

In 1952, in Maymyo, the Burma Army Engineering Corps Centre was established by transforming the Engineering Training Battalion. Having undergone various stages of restructuring, the Burma Army Engineering Corps Centre was renamed the Defence Services Engineering School (DSES) in January 1997. Out of a total of twenty-five different courses for officers and those of other ranks in the Engineering Corps, mine operations, field engineering, tunnel warfare, and civil engineering courses for officers are noteworthy.[56] For example, eight subjects are taught in the platoon engineering officer course: battlefield defence planning, mines and traps, explosives, roads and airfields, bridges, river crossing, water distribution, and field engineering.[57] The Defence Services Mechanical and Electrical Engineering School was opened in March 1990, after several stages of transformation since its establishment in 1958 as No. 2 Work Station in Maymyo. The school offers platoon- and company-level courses for officers. They include maintenance and repair of weapons systems, radar inspection, missile maintenance, electronic equipment maintenance, and so on. However, these courses are designed only for officers in the Mechanical and Electrical Engineering Corps.[58]

Officers in the air force and the navy have special-to-corps training centres. The air force runs two training schools: the Flying Training Base and Ground Training Base. The Flying Training Base has No. 1 Flying School (basic) and No. 2 Flying School (advanced) in addition to an interceptor squadron, a fighter squadron, a radar squadron, a mechanical unit, an administrative unit, and a flight navigational coordination unit. Training programmes include the basic flying course, navigation, air traffic and control tower operation, transport aircraft flying, helicopter flying, the air defence system, and so on. Up to 2001, the Flying Training Base had produced about 1,290 pilots for the air force in sixty-four batches. Although each intake was small in number, the No. 63 and No. 64 flying courses produced 215 and 218 pilots respectively. However, later intakes have roughly around seventy pilots per batch. No. 68 Flying course was completed on 17 November 2006. The Ground Training Base is comprised of the Administrative Training School, Technical Training School, Electronic Training School, and Central Inspection Unit. The navy has the Naval Training Command in Seikgyi. Courses at the training command include junior and senior naval officer courses, electronic intelligence, mine and torpedo operations, mine-sweeping, navigation, survey, naval commando, naval artillery, and so on. The passing out parades for No. 67 Junior Naval Officer Course and No. 41 Junior Naval Engineer Course were held on 23 January 2007.

For the political education of officers and other ranks of the Tatmadaw, a number of Combat Related Organisational Activities Training Centres (CROATC), known in Myanmar as *Taik-pwe-win-si-yone-ye-thin-dan-kyaung* (တိုက်ပွဲဝင်စည်းရုံးရေးသင်တန်းကျောင်း), were opened in the early 1990s. All armed forces personnel must take a three-month course at the CROATC. It is a replacement for the Central School of Political Science, the ideological training centre of the defunct Burma Socialist Programme Party (BSPP), which was the sole political party in Myanmar for twenty-four years from 1964, and led the state for fourteen years since 1974 and which ran Centres for Ideological Education at regional commands.

The Burma Army Staff College (BASC) was opened on 1 August 1948 in Maymyo. The first commandant was Brigadier General Sir James Roderick Sinclair, nineteenth Earl of Caithness, from the British Service Mission of Burma. Most of the instructors were from the British Service Mission and there was only one major from the Burma Army. The first two batches studied in Maymyo. The BASC was then moved to Mingalardon in January 1950 and before it was moved again to Kalaw in April 1954, it trained four batches of officers. Then, in 1966, the BASC was relocated to Bahtoo, a year before it was renamed the Command and General Staff College (CGSC). The CGSC was moved back to Kalaw in 1990. A number of junior officers, both majors and lieutenant colonels from the three services of the armed forces, plus a few police officers, are selected each year to be trained for about twelve months at the Command and General Staff College at Kalaw. Most of the trainees are from the army, with only a few officers come from the air force, navy, and police. Most of those who attend the CGSC are selected for promotion to colonel. Up until the late 1990s, medical officers were exempted from taking courses at the CGSC. The CGSC provides a mixture of training and education. Among the stated missions and tasks of the CGSC the following two are noteworthy:

- to train officers to be able to command infantry divisions and to perform staff duties of regional commands;
- to train officers to enable them to find quick and correct solutions to military issues within the framework of correlation between Myanmar defence policy, military doctrine, international and regional politics, military science, geopolitics and the current political, and socio-economic situation of Myanmar.[59]

The training provides an understanding of Myanmar's security interests, a general understanding of Myanmar's defence capabilities and their deployment within a framework of national security and defence policy. The focus of the study is on both the strategy and the tactics of four major principles of warfare: advance, attack, defence, and withdrawal. The training programme also involves students discussing their individual battle experiences and preparing a defence plan. Some of these defence plans are based on tactical aspects of defence, such as a defence plan for Kunlong or for the complete eradication of a certain insurgent group in a certain area. A large portion of the training is based on counter-insurgency operations. Among the subjects taught at the CGSC are command, military leadership, staff duties, special tactics in jungle warfare, river-crossing warfare, mountain range warfare, lowland warfare, tunnel warfare, guerrilla warfare, commando, ABC (atomic, biological, and chemical) warfare, joint services operations, people's war strategy, intelligence-gathering techniques, and the functions of support corps (such as signals and artillery).[60] The training programme is designed for fighting both conventional and counter-insurgency warfare. By early 2008, a total of 58 intakes were trained at CGSC.

In 1955, the Tatmadaw leadership planned to open a defence college for both military and civilian officials. On 24 November 1958, the National Defence College (NDC) was formally established in Yangon. However, a pilot course for twenty-nine senior military and civilian officials had been opened in August 1957. Between 1958 and March 1994, 1,489 officers were trained in twenty-seven batches doing short-term courses. From more than a dozen missions and tasks, the NDC intends to produce trainees:

- able to research and develop the appropriate military doctrine and public policy for the perpetuation of national independence and sovereignty, national solidarity, and development and progress of the Union of Myanmar;
- able to understand military affairs, domestic politics, economic issues and national policy aims, which are closely related to national security;
- able to analyse and efficiently make use of the military, political, logistical, managerial, and psychological factors that are interrelated and important in determining international and domestic policy for the building of a modern developed nation;
- able to develop a national grand strategy for the future, in both peace and war, in support of national objectives, by analysing national defence and security objectives and national policy aims.[61]

The NDC courses are designed to provide education for senior officers. Only in March 1994 did the NDC begin to offer a one-year programme and open the first regular course with twenty-nine senior officers. All candidates were colonels in rank. Then in 1998, the NDC introduced a Master's programme. So far, a total of 350 senior officers have completed the one-year regular course in seven intakes, of which 292 were awarded M.A (Defence Studies). Final research papers for graduation cover a wide range of subjects. The trainees are also required to draw up a national security plan as part of their exercises. Most of the trainees are colonels. Those who graduate from the NDC are considered for further promotion to brigadier general and above for both command and staff positions. The No. 8th Intake with forty-four students began its course on 30 January 2007. See Table 5.4.

Among the subjects taught at the NDC, the national interests and basic principles of the Union of Myanmar, allocation and employment of national resources, the strategic concepts of people's war and people's militias, and the appraisal and formulation of future national strategy for the Union of Myanmar are important subjects. Since late 1990s, joint services exercise has been an important part of the course at the NDC. The trainees are also taught international relations, international law, international economics, defence policies and defence planning in Asia and the Pacific, the revolution in military affairs, and the military strategies, national interests and national power of other countries.[62] According to "NDC Magazines" published at the end of every intake, among the 292 theses done, ninety-four were on the

TABLE 5.4
NDC Intakes and Trainees

Sr.	*Intake*	*From*	*To*	*No. of Candidates*	*Remark*
1	Intake-1	21-03-94	18-11-94	29	Diploma
2	Intake-2	11-11-96	18-07-97	29	Diploma
3	Intake-3	10-08-98	06-08-99	40	M.A (DS)
4	Intake-4	15-02-00	09-03-01	46	M.A (DS)
5	Intake-5	26-08-02	19-09-03	78	M.A (DS)
6	Intake-6	01-12-03	04-12-04	73	M.A (DS)
7	Intake-7	11-07-05	14-07-06	55	M.A (DS)

Source: NDC magazines for various years.

political issues, ninety-seven on the economic, seventy-five on the military, and twenty-six are on corps-related issues.

CONCLUSION

Military training and officer education in Myanmar is provided most importantly by the training schools under the Directorate of Military Training. The creation of the Chief of Armed Forces Training post at the General Staff Office in 1995 indicates the increasingly important role of the DMT in the Tatmadaw. Since 1989, the Tatmadaw has recruited more officers and trained them at the OTS and the DSA. Furthermore, it has established three new pre-commission training schools to produce medical, engineering, and nursing officers. Between September 1988 and December 1999, altogether 11,304 officers were commissioned into the three services of the Tatmadaw (10,391 into the army, 546 into the navy, and 368 into the air force). (This figure includes long-service commissions and commissions through young officer courses.) Through OTS, DSA, Teza, DSIM, and DSIT programmes, 10,052 officers were commissioned (9,331 into the army, 482 into the navy, and 239 into the air force). It is also noteworthy that the training programmes in both pre- and post-commission periods are designed to produce unity among officers. In order to provide training and education for officers of the ever-expanding and modernizing Tatmadaw, the DMT has opened new training facilities and introduced new training programmes.

The opening of the regular course in 1994 and a Master's degree programme, with special emphasis on international relations and strategic studies, in 1998 at the NDC, also indicates that the Tatmadaw is fully aware of the need to produce capable commanders and policy-makers for the future

Tatmadaw as well as for the future state. This is a new development for the Tatmadaw, as its leadership training in the past has centred mostly on military leadership. Whether the officer education and leadership training of the Tatmadaw will produce people capable of good governance in the future is a question beyond the scope of this chapter. Besides, since the interdisciplinary post-graduate (political) leadership training programme began only in 1998, it is still too early to see any impact or change in perceptions of the officer corps. Yet it is certain that the officers have a strong conviction that the officer education and (military) leadership training programmes of the Tatmadaw make them capable of holding the state intact and keeping the Union from disintegration, which in itself is a remarkable achievement for the Tatmadaw.

Notes

1 DR. 9692, History of the Directorate of Military Training.

2 DR. 876, The 1953 Tatmadaw Conference.

3 Ibid.

4 Later known as Brigadier Maung Maung.

5 DR. 876, The 1953 Tatmadaw Conference.

6 DR. 9692, History of the Directorate of Military Training.

7 ဒုဗိုလ်မှူးကြီးသောင်းထိုက် (ငြိမ်း)၊ *ဂျပန်ခေတ်စစ်တက္ကသိုလ်နှင့်ဗြိတိသျှဆင်းဟတ်စစ်တက္ကသိုလ်* (ရန်ကုန်၊ ဘဝတက္ကသိုလ်စာပေ၊ ၁၉၈၅) Lieutenant Colonel Thaung Htike (retired), *At the Military Academy of the Japanese Occupation Period and the Britain's Sandhurst Academy* (Bawathetkatho, Yangon, 1985).

8 A total of six Myanmar officers were sent to Fort Queenscliff in the 1950s. Lieutenant Colonel Kyi Win (1953 course) became a brigade commander, Lieutenant Colonel Bo Win (1954 course) became a director in the war office, Major San Kyi (1955 course) became a regional commander and Major Ye Gaung (1956 course) became foreign minister. However, I do not have information about Captain Aung Soe Myint (1957 course) and Captain Wing Maung (1959 course). Among the officers who attended the Fort Leavenworth Staff College, Colonel Kyaw Soe (1953) became a key figure in the Revolutionary Council and a minister, Colonel San Yu (1954) became a commander-in-chief and president, Colonel Kyi Maung (1955) became a regional commander, and Colonel Kyaw Htin (1962) became a commander-in-chief. For example, Major General Pe Myaing (OTS-7) attended Kimberley Staff College.

9 ဒုဗိုလ်မှူးကြီးသောင်းထိုက် (ငြိမ်း)၊ *ဖို့ဒ်လီဗင်ဝပ် အမေရိကန်စစ်ဦးစီးတက္ကသိုလ်* (ရန်ကုန်၊ ဘဝတက္ကသိုလ်စာပေ၊ ၁၉၈၇) Lieutenant Colonel Thaung Htike (retired), *The American Staff College at Fort Leavenworth* (Bawathetkathi, Yangon, 1987).

10 DR. 9692, History of the Directorate of Military Training.

11 For details of the doctrinal development of the Tatmadaw, see Maung Aung Myoe, *Military Doctrine and Strategy in Myanmar: A Historical Perspective* (Strategic and Defence Studies Centre, Canberra, 1999).

12 ဒေါက်တာမောင်မောင်၊ *သားမောင်စစ်သည်သို့* (ရန်ကုန်၊ ဝင်းမြင့်အောင်စာပေ၊ တကြိမ်၊ ၁၉၉၉). Dr Maung Maung, *To My Son, A Soldier*, 3rd printing (Win Myint Aung Sarpay, Yangon, 1999), p. 5.

13 DR. 9692, History of the Directorate of Military Training.

14 Ibid.

15 This figure does not include armed forces personnel who went abroad for training under directorates other than the Military Training. The most obvious case are medical officers studying abroad for advanced degrees.

16 DMT showroom at the Defence Services Museum.

17 The Tatmadaw sent Colonel Moe Hein (35/1995), Colonel Ba Nyunt (37/1997), Colonel Nyan Win (39/1998), Colonel Htay Aung (39/1999), Colonel Zaw Min (40/2000), Colonel Maung Myint (41/2001), Colonel Ohn Myint (42/2002), Colonel Khin Maung Thein (44/2004), and Colonel Soe Win Tint (45/2005) to the National Defence College.

18 Major Myint Aung (19/1990), Major Chit Naing (21/1992), Major Kyaw Win (23/1994), Major Kyaw Aung (25/1996), Major Win Naing (26/1997), Major Zaw Thin Myint (27/1998), Major Soe Htut (28/1999), and Major Htin Zaw Lwin (34/2005) attended the college.

19 Novosti (2 April 2006).

20 New training schools included the Defence Services (Army) Non-Commissioned Officer School, the Defence Services (Army) Infantry Artillery Schools, the Defence Services Physical Education and Training School, and the Defence Services (Army) Combat Forces School, in addition to a number of training battalions.

21 Most of the military training schools teach officers how to command and control. But it is only at the command training centres that officers actually exercise with troops.

22 Armed Forces Day Address (27 March 2000) by the Commander-in-Chief Senior General Than Shwe.

23 Ibid.

24 General Maung Aye's address at the passing out parade of No. 29th Intake of Under-Officer course (18 September 2001).

25 *Sitpyinnyar* Journal, vol. 38, no. 2, May 2004.

26 Among the publications noteworthy were: The Second World War — in five volumes (1955–1960); History of No. 17 Indian Division — 1941–1945 (1956); Report of Mountbatten (1957); Abstract from Landon Gazette — Assam and Burma Campaigns (1957); Military Doctrines (1957); Burma Campaign (1957); The Art of War by Sun Tzu (1959); German Army (1958); and German General Staff (1960).

27 Among these articles, two articles were concerned with Effect-Based Operations, three with Asymmetric Warfare, one with AirLand Battle Doctrine, one with Centre of Gravity, six with the Chinese Military, four with the Thai military, and three with the Indian military. There are two articles on military operations in Myanmar: Wakhathit Battle (32:2) and Minthami Battle (35:1).

28 Most noteworthy are: 75-mm Recoilless Gun, 2nd printing (1990), .38 Revolver and 9-mm Pistol, 3rd printing (1990), .30 Carbine, 3rd printing (1990), 4th printing (1994), Individual Battle, 3rd printing (1990), Mountain Operations, 3rd printing (1990), Air-Pressured Training Mortar (1991), BA-103/ 73-mm Rocket Launcher (1992), 120-mm Mortar (Light) K-6 (1992), Battlecraft, 5th printing (1992), Counter-insurgency Warfare Manual, 4th printing (1992), Watch Manual, 2nd printing (1992), Infantry Battalion — Field Manual, 3rd printing (1993), Weapon Maintenance and Repair, 3rd printing (1993), Bayonet Charge Training, 2nd printing (1993), Field Patrols, 4th printing (1993), 106-mm Recoilless Gun — M40A2 (1993), Type 69-1 (40-mm) Rocket Launcher (1994), Joint Warfare — with Air Force, 2nd printing (1994), 5.56-mm (MAC-1/2/3/4) Rifles (1994), 84-mm Recoilless Gun — Manual for Instructor (1994).

29 Some of the selected manuals are Mine Warfare (1997), Manual for Company Level Defense (1997), Anti-Personal Landmines and Anti-tank Mines (1998), Mine and Anti-Mine Operations for Infantry Battalion (1998), MA-11 5.56-mm Assault Rifle (1998), MA-12 5.56-mm Sub-machine Gun (1998), MA-13 9-mm Sub-machine Gun (1999), MA-4 5.56-mm Assault Rifle — with 40-mm Grenade Launcher (1999), Plastic Hand Grenade — MG-1 (2000), 12.7-mm Anti-Aircraft Gun — Type-85 (2000), .50 Browning Machine Gun — M-2 HB (2000), Plastic Mines and Anti-Tank Mines (2001), 81-mm Recoilless Gun — MA-14 (2002), 14.5-mm Anti-Aircraft Gun — Single Barrel (2002), 81-mm Mortar — BA-90 and 81-mm Mortar-long barrel — MA-8 (2003), BA-100 (60-mm) Commando Mortar No. 1 and MA-9 (2003), and Infantry Weapon System: Anti-Aircraft Guided Missiles and Anti-Tank Guided Missile (2004). It is also known that the instruction manual for 60-mm Mortar (BA-89) and 60-mm Mortar-long barrel (MA-7) is underway.

30 Five forms of manoeuvre are: Envelopment, Turning Movement, Infiltration, Penetration, and Frontal Attack. Patterns of offensive battle are: offensive against enemy's hasty defence, offensive against enemy's fielded positional defence, offensive against enemy's solid positional defence, raid on the halting enemy, offensive against the enemy in movement, and offensive against the air-landing enemy. Techniques for attack are: Baited Attack, Raid Attack, Searching Attack, Stalking Attack, Feint and Demonstration Attack, and Breaching Attack (MACFS Annual Magazine).

31 For positional defence, there are four forms: seamless web defence, perimeter defence, defence of a strong point, and linear defence. For mobile defence, there are five forms: gap filler defence, elastic defence, reserve slope defence, non-linear defence, and defence in sector. For retrograde operations, there are three forms: delay, withdrawal, and retirement.

32 *Sitpyinnyar* Journal, vol. 37, no. 3, September 2003.
33 DR. 9692, History of the Directorate of Military Training.
34 Maung Hla Paw (Mandalay), "I Will Look at the Mirror", *New Taryi Magazine*, vol. 458, September 1998.
35 For details, see Appendix (8).
36 *Annual Air Force Magazine* (1999).
37 Salaing Nwe, "The Academy that Produces Good Officers", *People's Armed Forces Journal*, vol. 35, no. 8, 15 August 1999.
38 For details, see Appendix (8).
39 *DSA Annual Magazine 2005*, p. 58.
40 *NLM*, 16 December 2006
41 *DSA Annual Magazine 2005*, p. 24.
42 DR. 9349, Medical Corps Centre.
43 For details of the birth of the DSIT, see Colonel Win Myint, "The Making of D.S.I.T.", *Annual Magazine of the Defence Services Institute of Technology*, 1999.
44 Kyaw Win Naing, "Our Institute- Welcoming the New Age", *Annual Magazine of the Defence Services Institute of Technology*, 1998.
45 General Maung Aye, Speech at the opening ceremony of the DSIT on 4 July 1994.
46 For details of the training programme, see Cadet Thein Thant Zaw, "An Introduction to D.S.I.T.", *Annual Magazine of the Defence Services Institute of Technology*, 1997.
47 DR. 9447, Nurses Training Wing.
48 MACFS 49th Anniversary Magazine, pp. 129–31.
49 DR. 9653, Burma Army Combat Forces School.
50 DR. 9692, History of the Directorate of Military Training.
51 DR. 10266, Land/Air Warfare and Paratroops School.
52 DR. 9692, History of the Directorate of Military Training.
53 History of the Armour and Artillery School (July 1999).
54 History of Defence Services Signals and Electronic School (July 1999).
55 The showroom of the Directorate of Signals displays a picture of an electronic warfare class.
56 History of the Defence Services Engineering Training School (July 1999).
57 For details, see Win Aye Hla, "Field Engineering", *Annual Magazine of the Defence Services Institute of Technology*, 1997.
58 History of the Defence Services Mechanical and Electrical Engineering School (July 1999).
59 DR. 9656, Command and General Staff College.
60 Ibid.
61 DR. 10600, The National Defence College.
62 Ibid.

6

FINANCING FORCE MODERNIZATION AND TROOPS WELFARE

Although the national budget and government expenditure have never been a secret in Myanmar, any attempt to calculate Myanmar defence expenditure is fraught with peril. This is particularly true since 1988. The published figures are unreliable. Besides, there are several other factors that should be considered in calculating Myanmar defence expenditure. First, the defence expenditure itself is underestimated. There is heavy state subsidization coming from other ministries and agencies, rather than the Ministry of Defence. For example, the armed forces get subsidized fuel from Ministry of Energy. Second, some of the expenditure in foreign currencies is calculated on the basis of the official exchange rate, which is more than 200 times lower than the market rate in early 2000s. Third, some expenditure comes from other agencies, such as home affairs and forestry. And fourth, some expenditures are paid by military businesses. Finally, some expenditures, such as payment for overseas suppliers, are made in kind under a barter system. (Some claim that some of the military hardware bought from the PRC are paid for in teak and other natural resources.)

DEFENCE EXPENDITURE

Financing the force modernization programme in Myanmar has always been a major issue. The defence budget takes the lion's share in the Total Government Expenditure (TGE) or Central Government Expenditure (CGE). In the first two years immediately after the nation's independence in 1948, the defence expenditure in momentary terms amounted to 40 per cent of the TGE. And it remained relatively high throughout 1950s — about 32 per cent of the TGE. Between 1948 and 1961, the Myanmar government spent Kyat 4,067.7 million (in current price terms) or Kyat 880.8 million (in 1960 constant price) on the defence. This budget was used mostly for equipment, salaries, rations, and medical facilities for the troops. The calculation of the percentage of defence expenditure to the TGE or CGE was simply for the period between 1948 and 1962 when there was little state-owned economic enterprises (SEE). In the early 1950s, the Tatmadaw found a way to provide welfare services for its members and their families; it established a number of business firms, including stores to sell subsidized commodities for Tatmadaw members. The issue of military business will be discussed later in the chapter.

Between 1962 and 1974, according to the SIPRI (Stockholm International Peace Research Institute), Myanmar's military expenditure in current price amounted to about Kyat 7,055 millions; it was US$1,425.1 million in the 1970 constant price (see Table 6.1). The percentage of defence expenditure

TABLE 6.1
Defence Expenditure (1962–74)

Year	*Current Price Kyat Million*	*1970 Constant Price US$ Million*	*% GDP*
1962	432.0	89.5	6.3%
1963	478.0	90.5	6.4%
1964	455.0	97.7	6.5%
1965	511.0	107.0	6.6%
1966	502.0	105.2	5.7%
1967	486.0	101.8	5.7%
1968	498.0	104.3	5.3%
1969	545.0	114.1	5.4%
1970	582.0	121.9	5.7%
1971	599.0	125.5	5.7%
1972	581.0	121.7	5.3%
1973	739.0	117.1	5.9%
1974	647.0	128.8	4.3%
TOTAL	7,055.0	1,425.1	—

Source: SIPRI Yearbooks.

in the GDP declined from an average of 6.5 per cent in early 1960s to an average of 5.5 per cent in the late 1960s and early 1970s, despite heavy military operations in the central or lower and northeast Myanmar, while the absolute of expenditure had steadily increased. In terms of the percentage of the defence expenditure in the TGE, the estimation varied, reflecting the different ways of calculation. In terms of expenditure by State Administrative Organizations (SAO), the military expenditure stayed an average of over 30 per cent.

In the period between 1975 and 1980, while the defence expenditure continued to grow in both current and constant price terms, its share of the GDP declined and remained on average of about 4 per cent (see Table 6.2).

TABLE 6.2
Defence Expenditure (1975–80)

Year	*Current Price Kyat Million*	*1980 Constant Price US$ Million*	*% GDP*
1975	886.0	162.0	3.9%
1976	1,041.0	156.0	3.9%
1977	1,197.0	181.0	4.1%
1978	1,320.0	213.0	4.2%
1979	1,491.0	227.0	4.3%
1980	1,622.0	246.0	4.3%

Source: SIPRI Yearbooks.

Before we proceed with the defence expenditure since 1980, it is important to clarify the method of calculating the percentage of defence expenditure in the TGE/CGE. Since the 1978–79 fiscal year (April–March), the Myanmar government statistics showed two types of expenditure: State Administrative Organizations and the Union Government. The expenditure by the SAO did not cover the expenditure on state economic enterprises, such as factories under various ministries. This point will be illustrated in Table 6.3.

The table suggests that the calculation should be done on the basis of Union Government expenditure. For example, thousands of people were working in the state-owned factories under ministries of industry-1 and industry-2. The expenditure of just Kyat 12.7 million under the SAO was impossible for the whole industry sector. The amount was merely for administrative costs, including pay and maintenance, mostly at the central

TABLE 6.3
Expenditure in the 1980–81 Fiscal Year

In Kyat Million

Sector	*SAO*		*Union Government*	
	current	*capital*	*current*	*capital*
Agriculture	298.2	506.9	1,045.4	617.5
Livestock and Fishery	17.0	19.5	330.6	368.0
Forestry	53.0	22.7	836.2	188.6
Mines	18.4	53.3	370.3	397.6
Industry	9.9	2.8	6,746.2	1,939.6
Energy	—	—	187.1	283.9
Construction	159.6	140.8	968.7	192.5
Transportation and Communication	39.7	55.9	1,191.0	677.6
Social Services (health, education, etc.)	927.1	113.8	1,224.6	125.9
Finance	60.1	5.3	1,451.3	24.3
Trade	75.0	1.3	5,230.4	120.0
Defence	1,153.8	187.7	1,281.3	255.8
Administration (council/home affairs)	1,268.9	108.7	1,268.9	108.7
Development Committees	129.0	70.6	129.0	70.6
TOTAL	4,209.7	1,289.3	2,2262.0	5,370.6

Note: current = current expenditure
capital = capital expenditure
Source: Central Statistical Organization.

level. We also see the difference in the defence expenditure; the amount spent by the Union Government was slightly higher. It explains that some money was spent by the state, not by the ministry of defence, for defence purposes, such as militias training and resettlement programmes. The 1999–2000 expenditure also demonstrates the same point (see Table 6.4).

Therefore, the defence expenditure should be calculated on the basis of the expenditure by the Union Government rather than by the State Administrative Organizations. Yet, for the benefit of readers, I would like to provide both sets of data here (see Tables 6.5 and 6.6).

Between 1980–81 and 1987–88, the percentage of defence expenditure in terms of the Union Government was about 5.5 per cent while it amounted to nearly an average of 22 per cent in the SAO. Its GDP share was an average of 3.6 per cent, with the lowest at 3.04 per cent in 1987–88 (see Table 6.7).

Throughout the Revolutionary Council period and the BSPP period, despite its growth in manpower, the Tatmadaw maintained a lightly equipped

TABLE 6.4
Expenditure in the 1999–2000 Fiscal Year

In Kyat Million

Sector	*SAO*		*Union Government*	
	current	*capital*	*current*	*capital*
Agriculture	6,638.4	8,519.2	53,150.5	11,609.1
Livestock and Fishery	406.0	93.2	1,641.7	121.1
Forestry	790.1	868.5	11,673.2	1,225.4
Mines	79.8	6.0	3,634.6	33.6
Industry	443.8	1,659.7	33,713.4	4,629.3
Energy	18.5	7.1	136,268.9	5,408.9
Construction	5,941.0	16,443.7	37,095.8	16,570.5
Transportation and Communication	405.6	3,821.8	16,985.6	12,273.4
Social Services (health, education, etc.)	24,272.9	6,390.6	25,515.9	6,559.4
Finance	779.2	558.9	24,428.2	870.8
Trade	417.0	199.4	61,779.7	667.3
Defence	19,279.5	18,758.0	19,279.5	18,758.0
Administration (SPDC/home affairs)	25,151.6	3,070.0	25,151.6	3,070.0
Development Committees*	23.2	8.6	23.2	8.6
TOTAL	84,646.6	60,404.7	450,341.8	81,805.5

Note: * Yangon and Mandalay City Development Committees have their own budgeting.
Source: Central Statistical Organization.

army suitable for anti-guerrilla warfare. The defence expenditure had been tightly constrained by the economic and budgetary realities of the country. The major portion of the spending went to manpower and the maintenance of forces. Government arms import was also limited. In terms of welfare for the Tatmadaw, there were no more special privileges exclusively for its service personnel. There were no more military businesses. Senior officers were allowed to buy subsidized commodities at two state-owned shops in Yangon, like any other senior party officials. Lower ranking officials could apply for permits for certain household items at state-owned corporations; but it was by no means a right. Generally speaking, Tatmadaw members did not enjoy special privileges. However, they were entitled to uniforms and other personal items, pays and rations (wet and dry), housing facilities or allowance, and medical services (even for immediate family members). Generally, despite the lack of off-budget welfare subsidies, soldiers were better off than their civilian counterparts and even more so compared with ordinary citizens.

TABLE 6.5
Percentage of Defence in the Union Government Expenditure (1980–88)

Kyat in Million (current price)

Year	*Current*			*Capital*			*Total*		
	Total	*Defence*	*Percentage*	*Total*	*Defence*	*Percentage*	*Total*	*Defence*	*Percentage*
1980–81	22,262.0	1,282.3	5.8	5,370.6	255.8	4.8	27,632.6	1,538.1	5.6
1981–82	25,185.3	1,460.4	5.8	6,563.6	270.4	4.1	31,748.9	1,730.8	5.5
1982–83	26,690.0	1,451.2	5.4	7,854.6	322.0	4.1	34,544.6	1,773.2	5.1
1983–84	26,249.0	1,470.8	5.6	6,935.9	324.9	4.6	33,184.9	1,795.7	5.4
1984–85	28,294.0	1,509.8	5.3	6,377.5	316.5	5.0	34,671.5	1,826.3	5.3
1985–86	28,271.2	1,565.1	5.5	6,397.4	359.8	5.6	34,668.6	1,924.9	5.6
1986–87	26,863.3	1,545.6	5.8	6,331.0	322.6	5.1	33,194.3	1,868.2	5.6
1987–88	25,178.4	1,699.7	6.8	7,873.6	389.9	5.0	33,052.0	2,089.6	6.3

Source: Central Statistical Organization.

TABLE 6.6
Percentage of Defence in the State Administrative Organization Expenditure (1980–88)

Kyat in Million (Current Price)

Year	*Current*			*Capital*			*Total*		
	Total	*Defence*	*Percentage*	*Total*	*Defence*	*Percentage*	*Total*	*Defence*	*Percentage*
1980–81	4,209.7	1,153.5	27.4%	1,289.3	187.7	14.6%	5,499.0	1,341.2	24.4%
1981–82	4,809.4	1,320.9	27.5%	1,337.0	179.2	13.2%	6,146.4	1,500.1	24.4%
1982–83	4,954.9	1,310.8	26.5%	2,006.1	187.9	9.4%	6,961.0	1,498.7	21.5%
1983–84	5,143.5	1,344.9	26.1%	1,979.6	195.2	9.9%	7,123.1	1,540.1	21.6%
1984–85	5,464.7	1,361.6	24.9%	1,999.1	214.4	11.4%	7,463.8	1,576.0	21.1%
1985–86	5,787.9	1,413.3	24.2%	2,098.6	284.7	13.6%	7,886.5	1,698.0	21.5%
1986–87	6,237.2	1,415.9	22.7%	2,454.5	283.9	11.6%	8,691.7	1,699.8	19.6%
1987–88	6,151.7	1,080.2	17.6%	2,302.1	159.7	6.9%	8,453.8	1,239.9	14.7%

Source: Central Statistical Organization.

TABLE 6.7
Defence Expenditure as Percentage of GDP

Year	*GDP current price Kyat Million*	*Defence current price Kyat Million*	*% GDP*
1980–81	38,609	1,538.1	3.98%
1981–82	42,879	1,730.8	4.04%
1982–83	46,811	1,773.2	3.79%
1983–84	49,823	1,795.7	3.60%
1984–85	53,597	1,826.3	3.41%
1985–86	55,989	1,924.9	3.44%
1986–87	59,025	1,868.2	3.17%
1987–88	68,698	2,089.6	3.04%

Source: Central Statistical Organization.

Although the SLORC came to power in September 1988, it did not immediately expand the armed forces. But more arms were procured, mainly from China, in the early 1990s. Thus, the defence expenditure greatly increased. In terms of percentage, the defence expenditure went up to two digit figures in both the Union Government and the SAO. While the percentage in the Union Government expenditure reached 14.4 per cent in the 1995–96 fiscal year, it was about 39 per cent of the SAO in the 1993–94 fiscal year. Its defence expenditure in early 1990s was about one-third of the SAO expenditure (see Tables 6.8 and 6.9).

However, it is interesting to note that the percentage of defence expenditure in the GDP remained relatively low and stayed below 4 per cent of the GDP. Considering its large military build-up and hardware procurement, some observers believe that there were off-budget measures to finance the Tatmadaw's force modernization programme. As mentioned earlier, different methods of calculation also played a role in underestimating the defence budget. See Table 6.10.

To cushion the defence budget and to provide welfare for its personnel, the Tatmadaw began to build up businesses. Welfare became particularly important since the state introduced a market economic system. The Tatmadaw has greatly reduced the amount of dry ration for the soldier since the early 1990s. Cash supplements for the officers and rank-and-files became compulsory for the Tatmadaw; therefore, the military businesses were part of the Tatmadaw's activities.

TABLE 6.8
Defence as a Percentage of Union Government Expenditure

Kyat in Million (current price)

Year	*Current*			*Capital*			*Total*		
	Total	*Defence*	*Percentage*	*Total*	*Defence*	*Percentage*	*Total*	*Defence*	*Percentage*
1988–89	27,085.9	1,852.1	6.8	4,365.7	279.3	6.4	31,451.6	2,131.4	6.8
1989–90	39,157.6	3,968.7	10.1	6,498.5	646.1	9.9	45,656.1	4,614.8	10.1
1990–91	48,771.2	3,845.8	7.9	10,209.9	1,590.4	15.6	58,981.1	5,436.2	9.2
1991–92	53,934.4	4,427.2	8.2	12,444.8	1,659.0	13.3	66,379.2	6,086.2	9.2
1992–93	62,237.2	5,894.1	9.5	13,455.6	3,232.6	24.0	75,692.8	9,126.7	12.1
1993–94	80,132.8	7,881.7	9.8	15,678.4	6,002.4	38.3	95,811.2	13,884.1	14.5
1994–95	108,718.9	9,273.0	8.5	25,782.5	8,421.1	32.6	134,501.4	17,694.1	13.2
1995–96	124,523.2	10,715.8	8.6	41,034.9	13,097.0	31.9	165,558.1	23,812.8	14.4
1996–97	156,958.4	11,485.8	7.3	57,275.2	17,465.7	30.5	214,233.6	28,951.5	13.5
1997–98	262,491.9	14,655.7	5.6	68,402.4	15,479.3	22.6	330,894.3	30,135.0	9.1
1998–99	372,563.2	15,984.0	4.3	79,598.3	23,642.6	29.7	452,161.5	39,626.6	8.8
1999–2000	450,341.8	19,279.5	4.3	81,805.5	18,758.0	22.9	532,147.3	38,037.5	7.1

Source: Central Statistical Organization.

TABLE 6.9
Defence as a Percentage of State Administrative Organization Expenditure

Kyat in Million (current price)

Year	*Current*			*Capital*			*Total*		
	Total	*Defence*	*Percentage*	*Total*	*Defence*	*Percentage*	*Total*	*Defence*	*Percentage*
1988–89	6,618.0	1,532.6	23.2%	1,744.6	230.3	13.2%	8,362.6	1,762.9	21.1%
1989–90	13,561.2	3,697.6	27.3%	3,398.3	633.2	18.6%	16,959.5	4,330.8	25.5%
1990–91	16,552.1	3,845.8	23.2%	6,815.4	1,590.4	23.3%	23,367.5	5,436.2	23.3%
1991–92	17,880.0	4,427.2	24.8%	9,098.0	1,659.0	18.2%	26,978.0	6,086.2	22.6%
1992–93	18,067.4	5,894.1	32.6%	9,760.0	3,232.6	33.1%	27,827.4	9,126.7	32.8%
1993–94	23,289.7	7,881.7	33.9%	12,304.9	6,002.4	48.8%	35,594.6	13,884.1	39.0%
1994–95	27,741.4	9,273.0	33.4%	20,146.4	8,421.1	41.8%	47,887.8	17,694.1	36.9%
1995–96	32,898.6	10,715.8	32.6%	31,825.3	13,097.0	41.2%	64,723.9	23,812.8	36.8%
1996–97	37,021.9	11,485.8	31.0%	42,923.9	17,465.7	40.7%	79,945.5	28,951.5	36.2%
1997–98	47,852.2	14,655.7	30.6%	50,379.8	15,479.3	30.7%	98,232.0	30,135.0	30.7%
1998–99	62,976.1	15,984.0	25.4%	60,930.6	23,642.6	38.8%	123,906.7	39,626.6	32.0%
1999–2000	84,646.6	19,279.5	22.8%	60,404.7	18,758.0	31.1%	145,051.3	38,037.5	26.2%

Source: Central Statistical Organization.

TABLE 6.10
Defence Expenditure

Year	*GDP current price Kyat Million*	*Defence current price Kyat Million*	*% GDP*
1988–89	76,243	2,131.4	2.80%
1989–90	124,666	4,614.8	3.70%
1990–91	151,941	5,436.1	3.58%
1991–92	186,802	6,086.2	3.26%
1992–93	249,395	9,126.7	3.66%
1993–94	360,321	13,884.1	3.85%
1994–95	472,774	17,694.1	3.74%
1995–96	604,729	23,812.8	3.94%
1996–97	791,980	28,951.5	3.66%
1997–98	1,119,509	30,135.0	2.69%
1998–99	1,609,776	39,626.6	2.46%
1999–2000	2,190,320	38,037.5	1.74%

Source: Central Statistical Organization.

TATMADAW'S ECONOMIC ACTIVITIES

The participation of the military in the national economy is not a new phenomenon, especially in third world countries. In what is known as "old professionalism", the role of the military is solely confined to the management of external defence. However, in some countries, this role has been expanded to cover the conduct of internal security operations and active participation in political and socio-economic domains of the state; it is now known as "new professionalism". Many Southeast Asian militaries — Thailand, Indonesia, Vietnam, and Laos — also engage in a wide range of businesses. The Tatmadaw is not an exception; it has a long tradition of participation in the national economy. It engages in a wide range of commercial activities: manufacturing, services, and so on.

The origins of the Tatmadaw's commercial interest in Myanmar can be found in both its ideological conviction and practical purpose. Ideologically, it is part of its dual functions; thus, it is "new professionalism". In Myanmar, the Tatmadaw has been an important part of nation building, state building, and infrastructure building. In this sense, the Tatmadaw's participation in the national economy is a natural process and legitimate business in its view. In practical terms, the financial incentive to cushion up its budgetary constraints, enhance the welfare and well-being of its service personnel and their families, and strengthen the corporate interest of the military as a viable and credible national institution are to primary rationales.

The Tatmadaw's Commercial Activities Before 1988

In the early 1950s, the Tatmadaw established the Defence Services Institute (DSI) to provide inexpensive consumer goods to the members of the armed forces; but this line of business was expanded to incorporate a wider range of economic activities. By the late 1950s, the DSI had probably become the largest commercial enterprise in Myanmar. Many military businesses were rather successful in those days, partly due to its special status under the Special Company Act of 1950. The DSI ran banking, shipping,[1] trading, manufacturing, publishing, and retail businesses, among others. Income generated from these commercial enterprises was used for the welfare and well-being of its service personnel and their families. Some of its business ventures served as vehicles to advance the Tatmadaw's political agenda. In the early 1950s, for example, the DSI-owned "Myawaddy Press" published two monthly magazines: *Myawaddy* and *Ngwetaryi*. The *Myawaddy* magazine, first published in 1952, was an instrument of psychological warfare to voice the interest of the military.[2] The Tatmadaw also published the "*Guardian Newspaper*" and "*Guardian Magazine*", reflecting a pro-military view, with a substantial circulations each, on a commercial basis.[3]

In the early 1960s, while a few enterprises remained under the DSI, many enterprises were placed under the newly formed Burma Economic Development Corporation (BEDC), which was effectively under the management of the Tatmadaw. Yet, when the Tatmadaw staged a military *coup d'etat* on 2 March 1962, in the name of the Revolutionary Council, and eventually introduced a state-owned socialist economic system under the Burmese Way to Socialism, these military commercial enterprises were the first to fall under the state's nationalization programme. On 20 October 1963, the Revolutionary Council government nationalized all assets and firms owned by DSI and BEDC: forty-seven in total.

At the time of nationalization, there were five firms under the DSI: Defence Services Institute Head Office; DSI No.1 and General Provision Store and Canteen; Beatrice Foods (Burma) Ltd.; Burma Orchid Ltd.; and Burma International Inspection Co. Ltd. Forty-two firms under the BEDC were as follows: BEDC Head Office; Burma Beverage Co.; Mandalay Brewery and Distillery; Burma Chemical Industries Ltd.; Burma Paints Ltd.; Burma Pharmaceutical Industries; Centrade Polyproducts Ltd.; Burma Canning

Factory; Burma Shoes Ltd.; Garment Factory Ltd.; Lodge Plug (Burma) Ltd.; Mechanical and Electrical Ltd.; Multitex Co. Ltd.; Burma Farms Ltd.; Burma Fisheries Ltd.; Burma National Housing and Construction Co. Ltd.; Ava House (Bookstore); Myawaddy Press; Burma Five Star Line Ltd.; Rangoon Agencies Ltd.; Diesel and General Services Ltd.; Burma Hotels Ltd.; Hotel International Ltd.; Tourist (Burma) Ltd.; Strand Hotel Ltd.; Ava Insurance Ltd.; People's Loan Co. Ltd.; Rangoon Drug House; Rowe & Company Ltd.; Burma Asiatic Co. Ltd.; Burma Teak and Plywood Trading Co. Ltd.; Continental Trading House; Burma Trading House Ltd.; Dalhousie Stores Ltd.; General Trading House Co. Ltd.; International Trading House Co. Ltd.; Motor House Co. Ltd.; S. Openheimer & Co. Ltd.; United Coal and Coke Suppliers and General Trading Co. Ltd.; Economic Development Fisheries Ltd.; Burma Trade (London); and BEDC Branch Office (Tokyo, Japan). Moreover, the Ava Bank was also nationalized at an earlier date and both the *Guardian Newspaper* and *Guardian Magazine* were also nationalized later in 1964.

Throughout what is known as the socialist era (1962 to 1988), the Tatmadaw was required to refrain from engaging in commercial activities. Thus, there were no commercial military enterprises; but the Tatmadaw was involved in the production of basic commodities, mostly for the welfare of its members and their families, and essentially on an individual unit basis, on a much smaller scale, and drawing financial support from Regimental Fund (RF). Military units, such as a battalion, for example, would grow rice and vegetables and raise poultry and fish, operate canteen, liquor house, and video house, and run cottage industries, such as a candle factory, all funded by the Regimental Fund.[4] Only after the Tatmadaw's takeover of the State in September 1988 was the military's commercial interest revived on a large scale.

The Tatmadaw's Commercial Activities since 1988

Throughout the 1990s, the Tatmadaw leadership repeatedly reminded its commanders that the Tatmadaw had to be built through four means: training, administration, welfare, and morale. These four means are referred to as the four main tasks of a commander. These four tasks, in their eyes, will strengthen the three capabilities of the Tatmadaw (military, administrative, and organizational) so the Tatmadaw would become "modern, strong and highly capable". In his address at the 54th anniversary of the Armed Forces Day Parade, Senior General Than Shwe explained what he meant by building the Tatmadaw through welfare. He said:

> Welfare is also an organizational activity. It supplements discipline. It also boosts morale. Therefore, welfare is essential in strengthening the Tatmadaw's capabilities. Welfare must be properly and correctly provided for Tatmadaw personnel who not only have to sacrifice life and limb but also have to stay away from their families, going through much hardship, and also for their families in the units.[5]

Building the Tatmadaw through welfare involved a number of measures, ranging from forming military-managed or military-back companies at the ministry level to running small-scale businesses, funded by the RF of individual military units, including renting regimental facilities, such as premises and electricity. Moreover, it also included the commercial aspect of factories and enterprises, run by various directorates under the Ministry of Defence, for military use.

Union of Myanmar Economic Holding Limited

The Union of Myanmar Economic Holding Ltd. (UMEHL) is the first business venture established by the Tatmadaw after its takeover of the state in 1988. Formed in 1990, under the 1950 Special Company Act, the UMEHL is a military-managed business engaged in small and medium-sized commercial enterprises and industries. As a special company, the UMEHL enjoys the privilege of tax exemption for its fully owned and subsidiary firms, but affiliated firms are not included. One of the main objectives is to support regimental welfare organizations, in-service and retired military personnel, and veteran organizations. In 2007, UMEHL had an authorized capital of 40,000 million kyats and an allotted capital of 39,000 million kyats. The Ministry of Defence and Directorate of Procurement invests 808.33 million kyats and 330 million kyats respectively as "A" shareholders, while 35,544 in-service military personnel with 1,916.81 million kyats, 1,467 military units with 33,745.31 million kyats, 6,069 retired military personnel with 1,265.53 million kyats, and eighty-nine veteran organizing committees with 427.96 million kyats hold stakes as "B" shareholders.[6] This is a remarkable expansion of UMEHL business activities within the two years from 2005. In 2005, the UMEHL had an authorized capital of just 30,000 million kyats with an allotted capital of 21,000 million kyats; while the amount of capital by "A" shareholders remained unchanged, among the "B" shareholders, 24,973 in-service military personnel invest 1,759.57 million kyat, 1,308 military units 17,846.01 million kyats, 3,437 retired military personnel, 671.19 million kyats, and eighty-two veteran organizing committees, 352.89

million kyats.[7] The major increases of "B" shareholders were military units and retired military personnel.

In 2007, the UMEHL is managed by a ten-member board of directors. The first chairman was Lieutenant General Myo Nyunt and the managing director was Brigadier General David Abel. They were succeeded in 1996 by Major General Than Oo and Brigadier General Win Hlaing respectively. While Major General Win Hlaing has remained the managing director up to the present, Adjutant General Lieutenant General Win Myint took up the chairmanship in 1998 and Lieutenant General Tin Aye in 2002.[8] It used to be under the Adjutant General Office, but is now under the Office of Defence Industries. Between 1990 and early 2007, the UMEHL formed a total of seventy-seven firms. UMEHL's firms can generally be classified as fully owned firms, subsidiary firms, and affiliated firms. However, by 2007, it only has a total of fifty-one firms: thirty-five fully owned enterprises, nine subsidiary firms, and seven affiliated firms. In the 2001–02 fiscal year, the UMEHL ran a total of forty-eight firms. However, since then many subsidiary firms and affiliated firms have been liquidated. So far, a total of twenty-six firms have been liquidated (see Table 6.11 and Appendix (9)).

The UMEHL proper earned 55,462.66 million kyats as profit between 1990 and March 2007, of which 789.73 million kyats and 43,885.52 million kyats were distributed to "A" and "B" shareholders respectively. It is, however, known that for the last five years, profit distribution towards military units has been suspended for reinvestment. In general, since the 1995–96 fiscal year, "B" shareholders have enjoyed a 30 per cent per annum turnover rate from their investment; even the interest rate for fixed deposit in a bank is just 10 per cent per annum. See Table 6.12.

Between April 1999 and March 2004, the UMEHL and all its fully owned, subsidiary, and affiliated firms made a profit of 74,561.05 million kyats (or K 74,106.81 million plus US$71.89 million). In the 2006–07

TABLE 6.11
Number of Firms under the UMEHL

Sr.	*Type of Firm*	*1999–2000*	*2001–02*	*2003–04*	*2006–07*
1	100% UMEHL-owned	15	16	17	35
2	Partnership (Subsidiary)	18	21	11	9
3	Partnership (Affiliation)	7	11	8	7
	TOTAL	40	48	36	51

Source: UMEHL Director's Report (various years).

TABLE 6.12
Profit Making and Distribution of the UMEHL

(Kyats in Million)

Sr.	*Fiscal Year*	*Profit*	*"A" Shareholder*		*"B" Shareholder*	
			Percentage	*Amount*	*Percentage*	*Amount*
1	1990–91	0.61	—	—	—	—
2	1991–92	6.67	10	4.00	10	2.02
3	1992–93	5.99	40	2.47	10	3.62
4	1993–94	25.12	40	5.07	15	7.58
5	1994–95	52.89	40	13.11	15	19.66
6	1995–96	218.62	12.5	41.25	30	107.90
7	1996–97	733.17	30	99.00	30	316.67
8	1997–98	1,225.83	30	64.00	30	651.83
9	1998–99	1,184.19	30	28.75	30	949.40
10	1999–2000	2,634.86	12.5	41.25	30	1,429.65
11	2000–01	3,433.17	12.5	41.25	30	2,133.69
12	2001–02	3,254.18	12.5	41.25	30	2,889.35
13	2002–03	4,792.41	12.5	41.25	30	3,960.48
14	2003–04	6,959.16	12.5	41.25	30	5,040.51
15	2004–05	8,943.97	12.5	41.25	30	7,266.54
16	2005–06	9,981.12	12.5	142.29	30	8,837.97
17	2006–07	12,010.70	12.5	142.29	30	10,268.65
	TOTAL	55,462.66	—	789.73	—	43,885.52

Source: UMEHL Director's Report (various years).

fiscal year alone, the UMEHL made a profit of 49,968.98 million kyats (or €0.2 million, US$30.53 million, and K 49,789.51 million). However, not all UMEHL firms are making a profit.[9]

UMEHL's commercial interests include gem production and marketing, garment factories, wood and wood-based industries, food and beverage and other trading, and supermarkets, banking, hotels and tourism, transportation, telecommunications and electronic equipment, computer, construction and real estate, the steel industry, cement production, automobiles, cosmetics, and stationery. In 2006–07 fiscal year, the UMEHL operated thirty-five firms; it has liquidated six firms since 1999.[10] Under the UMEHL, Myanmar Ruby Enterprise operates Mogoke mine, Mongshu mine, Nanyar mine, Mawchi mine, and a gold mine in the Thabeikkyin area. Nanyar mine was subcontracted to World Precious Gems Co. Ltd. in 2002, on the basis of profit sharing. The gold mine was also subcontracted to five domestic companies. Myanmar Imperial Jade Co. Ltd. has a jade mine in Sarhmaw, Kachin State; five sub-contractors are also working for the company. Myawaddy Trading is perhaps the best known firm of the UMEHL. It imports edible oil, diesel, automobiles, and steel, and it exports beans and pulses, cigarettes, and beer cans. It also engages in foreign currency exchange service. Myawaddy Bank Ltd. has branches in Mandalay, Monywa, Taunggyi, Phakent, and Bayintnaung, with 391 employees. It has an authorized capital of 5,000 million kyats and a paid-up capital of 4,000 million kyats. Bandoola Transportation owns 1,659 coaches and trucks. A total of 473 coaches are used for local bus services in Yangon under the name of "Parami" Transportation. Another 357 coaches are for highway travel and transportation services under various names, such as Shanmalay, Shwemanthu, and Patheinthu. Another 527 trucks are for the transportation of commodities. In Mandalay, 246 coaches and trucks are used for rental and transportation services and fifty-six buses are in Naypyitaw. Moreover, Bandoola Transportation sold 369 coaches to various government departments and private individuals. Myawaddy Travel and Tours used to run Myawaddy Airways with MI-17 helicopters for air travel between Mandalay, Mogoke and Muse. But this air travel service was transferred to the Myanmar Economic Corporation in 1997. Myawaddy Travel and Tours offers package tours in Myanmar. Nawaday Hotel and Travel Ltd. runs three hotels and one travel agency: Central Hotel, Ngwe Saung Beach Hotel, Mogoke Motel, and Nawaday Hotel and Travel Agency. Myanmar Arh Construction was established to engage in construction business. In 2004, the company completed the upgrading of Pathein Airport. There were, however, four UMEHL fully owned firms that were either merged with other firms or liquidated.

At the end of the 2006–07 fiscal year, the UMEHL had nine subsidiary firms while it had dissolved sixteen firms by then.[11] Myanmar Segye International Ltd. was formed as a subsidiary firm of Segye Corporation of Korea. Myanmar Daewoo International Ltd. was also formed as a subsidiary firm of Daewoo Corporation of Korea. These two firms are very first of their kind in the garment industry in Myanmar. Rothmans of Pall Mall Myanmar Pte. Ltd. is a subsidiary firm formed with Rothmans Myanmar Holding Pte. Ltd. of Singapore. Its best known product is "LONDON" cigarettes. Myanmar Brewery Ltd. is also a subsidiary firm of a Singaporean company, called Fraser & Neave. Myanmar Brewery produces "MYANMAR BEER" which wins many international prizes and holds a high reputation among customers. In 2003–04 fiscal year alone, Myanmar Brewery made a profit of US$9.9 million and K 462.47 million. Myanmar Posco Steel Co. Ltd. was formed with Korea-based Pohon Iron and Steel Co. Ltd. to build a factory to produce corrugated or plain galvanized iron sheets. Another factory that produces galvanized iron sheet is under Myanmar Nouveau Steel Co. Ltd., a subsidiary firm of the local Myanmar One Co. Ltd. These two factories are not really making a profit. The First Automotive Co. Ltd., with a paid-up capital of US$3.5 million, was formed with Mitsugi Corporation of Japan to assemble light trucks and cars in Myanmar. The first roll-off ceremony was held on 17 December 1999. Up to the end of March 2004, it had sold 536 vehicles, making a profit of US$1.06 million and K 43.53 million. Hanthawaddy Golf Course and City Club is a subsidiary firm formed with Nikko Shoji Co. Ltd. of Japan to build an eighty-room three-star hotel and a golf course in Bago area. But it is not functioning well at present. National Development Corporation was formed with a local company named Myanmar Golden Star Co. Ltd. Its main business activities are landscaping, real estate development, and road construction. One of the main reasons for firms being liquidated was the investment sanction imposed by Western governments on Myanmar. Another possible reason could be structural problems relating to the poor macroeconomic policies and business environment in Myanmar.

At the end of the 2006–07 fiscal year, the UMEHL had seven affiliated firms and had liquidated four firms.[12] Mercury Manufacturing Co. Ltd. is a Myanmar private company affiliated with the UMEHL. Its main line of business is the production of plastic ware, mostly for agricultural use. Myanmar Hwa Fuh International Ltd. is owned by a Hong Kong-based company that engages in the production of garments for export. The UMEHL receives US$314,737 annually as land use premium from Myanmar Hwa Fuh. Myanmar Samgong Industrial Co. Ltd. was established by a Korea-based company. The company pays US$30,780 annually to the UMEHL as land use premium. Myanmar Mamee Double Decker Ltd., known for its instant noodle packs, is run by a Malaysia-based company. The UMEHL receives US$51,034 annually as land use premium. Another well known affiliated company of the UMEHL is Myanmar Tokiwa Corporation that produces pencils and cosmetics. The UMEHL also receives US$38,485 annually as land use premium from Myanmar Tokiwa. Myanmar Kurosawa Trust Co. Ltd., which engages in the jewellery business, pays US$18,000 annually as building use premium to the UMEHL. Diamond Dragon Co. Ltd. is a local company affiliated with the UMEHL. It has to pay K 230,000 monthly to the UMEHL as land use premium. Between April 1999 and March 2004, affiliated firms of the UMEHL paid K 1,229.44 million (or US$4.25 million and K 1,203.98 million) as tax to the government. In the 2006–07 fiscal year alone, the affiliated firms paid US$3.4 million and Kyat 15.17 million as tax.

The UMEHL and its subsidiary and affiliated firms engage in trading activities. The largest trading partners are Singapore, Japan, Malaysia, China, South Korea, and India. The most well known imports are edible oil, fuel oil, and automobiles while exports are cigarettes, beans and pulses, and gems, in addition to the re-export of garments which always stands at top.[13] In addition, the UMEHL is one of the very few enterprises that import cars from overseas, generating a huge income.[14] In term of assets and liabilities, both the UMEHL and its subsidiary and affiliated firms are impressive. In the 2006–07 fiscal year, UMEHL and its fully owned companies had total assets of €17.72 million, US$119.15 million, and Kyat 45,4717.74 million, while its subsidiary and affiliated firms had €19.69 million, US$107.04 million, and Kyat 16,493.18 million.[15] After a brief period of slowdown resulting from the 1997 economic crisis, the UMEHL has been expanding its business activities since 2005; it plans to build new factories, including a new cement factory, a dockyard, and a logistic transport company. In mid-2007, the UMEHL bought factories under Ministry of Industry-2 to help the government resolve the budget deficit.

Myanmar Economic Corporation

Myanmar Economic Corporation (MEC) is another military-managed economic organization. It is perhaps the most secretive business organization of the Tatmadaw. In March 1989, the SLORC government enacted the State-Owned Economic Enterprise Law, which states that the government has the sole right to carry out twelve broad economic enterprises as state-owned economic enterprises, but it can form joint ventures with any other person or any other economic organization. According to the SLORC Law No. 9/89, these economic enterprises are for the extraction of teak and sale of the same in the country and abroad; cultivation and conservation of forest plantations with the exception of village-owned firewood plantations cultivated by the villagers for their personal use; exploration, extraction and sale of petroleum and natural gas, and production of products of the same; exploration and extraction of pearls, jade, and precious stones and export of the same; breeding and production of fish and prawns in fisheries that have been reserved for research by the government; postal and telecommunications services; air transport and railway transport services; banking and insurance services; broadcasting and television services; exploration and extraction of metals and export of the same; electricity-generating services other than those permitted by law to private and cooperative electricity-generating organizations; and manufacture of products relating to security and defence which the government has, from time to time, prescribed by notification. However, this law was amended on 4 March 1997 by the SLORC Law No. 6/97, with a new clause inserted that states:

> In order to contribute towards the development of State economy, to mitigate the expenditure from State finances and in the interests of the welfare of State employees, the Government may, by notification constitute any organization to enable economic enterprises to be carried out without subscribing from State finances but by causing investment [to] be made from the funds owned by the relevant employees' organization.

A couple of days later, the government issued SLORC Notification No. 4/97 to form Myanmar Economic Corporation (MEC) under the Ministry of Defence. It states its purpose as follows:

> In order to contribute towards the development of the State economy, to decrease defence expenditure by fulfilling the needs of the Tatmadaw, to carry out the welfare of the Tatmadaw service personnel and to implement other necessary matters for the Tatmadaw.

Initially, while the UMEHL was under the Adjutant General Office, the MEC was under the Quartermaster General (QMG) Office cum, no defunct, Ministry of Military Affairs. Then the removal of Adjutant General Lieutenant General Win Myint and Quartermaster General Lieutenant General Tin Hla, as well as the new set-up of the Ministry of Defence, has placed the UMEHL under the newly created Bureau of Defence Industries while the MEC remained under the QMG office. The government authorized MEC to undertake a wide range of economic activities (see Table 6.13). These include trading and commercial enterprises; agricultural produce trading enterprises; services enterprises; industrial, commodity production enterprises, and construction enterprises; hotel and tourism enterprises; air, rail, and other transport enterprises; gem and metal extraction enterprises; banking, finance, and insurance; exploration, extraction, and sale of petroleum and natural gas, and manufacture of products of petroleum and natural gas; telecommunication enterprises; and all other economic enterprises which were government monopolies under the State-Owned Economic Enterprise Law of 1989. The MEC was also designed to help the Tatmadaw build its own industrial and technological base.[16] MEC has an initial investment capital of 10 billion kyats. This amount of investment capital has been significantly expanded since its business activities have expanded in recent years.

TABLE 6.13
Factories under the MEC in 2006

Factory/Plant	*Location*	*Products/Remark*
Steel Plant (1)	Aung Lan	Iron nails
Steel Plant (2)	Myaung Dagar	Bridge frames
Steel Plant (3)	Insein (Ywama)	Iron nails, square-match, bulb wire
Steel Plant (4)	Myingyan	Iron ore (project underway)
Cement Factory	Myaing Gale	Cement
Cement Factory	Kyaukse	Cement
Marble Slab Factory	Mandalay	Marble slabs
Granite Slab factory	Loikaw	Granite slabs
Oxygen Factory	Yangon (Mindama)	Oxygen Gas
No. 1 Sugar Factory	Kant Balu	Sugar
Methanol Factory	Kant Balu	Methanol (project underway)
Roofing Sheet Factory	Indagaw	Corrugated Zinc Sheet
Yangon Pharmaceutical Factory	Hmawbi	Syringe, household drugs
SIGMA Wire Factory	Hlaing Tharyar	Wire
Dagon Brewery	Shwe Pyithar	Beer (SKOL/DAGON)
Ship Scrapping Plant	Thilawa	Raw irons for Steel Plant (1)
Coal Production Plant	Maw Taung	Coal/mainly for export to Thailand
Gawdan Mine	Thibaw	Gypsum
Innwa Trading	Yangon	Export and Import (beans and pulses)
Innwa Bank	Yangon	Financial Services
Freight Handling Services	Yangon	Container Services

The *Innwa* Bank under the MEC has a circulating capital of 15 billion kyats while it has a deposit of 8 billion kyats and a loan of 4 billion kyats. The *Innwa* Bank issued financial loans totalling about 2 billion kyats to construction companies for the construction or extension of airports and runways in Magway, Lashio, and Heho. Another loan of 500 million kyats went to projects for developing fish ponds. Loans to the service and trading sector amounted to about 1.5 billion kyats. The MEC is also undertaking the construction of *Tarsan* Hydroelectric Power Plant, which could generate over 7,100 megawatt of electricity, with a Thai firm.

The most prominent and publicized business under the MEC was insurance. Until 1997, state-owned Myanmar Insurance was the only authorized life and general insurance company in Myanmar. However, with the introduction of the Myanmar Insurance Business Law (No. 6 of 1996) and Myanmar Insurance Rules (Notification No. 116 of 1997) on 24 June 1996 and 26 June 1997, respectively, the government issued an insurance licence to Myanmar Economic Corporation; it was probably the only firm to be issued such a licence. The MEC formed the Myanmar International Insurance Corporation (MIIC), as an insurer, and Myanmar International Insurance Service Corporation (MIISC), as an insurance broker, in August 1997 and entered the insurance market. Major shareholders in the MIIC were the MEC (55 per cent), Jarney Asia Bhd. of Malaysia (27 per cent), and Michael Nyunt & Company (18 per cent). The MIIC assigned Michael Nyunt & Co. and Swiss Underwriting Services Ltd. as its insurance agents. But on 1 August 1998, the MIIC withdrew the agent assignment and took over the operation. Later, Jarney Asia Bhd also transferred its shares to the Innwa Bank.[17] Though commercially successful, in accordance with the decision of the government, the MIIC was finally transferred to the Ministry of Finance and Revenue in the early 2000s. Moreover, some MEC factories and services were either liquidated or transferred to other government departments.[18]

Other Military-Managed Businesses

Up until 1989, even for its essential military supplies, the Tatmadaw had to rely on state-owned factories under the Ministry of Industry-1. On 31 July 1989, the Directorate of Ordnance took over the management of three factories from the Ministry of Industry-1. They were the *Tatmadaw* Garment Factory (Mingalardon), the *Tatmadaw* Waterproof Canvas Factory (Thamaing), and the *Tatmadaw* Shoe Factory (Indaing).[19] Six more factories were transferred to the directorate. These included the *Tatmadaw* Textile Factory (Meikhtilar), the *Tatmadaw* Textile Factory (Thamaing), the *Tatmadaw* Football Factory (Hmawbi), the *Tatmadaw* Metal Products Factory (Oakkyin), the *Tatmadaw* Leather Factory (Mandalay), and the *Tatmadaw* Pharmaceutical Factory (Hmawbi).[20] At present, therefore, the Directorate of Ordnance operates nine factories in addition to the production of arms and ammunition for military use.[21] Although many of them are exclusively for military use, some products are for non-military commercial purposes, the most prominent being those from the football factory and pharmaceutical factory. These industries generate some income for the Tatmadaw, and also provide jobs for many families of the Tatmadaw rank-and-file.

In addition to the Directorate of Ordnance, the Directorate of Supply and Transport also runs a number of factories. These factories are *Tatmadaw* Tea Factory (Nangsam), *Tatmadaw* Tea Factory (Thandaung), *Tatmadaw* Tea Factory (Yangon), *Tatmadaw* Canning Factory (Mandalay), *Tatmadaw* Canning Factory (Thandwe), *Tatmadaw* Shrimp-paste and Fish-sauce Factory (Hmawbi), *Tatmadaw* Biscuit and Noodle Factory (Hmawbi), and *Tatmadaw* Wheat Flour Factory (Aubar).[22] These factories produce a range of products not only for military ration, but also for commercial purposes. The directorate took over the Pyinmapin Diary Factory and then contracted this out to the private sector in May 1997 to produce "SUN" brand condensed milk cans for commercial purpose.[23]

The Directorate of Defence Services Intelligence (DDSI) engages in a wide range of business activities, which is not unusual in intelligence communities since they build up many front organizations to finance their covert operations. It is quite well known that the DDSI runs restaurants, publishes books and journals, and produces entertainment materials. In November 2004, the Ministry of Home Affairs abolished the DDSI-sponsored "*Say-Ta-Man*" Music Production Co. Ltd. and "*Myet-Khin-Thit*" Arts Forum.[24] Similarly, publication licences were withdrawn from bimonthly journals of the *Myanmar News Gazette* and *Wuntharnu*, the *Myet-Khin-Thit* monthly magazine, and *Myanmar Perspective* quarterly magazine.

The Directorate of People's Militias and Public Relations[25] took over the "Myawaddy Press" in the early 1990s. Although it published two monthly magazines, a monthly children's magazine, a weekly journal, and a few books, it appears that the press depends heavily on subsidization. "Myawaddy Television", which is also part of the directorate, runs an advertisement agency for TV commercials. That business might generate a certain amount of income, but this fell far short of production and transmission costs.[26]

Military units at various levels of command continued to engage in business activities and even expanded. In addition to its normal business activities of running canteen and other cottage industries, at the lower level of command, some battalions engaged in small-scale businesses, such as running an ice-block factory or road transportation. There were many cases where military units rented out the premises, electricity, and even military trucks for commercial purposes. However, there were apparently a widespread disparity among the military units of the benefits received and huge gaps in their subsidies. Some units can give quite a good amount of cash as a monthly allowance while many units, especially those in the far flung and remote areas, find it very difficult to meet the basic minimum requirements of a cash subsidy, which was about 1,500 kyat in 2,000 and about 3,000 kyat in 2003.

As this began to threaten institutional cohesion, and also encourage some units to engage in extra-legal business activities, such as storing unregistered cars in military barracks or carrying contraband goods on military trucks, the Tatmadaw leadership decided to end the commercial activities of individual units. General Thura Shwe Mann explained:

> On 30 September 2004, at the cabinet meeting, Senior General Than Shwe gave a guidance that ministries and departments should not set up business venture[s] to raise fund[s], giving welfare for service personnel as an excuse, and to terminate all business activities by the end of the year since the state has been giving [a] monthly extra allowance of Kyat 5000 per capita for all service personnel since December 2003. In December, the Ministry of Defense [sic] issued instruction[s] to all military units to end their business activities by 31 March 2004, except farm[ing] and officially sanctioned activities associated with [the] Regimental Fund. The order was to transfer some enterprises to respective ministries or organizations and to dismantle altogether for [sic] those were not transferable.[27]

The instruction was implemented more effectively after the dismantling of the DDSI. Therefore, all individual military units stopped their business ventures.

Military-Backed Business

Under the Adjutant-General Office, there are two business organizations for different ex-military service personnel. One is under the supervision of the Organizing Committee of the Myanmar War Veteran Organization (MWVO) and the other is under the supervision of Directorate of Resettlement. Under various names, the MWVO owns twenty-six businesses worth over K 9.6 billion; it provides state/division WVO Supervisory Committees with loans for doing business in their respective regions.[28] The most prominent business organizations under the MWVO are Shwe Innwa Job Agency and Shwe *Innwa* Bus Line, both established in 2001. In June 2002, the MWVO opened the "Thamadaw Special Clinic" in Yangon, staffed with in-service and retired medical personnel from the military hospitals, which provides good services at reasonably fair fees.[29] Between 2001 and 2004, within four years, the MWVO provided K 1,430.5 million for its members and their families. Moreover, it created job opportunities for fifty-six officers, 179 members and 182 family members at home, and 11,903 sons of family members in Malaysia. In addition, it built about 120 low-cost houses for its members for settlement.[30]

The Directorate of Resettlement oversees the Thanmyanthu Economic Enterprise, comprised of Thanmyanthu Bus Line and Thanmyanthu Construction Group, for the welfare of disabled military personnel. The directorate offers vocational courses and training for disabled military personnel to earn their living. The directorate has bought shares for 177 disabled military personnel at the UMEHL to provide long-term assistance for them and has rendered assistance to another 1,340 persons. Cash donation ceremonies for disabled soldiers are reported in the media from time to time. The Thanmyanthu Bus Line operates more than a dozen bus lines in Yangon and it has branches in Mawlamyaing, Monywa, Ba-an, and Loikaw, running highway bus services. Moreover, it has established the Thanmyanthu Inspection Service, Thanmyanthu Economic Development Company, and Thanmyanthu Construction Group.[31] It has also ventured into other businesses such as car servicing; car body repair workshop; car rental service; and car spare parts sales service. In March 2000, the Thanmyanthu Economic Enterprise opened a "Dental Clinic" in Yangon which provides dental care at a fairly reasonable price.[32] The directorate also runs a number of factories employing disabled military personnel, such as the chain-link and bulb-wire factory, brick factories, and firewood-substitute energy stick factories.

CONCLUSION

Until early 1990s, the force modernization programme in Myanmar was financed mostly through the annual defence budget. The defence budget amounted to an average of one-third of Total Government Expenditure (TGE) in the 1950s and 1960s. Due to the different methods of calculation, the defence budget in the TGE varied from an average of 5.5 per cent to an average of 20 per cent in the period between 1980 and 1988. The same situation persisted throughout 1990s; the percentages were much higher as they varied from an average of 10 per cent to an average of 30 per cent. In the 1993–94 fiscal year, the defence budget in the expenditure of Union Government Expenditure reached 14.5 per cent while its share in the expenditure of State Administrative Organizations came up to 39 per cent, clearly reflecting its aggressive force modernization programme. Yet most of the defence budget went to the pay and ration, and administrative expenses, rather than military hardware. The percentage of defence expenditure in the GDP steadily declined from an average of 6.5 per cent in the early 1960s to an average of 3.5 per cent in the 1980s. Even in the 1990s, the official figure claimed that it was just an average of 3.5 per cent of the GDP. Since 1990s, according to some knowledgeable observers, Myanmar's defence expenditure has been much higher than the officially stated figure. As mentioned earlier, there are several other factors that should be considered in estimating the defence expenditure of Myanmar.

Beginning from 1951, the Tatmadaw has been considering the expansion of its role beyond the traditional domain of defending the country from external aggression and the newly acquired role of suppressing insurgency. It has placed great emphasis on the socio-economic development of the country. At the 1952 COs' conference, the COs discussed economic development planning, land reform, health services, education, democratization of local administration, agricultural productivity, and the development of transportation and communication. Many of these discussions embraced the question of how the Tatmadaw could contribute to the socio-economic development of the nation.[33] This, however, required some form of ideological justification.

Having gone through several phases of ideological gestation and formulation, the Tatmadaw finally came up with what was known as "The National Ideology and Our Pledge" in October 1958; it was supplemented a year later with "The National Ideology and the Role of the Defence Services", which officially defined the Tatmadaw's attitudes towards politico-socio-economic issues of the state. Now, the Tatmadaw has decided to become an important socio-economic force in Myanmar. Thus, the Defence Service Institute, what was essentially a welfare institution in the early 1950s, has grown into the largest commercial enterprise, playing a very important role in the socio-economic development of Myanmar in the late 1950s. However, under the "Burmese Way to Socialism", the military's enterprises were considered unnecessary and against the principles of a socialist economic system; thus, all of them were nationalized. In fact, at the 1962 Tatmadaw conference, it was decided to transform the Tatmadaw into the People's Tatmadaw; a national army not only protecting a socialist economic system, but also building one. For the next twenty-six years, the Tatmadaw was a leading example of a revolutionary force. For that, the state took care of the welfare of the troops and looked after legitimate defence needs.

The collapse of the socialist regime in September 1988 opened an avenue for the Tatmadaw to revitalize its socio-economic role, independent of the state and its commercial interests, as it decided to play "a leading role in national politics". To be self-reliant and self-sufficient under a "multi-party political system" for the welfare of its troops, in addition to financing defence modernization as an off-budget measure, the Tatmadaw reasoned that it was necessary to build up commercial enterprises. As the case of the MEC indicated, the Tatmadaw financed large-scale infrastructure and industrial projects, for it was considered to be a player in the national economy. However, the problem with military commercial activities came with the decentralization of command and concentration of ministerial authorities in the hands of regional commanders in 1988, which opened up opportunities for regional commands to engage in various businesses. Soon after the military takeover in September 1988, regional commanders were authorized to raise fund to finance the repair of state-owned factories and to maintain these factories in running condition.[34] Moreover, the growing prices of consumer goods pushed the Tatmadaw to seek off-budget external income to finance its welfare activities at the regional and local levels. Initially, only the command headquarters level engaged in business. Later, all local military units commanded by either the Commanding Officer (CO) or the Officer in Command (OC) were allowed to do business in the name of welfare.[35] All COs and OCs were forced to find external income to finance welfare activities and to pay monthly cash subsidies for the troops; thus, it also opened up the opportunity to abuse the system, even for private gains. The problem of corruption was more serious and widespread among military units in the cities. In this way, under the banner of "welfare for the unit", many military officers engaged in business and became unusually rich. It appeared that this became particularly true for the people in the military intelligence corps since they were vested with immense authority. The scale of abuse of the system was recently revealed by non other than General Thura Shwe Mann; he explained that, in the period of about two or three months, a military intelligence unit based in Muse had got hold of all kinds of commercial goods worth over 3 billion kyats [US$3 million].[36] Moreover, as some units and officers were involved in extra-legal activities and showed abuse of power, in the name of welfare for the troops as mentioned earlier, some people began to see the military's commercial activities as being business above the law. Faced with unfair competition, monopoly, protection, and corruption, some people started seeing the Tatmadaw's commercial activities as vehicles for not only making the Tatmadaw a privileged institution, but also for paving the way for military personnel to make their personal gains, rather than contributing to the benefit of the state and society. This was despite the fact that the Tatmadaw's commercial activities created jobs and generate income for many families. Therefore, it seems to suggest that the ideological basis for military commercial activities has suffered a major setback.

The Tatmadaw's commercial interests and activities in Myanmar had revived after the military takeover of the state in 1988. The Tatmadaw's businesses served as instruments for political patronage and economic rent-seeking. At the same time, these commercial enterprises provided financial assistance to cushion up the budgetary constraints on defence expenditure, and contributed to the welfare and well-being of the Tatmadaw's personnel and their families, while creating employment opportunities and generating income for many families. Some of the commercial enterprises, especially under the MEC, were involved in large-scale infrastructure building projects and made long term investments, which could be done only by the government in Myanmar. But there was a problem of widespread corruption. Perhaps, though not desirable, such corruption might by a necessary evil in a business environment and system beset with economic irrationalities, plagued by inefficient bureaucracy, and conditioned by a heavily charged political atmosphere. Not all military businesses, especially under the UMEHL and MEC, are making profits. Recently, the UMEHL had to buy back some state-owned economic enterprises (SEEs), which were draining the state's coffers.

Initially, the unchecked business activities of individual military units created problems of disparity of benefits among troops, threatening institutional cohesion and undermining military efficiency. This problem was finally addressed in late 2004. Therefore, at present, only those commercial enterprises directly under the management of the War Office remain in business operation. Both UMEHL and MEC will continue to be a major player in Myanmar's economic life. For the MEC, it is a government within a government in reality. Through these two economic enterprises, the Tatmadaw will be able to maintain its hold on various sectors of the economy. For both ideological reason and practical purpose, the Tatmadaw will continue to keep its commercial interests and activities thriving, despite concerns among some societal groups. However, the question of ensuring the greater transparency and accountability of these enterprises will be a major challenge for the Tatmadaw leadership in the immediate future. Of course, at a more generic level, questions will eventually come up about the advisability and propensity of the military's commercial interests and activities when the country undergoes the process of liberalization, eventually leading to democratization. However, with its managed transition to a constitutional government, the Tatmadaw's commercial interests and activities are well protected, at least for the foreseeable future. What will eventually determine the future of Tatmadaw's business is the ability of the Tatmadaw's leadership to maintain institutional cohesion within the military and to influence the political process in Myanmar.

Notes

1 The DSI established Burma Five Star Line Co. Ltd. on 5 February 1959 with a paid-up capital of 1.2 million kyat. The management was contracted out to Zim Israel Navigation Co. Ltd., but it was terminated in 1963. Along with the Five Star Line, on 26 November 1959, the DSI formed the Rangoon Agency

Ltd. as a shipping agency, and Burma Trading House for trading. (See Ye Yint Sit Thu, *Performance of the Ministry of Transportation*, vol. 2 [Yangon: Ministry of Transportation, 1999], pp. 92–103.)

2 In fact, the very original version of the "Burmese Way to Socialism" (BWS) appeared in the *Myawaddy* Magazine (October 1957) under the name of "Namarupa Wada" (ideology of correlation between mind and matter) by U Chit Hlaing, an architect of the BWS.

3 The Tatmadaw's Psychological Warfare Department ran its own publications unit.

4 In the early 1980s, in the South West Command area (Ayerwaddy Division), many battalions ran candle factories and plants producing firewood substitute sticks made of husked paddy.

5 Senior General Than Shwe's address at the 54th Anniversary of Armed Forces Day (27 March 1999).

6 UMEHL Director's Report (2007).

7 UMEHL Director's Report (2005).

8 UMEHL Director's Report (various years).

9 UMEHL Report 2007.

10 See Appendix (9).

11 See Appendix (9).

12 See Appendix (9).

13 In fact, the UMEHL has a monopoly over the import of edible oil and fuel oil until very recently and still enjoys the privilege of tax free import on these items.

14 The UMEHL imports a few hundred cars per year for domestic sale by lucky draw. Since the import licence for cars is highly profitable, the sales of imported cars alone can generate a huge amount of profit.

15 UMEHL Director's Report (2007).

16 The MEC established "Cybermec" in 1999. The idea was to build up the Tatmadaw's own IT network for civilian use and a critical mass of talented IT experts who could become frontline defenders of the country's IT network in case of a military confrontation or national emergency. But the business did not survive in the fairly competitive market.

17 Han Htet Aung, "Prospect for Insurance", *Living Color Magazine* (November 1998), pp. 57–58.

18 This included the transfer of *Ohndan* Nilar Mine to the UMEH, *Mongshu* Jade Mine to Camp Commandant Office (under the War Office), Bird's Nest Production (Myeik) to the QMG Office, Confiscated Goods Sales Services to QMG office, and the liquidation of *Chinthe* Airline (Helicopter Service), the liquidation of the *Cybermec* Computer Sale Centre (Yangon), and the closure of Computer Assembly Plant (Pale).

19 Ministry of Information, *Taingkyo Pyipyu* (Nation-Building Endeavours), vol. 1, p. 167.

20 *Kyemon*, 27 April 2000, p. 12.

21 Ministry of Information, *Taingkyo Pyipyu* (Nation-Building Endeavours), vol. 4, p. 142.

22 Ministry of Information, *Taingkyo Pyipyu* (Nation-Building Endeavours), vol. 4, p. 141.

23 Ministry of Information, *Taingkyo Pyipyu* (Nation-Building Endeavours), vol. 3, p. 111.

24 The *Myanmar Times* (English), vol. 13, no. 249 (10 January 2005): 5.

25 In 1990, the Directorate of People's Militias and Public Relations was reorganized into two separate departments: (1) Directorate of Public Relations and Psychological Warfare (DPRPW) and (2) Directorate of People's Militias and Frontier Troops (DPMFT).

26 There was unconfirmed information that the DPRPW entered a business venture with a firm named "Ace Dragon" that engages in insurance and media advertising.

27 General Thura Shwe Mann's Explanation on 24 October 2004 (*NLM* Supplement).

28 Senior General Than Shwe's Address at the MWVO Conference (2005), *NLM* (30 June 2005).

29 *NLM*, 5 June 2002.

30 *NLM*, 29 June 2005.

31 From Thanmyanthu (booklet).

32 *NLM*, 31 March 2000.

33 CD. 351, Minutes of the Commanding Officers' Conference held on 21 July 1951.

34 For example, in the Southwest Command region, the commander had to raise funds and earn foreign exchange, by exporting marine products, to repair a glass factory which was shut down during the 1988 political upheaval. Then, from the income generated from this kind of commercial activities, the command imported coaches for highway services. It also donated medical instruments to the military hospital. Other regional commands also did similar things. A similar pattern could be found in the civil administration too, because the regional commanders were also the chairmen of their respective states or division. Many local projects were financed by the regional administrative bodies, rather than ministries through the state budget. (For example, the building of the Pyigyimon Royal Barge was financed by contributions from various states and divisions, which had income generated from commercial activities.)

35 In the civilian sector too, almost all offices and departments have so-called "Welfare for Service Personnel" (*Wunhtan-Thetthar*) and raised funds.

36 General Thura Shwe Mann's explanation of the situation on 24 October 2004, (*NLM*).

7

CONCLUSION

Building the Tatmadaw since 1948 has been a challenge. It has gone through various phases of development. In July 1947, Bogyoke Aung San, father of the present day Tatmadaw, expressed his view on the future of Myanmar's national defence and the armed forces in the following terms:

> Look at the national defence, our military is just enough for suppression of internal unrest. For national defence [against external threat], it is not sufficient. Army [infantry] is not enough. There are no armour[ed] battalions. [The] Navy is just for show. In reality, there is no way to defend this country. [The] Air force is just in the formative stage. In [the] air force, for this country, there should be at least 500 combat aircrafts [sic] for [the] first line of defence. That is not sufficient. While these 500 aircrafts [sic] are in frontline combat action, each aircraft should have three or four aircrafts [sic] in [the] rear for [sic] reserve. At least another 500 combat aircrafts [sic] is [sic] needed. Overall, this country needs at least one million soldiers at the time war begins. It is better to have an army of [a] million soldiers. Right now, we have just 20,000 soldiers.[1]

Over a period of nearly six decades, the small and lightly equipped Tatmadaw has grown in size, force structure, and technological sophistication. Largely as a result of recent force modernization and expansion, the Tatmadaw has transformed itself from essentially a counter-insurgency force into a force supported by tanks and artillery, capable of fighting a regular conventional war. It has now become Southeast Asia's second largest military force, next to Vietnam's. One of the declared missions of the Tatmadaw is to build a "strong, highly capable and modern armed forces", which, according to the rhetoric, "keeps up the twelve noble traditions of the Tatmadaw".[2] According to official statements, in building a strong, highly capable, and modern Tatmadaw, three capabilities — military, organization, and administrative, have to be achieved through four means — training, administration, welfare, and morale. While training is a key to enhance all capabilities, there are other factors that play an important role in building the Tatmadaw, especially in the field of military capability: military doctrine and strategy, force structure, armament and force modernization, and military training and officer education.

In the process of formulating its military doctrine and strategy, the Tatmadaw has undergone three phases in line with the changing threat perception. The first phase of the doctrine was to cope with external threats from more powerful enemies with a strategy of strategic denial under conventional warfare. The perception of threat to state security was more of external rather than internal threats. The internal threat to state security was managed through the use of a mixture of force and political persuasion. However, this did not resolve the internal threat to state security. The second phase of the doctrine was to suppress insurgency with the "people's war", and the perception of threat to state security was more of internal threats. During this stage, external linkage to internal problems, and direct external threats were minimized by a foreign policy of isolation. The third phase was to face lower-level external threats with a strategy of strategic denial under the "total people's defence". The SLORC/SPDC has successfully dealt with seventeen major insurgent groups, whose "return to the legal fold" in the past eighteen years has remarkably decreased internal threats to state security, at least for the short and medium terms. Moreover, there are some indications that some of the ceasefire troops will eventually become paramilitary or special police reserve in support of the Tatmadaw.[3] However, the threat perception of the possibility of external linkage to internal problems, perceived as being based on pretexts such as human rights violations and ethnic cleansing, remains high.

Myanmar's national objective, as declared by the SPDC, is to create a modern, peaceful, and prosperous nation in which 135 national races live in harmony. The role of the Tatmadaw, which must be a "strong, highly capable and modern" force, in this process has been prominent as political and social cleavages have been difficult to reconcile and have often resulted in violence. Since the day of independence, the Tatmadaw has been involved in restoring and maintaining internal security and suppressing insurgency. It was with this background that the defence policy was formulated. In this context, Myanmar's defence policy could, therefore, be argued to be multifaceted.

The Tatmadaw's force modernization programme appears to be a capability-based modernization as it aims to provide capabilities suitable for a wide range of future challenges and circumstances, in contrast to what is known as threat-based force modernization that identifies adversaries and detailed scenarios. The modernization effort suggests that the Tatmadaw is moving towards a mechanized army. Do all these new doctrines and strategies, organizational structure, armaments, and training and leadership programmes produce "desired" firepower, protection, intelligence gathering, and mobility? Do they produce combat efficiency and combat readiness? What about synchronization? Will they give the Tatmadaw an element of initiative? Many questions certainly remain. Acquiring more advanced warships and aircraft is becoming increasingly expensive; it is even difficult for a small country such as Myanmar to retain a basic defensive capability with the existing order of battle. With regard to the force modernization, a government spokesman argued that the Tatmadaw is "one of the most ill equipped armed forces in the world and it is just trying to modernize or mechanize the present armed forces, in [sic] which it is still not successful".[4] No single factor can explain the current force modernization programme in Myanmar. In reality, such a modernization programme has been long overdue, due to financial difficulties. However, it appears that the recent force modernization in Myanmar is closely linked to anxieties generated by the possibility of foreign invasion or invasion by proxy.

In Myanmar, the Tatmadaw has endorsed twelve principles of war: objective, morale, economy of force and mass, offensive, manoeuvre, security, surprise, intelligence, flexibility, coordination, logistics, and support of the entire population. It is in this context of the principles of war and threat environment that the Tatmadaw declared the "People's War Doctrine and Strategy", and organized, armed, and trained its troops. Myanmar's military doctrine could be interpreted as defence-in-depth. It was influenced by a number of factors such as history, geography, culture, economy, and sense of threats. Myanmar does not have the capabilities to be self-reliant in the adoption of conventional military strategies. The lack of infrastructure, low industrial base, and weak economy would likely undermine its capacity to conduct or sustain large-scale conventional military operations on a longer term or a continuous basis. As a result, it appears that the Tatmadaw has developed an "active defence" strategy, based on guerrilla warfare with limited conventional military capability, designed to cope with lower-level external threats and internal threats to state security. This strategy, as revealed in joint services and combined arms exercises, is built on a system of "total people's defence", where the armed forces provide the first line of defence, and the training and leadership of the nation in the matter of national defence. It is designed to deter potential aggressors by the knowledge that the defeat of Myanmar's regular force (the Tatmadaw) in conventional warfare would be followed by persistent guerrilla warfare in the occupied areas by militias and dispersed regular troops, who would eventually wear down the invader, both physically and psychologically, and leave it vulnerable to a counter-offensive. In other words, if the conventional strategy of strategic denial fails, then the Tatmadaw and its auxiliary forces will most likely follow Mao's strategic concepts of "strategic defensive", "strategic stalemate" and "strategic [counter] offensive". Therefore, the broad contours of Myanmar's military strategy are defensive, ensuring the security of land, sea, and air.

The "people's war" doctrine evolved through the military experience of the Tatmadaw in the Cold War period. While it has been modified in accordance with emerging threat perceptions in Myanmar's strategic and political environments, some key tenets of the doctrine remain unchanged. These enduring elements include the primacy of politics, the primacy of people over weapons, the strategy of using weak against strong, the mobilization of the masses to fight a protracted war against invasion, and the multiple role of the Tatmadaw. The adaptation of the Tatmadaw to "people's war under modern [high tech] conditions" has become the main preoccupation of the Tatmadaw. The "under modern conditions" indicates that "instead of luring the enemy deep into the country in the opening phase of the war, the Tatmadaw should firmly hold on to the positional defence in order to weaken the enemy's massive invasion and then wage counter-offensive campaigns with concentrated and combined forces". This "active defence" will prevent invaders from entering Myanmar's territories. When this failed, a "people's war" would be waged within the territory to wear down powerful enemies. In other words, active defence means holding invaders outside the country's key areas, beyond the borders if necessary. It also indicates a determination to launch large-scale counter-offensives after blunting the enemy's initial attack.

With "people's war under modern conditions", the Tatmadaw gives more attention to external security threats. In both the traditional "people's war" and "people's war under modern conditions", the battlespace is dominated by more civilians than regular soldiers. But there are differences between the two. The battlespace in the traditional "people's war" is mostly in the domestic sphere, dominated by peasants, and has three dimensions: land, sea, and air. But, in the "people's war under modern conditions", the battlespace is both domestic and foreign, dominated by more professionals, and have four dimensions: an extra dimension is the cyberspace, which is known as the fifth dimension of the war while space is considered the fourth dimension. Nevertheless, both the traditional "people's war" and the "people's war modern conditions" are essentially asymmetric warfare, known in strategic literature as the 4th Generation War (4GW). Thus, the fundamental principle of "you fight your kind of war and I will fight mine" will remain in the Tatmadaw's doctrine.

Regardless of the forms, at the grand strategy level, the centre of gravity in the "people's war" is domestic and international public opinion; thus the political context of the war is essential. At the strategy level, the centre of gravity is the link between the regular army and the people, and it is the political organization that serves as the link. An essential characteristic of the "people's war", regardless of traditional or modern conditions, is a just war. It is the war against foreign invasion, in defiance of an infringement on its independence, sovereignty, and territorial integrity. There is unity and collaboration between the people and the armed forces — it is the duty of the entire people to be involved in the national defence. The armed forces will be the core around which the people will revolve. The regular army and people will fight a war by joining hands. What is important in the "people's war", whether under "modern conditions" or otherwise, is the vitality of the support of the people. The guerrilla or regular army (fish) has to operate (swim) in the people (water); therefore, the control of the water temperature is important in the success of the "people's war". It is important not to mistake mirage for water and to keep the water cool. Taking the view of a multidimensional threat, Myanmar has turned to the "people's war under modern conditions", which combines regular conventional warfare with "unrestricted warfare" or asymmetric warfare, to address its defence needs.

As far as the Tatmadaw is concerned, until and unless one commits its ground force to capture its military headquarters, a war cannot be declared over. The moving of the capital and military high command from Yangon to Naypyitaw clearly reflects the underlying military thinking and warfighting strategy of the Tatmadaw. Although the new location of its military high command cannot escape from any decapitating strikes with cruise missiles, it can certainly provide defence-in-depth before any ground force invasion. In this context, the new location of the high command is less vulnerable to amphibious warfare. From the Tatmadaw's point of view, it is the trading of space for time. Being located in the vicinity of mountains and jungles, in a spot that sits on major communication links between upper and lower Myanmar, the Tatmadaw could mount considerable resistance against any invasion force, by using the military strategy of protracted people's guerrilla warfare of attrition. In this context, the surrounding areas of Naypyitaw can be considered the heartland or base area where the enemy should be "lured deep for annihilation". The Inchon landing of 1950 in Korea appears to offer military lessons for the Tatmadaw; an amphibious landing on the west coast of Myanmar [Rakhine State] and a land-based invasion from the east [Kayah State] will not only cut off Yangon from the Upper Myanmar, but also make it an encircled target for attacks from the south. The new location will give the military high command easy access to heavily forested mountainous areas in the north bordering China or India; this is vital for protracted guerrilla warfare.

Under the "people's war under modern conditions", the main thrust of its warfighting strategy remains relatively unchanged. The doctrine can be considered as centring around the concept of mass warfare. Armed with large quantities of low-technology hardware, the Tatmadaw continues to emphasize engagement with enemies at close range with infantry, though increased attention has been accorded to the idea of combined arms operations: the artillery and armour corps is greatly expanded. At the strategy level — perhaps some might call it the operational level — the Tatmadaw appears to focus on its offensive capability. But it was inadequate to hold back an invasion through positional defence in the border areas on a continuous sustained basis. With the advent of the RMA, the Tatmadaw will certainly face the challenge of the RMA-based warfare. Under "modern conditions", while the "four strengths" of the traditional "people's war" doctrine will be still valid, it is necessary to modify the "three masses" to include "cyberspace" or "information mass". In the near future, it might be a reality to develop capabilities for a "people's war in the cyberspace"; but the Tatmadaw needs to digest the concepts of "cyber-warrior", "cyber-guerrilla", and "cyber-militias", and to build up a critical mass for such a "people's war in the cyberspace". A number of things remain to be addressed to improve the military capability of the Tatmadaw. For strategic denial, it should develop a better command, control, communication, and intelligence system; (near) real-time intelligence; a formidable air defence system; and an early warning system. The Tatmadaw also needs to enhance its troop mobility. Although a number of light infantry divisions and military operation commands were formed in recent years, the force structure is still territorially organized.[5] However, for "total people's defence" to be effective, it requires not only a command and control system that can maintain contact with the people from national to village level, but also a nationwide mobilization programme to use local resources and the local environment to the best effect. Support of the masses, or mass mobilization is the most challenging task for the present day Tatmadaw.

Over the past fifty years, the Tatmadaw has gone through various stages of institution building. A relatively small, weak, and disunited Tatmadaw has emerged as a considerably large, strong, and more or less united one. Splits along the lines of racial background, organizational origins, and political affiliation have been resolved by the early 1960s. The gap between staff officers and field commanders has been bridged too. Competition between intelligence officers and field commanders has been more or less settled. There is no concrete evidence of discrimination against one school of graduates over another in promotions. Until the mid-1990s, there was no discrimination on racial or religious grounds in promotions. Many Christian officers were appointed to senior staff and command positions. Some Kayin, Kachin, and Chin officers were promoted to brigadier general and above ranks. However, there were some changes in both recruitment and promotion patterns for officers in the late 1990s. There has been no more recruitment of fresh university graduates since the early 2000s. Most officers come from the DSA and other ranks with university degree or high school certificate or distinguish services. New regulations require a university degree for promotion to lieutenant colonel and above ranks. In addition, unwritten regulations also require that the spouse of a company commander (major) must complete high school, and that of a battalion commander (lieutenant colonel) and above position or rank must have a university degree. This unstated policy of setting criteria for the spouse encourages military officers to marry women with middle-class background or from the educated class. Now, with very few exceptions, a division commander (brigadier general) and those with ranks above that must have a Master's degree from the NDC. Religious background appears to be an important criterion. Although there is no official regulation, non-Buddhist officers or officers with non-Buddhist spouses are unlikely to climb beyond the rank of major or hold important command positions. This is partly the result of a policy of building a patron-supporter relationship [*Sayar-Dagar-Setsanye* (ဆရာ-ဒကာဆက်ဆံရေး)] between Buddhist monasteries and battalions in their respective areas and a widely held view that a battalion commander and his wife are parents of the battalion who need to look after the majority rank and file who are Buddhists. Racial background or ethnicity, however, is not an important criterion. Officers with a non-Bamar ethnic background still make it to important positions, including division commanders. The political background of immediate family members (parents, wife, in-laws, sons, and daughters) is also very important. All of them must be free from party politics and must not be members of any political party. The social background of the officer seems to be important in promotion; the present leadership generally appears to favour a rural background; almost all senior commanders come from rural towns. Therefore, as a result of these measures, the present day Tatmadaw is commanded by educated Buddhist officers with a rural background, most of whom are ethnic Bamar. In early 2007, the Tatmadaw leadership implemented a three-decade-old policy of early retirement for officers who had not reached the rank of major by thirty-five years of age, lieutenant colonel by forty, and colonel by forty-five. But, it is not certain whether this policy will remain for long. In terms of the different services, the rivalry between the three services of the Tatmadaw has virtually been eliminated. Yet, the Tatmadaw has basically remained an army of infantry battalions while eliminating rivalries so prone to arise between services. In Myanmar, in 1988, out of a total of about 198,600 personnel in the Tatmadaw, the navy and air force only have 8,000 and 6,500 personnel respectively. Even at the present troop level, navy and air force only have a staff strength of 12,000 each. This is, by any Southeast Asian comparison, the highest ratio of army to the total number of armed forces personnel.

According to some observers, the War Establishment (WE) of the Tatmadaw has 600,000 personnel. However, its Implemented Strength (IS) is much below that of the WE. To some observers, it is no more than 60 per cent of the WE. When asked by a Japanese journalist, Myanmar military spokesman, Colonel Hla Min said that "the current Myanmar armed forces is totally 350,000 plus".[6] It is not clear whether the colonel was talking about the actual strength or the War Establishment. Considering the fact that the Tatmadaw has nearly 1,300 military units of various sizes, including 504 infantry battalions, its force structure is over 600,000 personnel. Yet there is no way to verify these facts. Although the colonel claimed that "Myanmar did not have any enemy or threat from outside",[7] he did not explain why the Tatmadaw needed so much manpower. In this context, one might wonder — given the lack of any immediate external threat although arming themselves with better equipment is understandable — why the Tatmadaw has expanded so much in structure. The official explanation is the fact that most of the troops were "Civilian Construction Corps".[8] To some analysts, however, it can be understood within the context of the doctrine of a "people's war". The expansion of force structure will allow the Tatmadaw (extensive) territorial representation and easy access for the mobilization of the local population for a war effort in times of emergency.[9] Yet, it also appears that the internal armed security threat and civil unrest continue to influence the Tatmadaw's security perception. There is no indication that the Tatmadaw will abandon its role in internal security operations in near future. Thus, in one sense, the force structure of the Tatmadaw demonstrates the continuity of its historical security perception.

But such a large-scale territorial force structure will likely undermine the Tatmadaw's mission of building "strong, highly capable and modern armed forces" since much of its scare resources have to be devoted to manpower and other non-combat necessities. Nevertheless, one has to take note that the organizational expansion of the Tatmadaw is not simply in the infantry, but in artillery, armour, and other support services, which indicates that the Tatmadaw has been in the process of building a force capable of fighting conventional warfare and coping with external security threats. In the meantime, the Tatmadaw faces problems with low morale among its troops. Foreign media frequently report the desertion and forced recruitment of child soldiers. The Tatmadaw troops operate in a very rough operational environment where there is no guarantee of a re-supply of rations and ammunition or medical evacuation. Logistics has always been an issue in the Tatmadaw, which also hampers the troops' mobility. This is particularly true in counter-insurgency operations. "Yeikkha-Santsar (ရိက္ခာဆန့်စား)" or stretching of the ration in the frontline has become a common phenomenon. A confidential document leaked to, and reported by, international media reveals that the Tatmadaw has a serious problem with low morale. According to this report, between May and August 2006, for four months, it has a total of 9,497 deserters; the situation seems to be rather persistent as it saw desertion of 7,761 personnel in the period between January and April 2000. Some estimates claim that the Tatmadaw has a monthly average rate of desertion of nearly 1,600 personnel.[10] The *Jane's Defence Weekly* (JDW) (4 April 2007) revealed that the Tatmadaw also has problems with personnel fitness; in mid-2006, more than 13,700 soldiers were HIV positive and another 2,000 plus were Hepatitis B positive. Discipline is also a serious issue. The leaked document indicated that officers are self-centred and involved in profit-making, and have problems with alcohol and womanizing. Military units filed false reports, maintained poor or incomplete records, and lacked proper inspection of their work.[11]

While most of the countries in the Southeast Asia region have transformed their armed forces into meaner and leaner forces, Myanmar is probably the only country where only the "meaner" bit is applicable, but not "leaner". For the present Tatmadaw leadership, "downsizing" the Tatmadaw is not an option in the foreseeable future. At present, it is estimated that the Tatmadaw has a ratio of 20:1:1 for its army, navy and air force personnel, and of 2:1 between infantry battalions and support battalions, such as artillery, armour, signal, supply and transport, medical, engineering, ordnance, and so on. The

Tatmadaw might consider a better tooth-to-tail ratio as the modernization of the armed forces is desirable.

Despite the current force modernization programme, the Tatmadaw-Kyi, particularly the infantry, is still armed with technologically less sophisticated weapons. Most of the infantry equipment is best suited to counter-insurgency warfare and the continental defence of Myanmar, and to cope with low-level contingencies along the border. But it has never lost sight of technological advancements and new forms of warfare as it has been in the process of developing electronic warfare and information warfare capability. The acquisition of Main Battle Tanks, Amphibious Light Tanks, Armoured Personnel Carriers, and various calibres of artillery have certainly boosted the army's firepower and mobility. For the first time in the history the Tatmadaw-Kyi is now capable of amphibious warfare. It becomes more capable of fighting a limited conventional warfare. Moreover, the Myanmar Armed Forces, for the first time, has built up a more or less elaborate system of air defence system. The newly procured signal intelligence equipment have also greatly enhanced the C^3I capabilities of the Tatmadaw. Once again, all these new inventories clearly indicate that the Tatmadaw is building up its military capabilities to deal with external security threats.

While the Tatmadaw continues to pursue a policy of self-sufficiency in small arms production, it procures most of its heavy artillery from overseas suppliers. But most of the overseas procurements were second-hand and they were modified to meet local operational requirements. The Defence Industries (DI) in Myanmar is still primitive in armament productions. They are only capable of manufacturing small arms, ammunitions, mines, and a few spare parts, and of maintaining and upgrading a few items of military hardware. Since some of the factories under the DI have been built in the 1950s and 1960s and their technologies are already outdated. The recent transfer of military technology from the PRC is not particularly advanced either. Although the Tatmadaw is planning to acquire modern technology, it does not have the industrial base and manufacturing capacity to produce modern armaments. In this respect, the Tatmadaw will continue to rely on foreign sources. The Tatamadaw lacks critical mass in science and technology to build its own defence industry.

The Myanmar navy is still a coastal navy. Little is known in terms of the naval operational doctrine, campaign theory, and tactics of the Myanmar navy. It is fairly obvious that concepts such as air superiority, long-distance missile strike, and electronic warfare in sea battle have no role in the maritime doctrine and naval strategy of Myanmar navy. Perhaps, for the Myanmar navy, its activities are restricted to short-range coastal defence, most possibly at the campaign level; it is based more or less on close coordination between the army and air force and the navy in littoral and coastal waters. This campaign level emphasis has significantly influenced its naval strategic objectives and battle tactics, weapon procurement, and training. The Navy's warfighting strategy will fall within the overall doctrine of "people's war under modern conditions". Instead of a maritime strategy, the Myanmar navy appears to pay much more attention to a naval strategy. One of the most important operational concepts is the "layered defence", comprised of three layers. The inner layer is up to twelve nautical miles from the shore; mostly inshore or internal waters and littoral or coastal waters. The middle layer is between territorial waters and EEZ waters, mostly offshore waters covering the contiguous zone. The outer layer covers the EEZ waters. With increasing capabilities, the Myanmar navy can expect to extend its operations into offshore waters, implementing the concept of "defence-in-depth". Although the Myanmar navy has no capability to develop the "forward defence" posture, in terms of command of the sea, it does intend to maintain some form of sea denial on offshore waters; this is apparent in its interest in building a submarine force. Sea control is apparently way beyond its capability. At this point in time, the Tatmadaw-Yay is capable of effective patrol over Myanmar's territorial waters. It is no doubt in the process of building blue water capability. Since it plans to move from brown water to blue water capability (as its motto goes — *Yay Nyo Hma Thi Yay Pyar Tho Chi*), more surface ships, such as frigates and corvettes, will be added to the list in the near future. Moreover, the Tatmadaw-Yay is also developing its shipbuilding facilities and technological base. For the time being, sea control is beyond its capability. From being a brown water navy to a blue water navy is indeed a very ambitious motto. Due to financial and technical reasons, the naval expansion programme will be halted or delayed for several years. Even for its sea denial in offshore waters operation, there are several limitations. Moreover, many warships in the naval inventory are very old and outdated, especially in terms of naval electronics and weaponry, and their seaworthiness is questionable. Naval personnel have very few hours at sea and they lack regular naval exercises, especially live firing ones. Although its surface capability has been considerably strengthened, the navy has no sub-surface and above-surface capabilities for practical purposes.

The Tatmadaw-Lay is still very much limited in its power projection. It is in the process of procuring air superiority aircraft and more advanced multi-role fighters. Though the Tatmadaw-Lay has absorbed such advanced aircraft as the MiG-29, it has problems with operational capability. The Tatmadaw-Lay appears to have neither the air supremacy nor air superiority over Myanmar's airspace. It is just good enough to provide close air support though it is quite capable of fighting a counter-insurgency war in cooperation with the army. It does not have the capability for defensive and offensive counter-air operations. Taking relevant geopolitical and geo-strategic factors into consideration, the Tatmadaw-Lay does not need bombers in its order of battle. The F-7 supersonic fighter has many weaknesses. It is only installed with Automatic Direction Finder (ADF) in the avionic system, thus making it just a "clear weather day fighter" rather than an "all weather fighter". Moreover, there is no Head-Up Display (HUD) unit. For Electronic Counter Measure, the F-7 does not have flare and chaff. Although the PL-5B missile has a radar range finder, it does not have radar display, and the pilot needs guidance from ground radar. In this area too, the F-7 has problems as its transponder and ground radar systems are not matched. Still worse is the absence of a radar warning receiver in the F-7 that makes the aircraft extremely vulnerable to enemy missiles. The same is true for the A-5 ground attack fighter: it is even worse in manoeuvre. The best the Tatmadaw-Lay can achieve is temporary and tactical air superiority in a certain battle direction. This tactical air superiority will even be hampered by an adversary's air defence systems and electronic warfare. It terms of air operations, the Tatmadaw-Lay has negligible capability to engage in offensive counter-air operation. Although some of its aircraft can engage in a ground attack role, their combat radius is rather small. Yet Tatmadaw-Lay can provide close air support and perform air interdiction at a certain level. But, it has problems with ageing aircraft. Due to the lack of spare parts, for example, all G-4 Super Galab aircraft were grounded. The airworthiness of some aircraft is questionable. Moreover, it has a serious shortage of trained pilots. According to some reports, the Tatmadaw-Lay does not even have enough trained pilots to man its MiG-29 aircraft. Therefore, the power projection capability of the Tatmadaw-Lay is questionable. Since both F-7 and A-5 have relatively small combat radius, these aircraft cannot be used for any air superiority or counter-air operations. The Tatmadaw-Lay pilots have few flying hours. What is more, Chinese-made aircraft have a reputation for bad performance and frequent air crashes. Chinese aircraft have shorter engine lives. They need to undergo the first engine overhaul between 300 to 350 flying hours, the second overhaul between 200 to 250 flying hours, and the last overhaul after another 150 flying hours. The Tatmadaw-Lay has suffered several air crashes, the most prominent case being the crash of MI-17 on 19 February 2001. The most recent air crashes were on 18 August 2004, 5 December 2006, and 17 December 2007.[12] According to some reports, in recent years, the Tatmadaw-lay has lost one MI-17 helicopter, one MI-2 helicopter, one Sokol helicopter, one PT-6 trainer, five F-7IIK fighters, and four A-5 attack aircraft.

As is always the case with Russian and Chinese aircraft, the Tatmadaw-Lay appears to have a low level of combat readiness.

Since military training is a key to achieving combat readiness and operational efficiency, the Tatmadaw in recent years has given much attention to training programmes. It is military training that will coordinate and integrate the doctrine, strategy, manpower, weaponry, and organization into a "strong, highly capable and modern" Tatmadaw. Through its training programme, the Tatmadaw plans to enhance its military, organizational, and administrative capabilities. It is believed by the Tatmadaw leadership that such a training programme would not only make every Tatmadaw personnel imbued with five basic attributes, namely, morale, discipline, loyalty, unity and the three capabilities [military, organizational, and administrative], but would also strengthen their four outlooks: political, military, economic, and administrative.

The training regime in the Tatmadaw resembles wartime Japanese-style instruction, such as highly centralized control, rigid discipline, unquestioning obedience, and strong respect for senior-junior relations. This strict military discipline and military courtesy have been passed on from one generation to another. Therefore, some Tatmadaw officers say that the Tatmadaw has a British structure with a Japanese heart. While the focus of the pre-commission training programmes is to produce junior officers with background knowledge in the operation of weapons, battlecraft, and fieldcraft skills, operational staff procedures, military history, military science and technology, military instruction and drill, military ethos, physical fitness, and military leadership, the post-commission training is to give officers both training and education, including a number of special-to-corps courses and political education. In addition, the extension of military training to cover political leadership training indicates that the Tatmadaw is fully aware of the need to produce capable commanders and policy-makers for the future Tatmadaw, as well as for the future state. Moreover, joint services training programmes, such as amphibious warfare and air-land warfare indicate that the Tatmadaw is preparing for a conventional warfare. However, it will take quite some time for the Tatmadaw to make full use of its military capabilities.

Until the early 1990s, the force modernization of the Tatmadaw was financed mostly through the annual defence budget. The defence budget amounted to an average of one-third of the Total Government Expenditure in the 1950s and 1960s. Depending on the different methods of calculation, the share of defence expenditure in the TGE varied between 5.5 per cent and 20 per cent in the period between 1980 and 1988, and 10 per cent and 30 per cent in 1990s. It terms of its percentage of GDP, available data indicate that it has been an average of 3.5 per cent since 1960s. However, it is important to note that there are extra-budget measures to finance the defence expenditure. Considering the large number of officers commissioned each year, which is about 3,000, we see that even monthly salaries will consume a huge amount of the defence budget; a second lieutenant receives a salary of about Kyat 100,000.

In the 1950s and early 1960s, the welfare for the troops was financed through military-owned businesses. But, military businesses were nationalized in 1963 and the state took care of the general welfare of the troops. By the early 1990s, the Tatmadaw re-established a number of military-owned businesses. These military-run businesses were not only for troop welfare, but also for off-budget defence expenditure. Military units at various levels also engaged in fund-raising businesses. As fund-raising business activities began to threaten the institutional unity of the Tatmadaw, the Tatmadaw leadership decided in 2004 to end all except those directly under UMEHL and MEC. The Tatmadaw will likely protect its commercial interests at least for the foreseeable future and military businesses will continue to grow.

In conclusion, despite all these efforts in transforming the Tatmadaw from essentially a counter-insurgency force into a conventional one to cope with any (real or imagined) external security threat, it is very much limited in power projection. The building or enhancing of its air power and sea denial, if not sea control, capabilities, shows that the Tatmadaw's threat perception is more external than internal; but it seriously worries about a proxy war sponsored and supported by external powers. Doctrinal modification, expansion of force structure, force modernization, and new training regimes indicate the significance of an external security threat in the Tatmadaw's perception. Whether its existing doctrine and strategy, organization and force structure, armament and force modernization, and its military training and officer education are in support of actual war fighting still remains to be seen.

Notes

1 စာပေဗိမာန်၊ *ဗိုလ်ချုပ်အောင်ဆန်း၏မိန့်ခွန်းများ* (ရန်ကုန်၊ စာပေဗိမာန်၊ ၁၉၇၀) [Sarpay Beikman, Speeches of Bogyoke Aung San (Yangon: Sarpay Beikman Press, 1970)], pp. 394–96. (It is also important to note that Myanmar had less than 18 million people in 1947.)

2 These are "a patriotic Tatmadaw; a disciplined Tatmadaw; a loyal Tatmadaw, a united Tatmadaw; an efficient Tatmadaw, a Tatmadaw which makes heroic sacrifices; a Tatmadaw which does not seek personal gain; a Tatmadaw of noble

spirit and high morale; a Tatmadaw which posses[es] courage and overcome[s] obstacles; a Tatmadaw which can endure hardships; a Tatmadaw of [sic] tenacious and persevering; and a Tatmadaw which perpetually upholds Our Three Main National Causes" (Armed Forces Day Speech [27 March 1998]).

3 For example, some ceasefire troops in the Kachin State are already transformed to special police reserve units.

4 Information Sheet C-2066/2068 (I), 29 and 30 December 2001 (Interview was done in August 2001).

5 Tin Maung Maung Than argued that the nature of the armed threat as well as resource constraints that precluded the acquisition of expensive weapons systems resulted in an overwhelmingly counter-insurgency force structure. See Tin Maung Maung Than, "Myanmar: Myanmar-ness and Realism in Historical Perspective", p. 171.

6 Information Sheet C-2066/2068 (I), 29 and 30 December 2001 (Interview was done in August 2001).

7 Ibid.

8 Ibid.

9 It seems to me that almost all the cities in Myanmar have one or more battalions in their locality.

10 BBC (Burmese Service) 29 March 2007 (20:15 Myanmar Time); RFA (Burmese) 29 March 2007 (19:00 Myanmar Time).

11 Ibid.

12 DVB (7 and 8 December 2006); NLM 4 January 2007 [Pilot Major Thant Zaw Lin, who was killed in the crash on 5 December 2006, was posthumously awarded the gallantry medal.] The air crash on 17 December 2007 was reported in state-owned newspapers.

APPENDICES

APPENDIX (1)

TABLE I (i)
Ethnic and Army Composition of the Tatmadaw in 1948

No.	*Battalion*	*Ethnic / Army Composition*
1	No. (1) Burma Rifles	Bamar (Burma Military Police)
2	No. (2) Burma Rifles	Kayin Majority + Other Non-Bamar Nationalities
3	No. (3) Burma Rifles	Bamar / BPF members
4	No. (4) Burma Rifles	Bamar / BPF members
5	No. (5) Burma Rifles	Bamar / BPF members
6	No. (6) Burma Rifles	Bamar / BPF members
7	No. (1) Karen Rifles	Karen / Burma Army
8	No. (2) Karen Rifles	Karen / Burma Army
9	No. (3) Karen Rifles	Karen / Burma Army
10	No. (1) Kachin Rifles	Kachin / Burma Army
11	No. (2) Kachin Rifles	Kachin / Burma Army
12	No. (1) Chin Rifles	Chin / Burma Army
13	No. (2) Chin Rifles	Chin / Burma Army
14	No. (4) Burma Regiment	Gorkha
15	Chin Hill Battalion	Chin

TABLE I (ii)
Staff and Command Positions as of 1948

Chief of Staff	*Lt. Gen. Smith Dun*	*Karen*
Vice-Chief of Staff	Brigadier Saw Kyar Doe	Karen (ex-ABRO/PBF)
Chief of Air Staff	Lt. Col. Shi Sho	Karen
Chief of Naval Staff	Commander Khin Maung Bo	Pro-West
Commander, NBSD	Brigadier Ne Win	Ex-PBF
Commander, SBSD	Brigadier Aung Thin	Ex-ABRO
No. 1 Infantry Division	Brigadier Saw Chit Khin	Karen
Adjutant General	Lt. Col. Kyaw Win	Ex-PBF
Quarter Master General	Lt. Col. Saw Donny	Karen

TABLE I (iii)
Participants at the 1948 COs' Meeting

Hon. Bo Let Ya	Minister for Defence
General Smith Dun	Chief of Staff
Brigadier Ne Win	Commander, NBSD
Brigadier Aung Thin	Commander, SBSD
Brigadier Saw Kyar Doe	Vice-Chief of Staff
Lt. Col. Ze Ya	General Staff Officer-1 (War Office)
Lt. Col. Saw Tun Sein	1 Burma Regiment
Maj. Tun Sein	2 Burma Regiment
Capt. Thet Tun	1 Burma Rifles
Maj. Chit Myaing	3 Burma Rifles
Maj. Thaung Kyi	3 Burma Rifles
Lt. Col. Tin Oo	6 Burma Rifles
Maj. Tin Maung	6 Burma Rifles
Lt. Col. Ye Htut	3 Burma Rifles
Maj. Saw Myint	5 Burma Rifles
Lt. Col. Maung Maung	Burma Army Officers Training School
2/Lt. Ba Thein	4 Burma Rifles
W.O II Than Nyunt	4 Burma Rifles
W.O II Aye Ko	4 Burma Rifles
Capt. Bo Lwin	Assistant Adjutant & Quartermaster, NBSD

Source: DR. 497.

APPENDIX (2)

TABLE II (i)
Officers Commissioned in 1959 and 1960

No.	*Intake*	*Cadet*	*D/C*	*Remark*
1	DSA-1	40	1 June 1959	Army (31)/Navy (4)/Air Force (5)
2	OTS-21	263	22 June 1959	
3	OTS-22	109	4 July 1959	
4	OTS-23	72	28 October 1959	
5	OTS-24	43	13 February 1960	
6	DSA-2	25	23 April 1960	Army (14)/Navy (3)/Air Force (8)
7	OTS-25	107	24 May 1960	
8	OTS-26	94	16 July 1960	
9	OTS-27	52	8 October 1960	
10	Total	805		

Source: Myanmar Gazette.

TABLE II (ii)
Officers Commissioned in 1964 and 1965

No.	*Intake*	*Cadet*	*D/C*	*Remark*
1	DSA-6	29	27 April 1964	Army (12)/Navy (16)/Air Force (1)
2	OTS-29	163	17 October 1964	
3	OTS-30	172	12 December 1964	
4	OTS-31	187	6 February 1965	
5	DSA-7	57	28 April 1965	Army (34)/Navy (14)/Air Force (9)
6	OTS-32	173	25 September 1965	
7	OTS-33	127	10 December 1965	Course began on 15 February 1965
8	OTS-34	134	6 November 1965	Course began on 5 April 1965
9	Total	1,041		

Source: Myanmar Gazette.

TABLE II (iii)
Officers Commissioned in 1997

No.	*Intake*	*Cadet*	*D/C*	*Remark*
1	DAS-38	227	11 April 1997	Army (171)/Navy (34)/Air Force (22)
2	OTS-96	82	2 May 1997	Army (67)/Navy (3)/Air Force (12)
3	OTS-97	474	11 July 1997	
4	OTS-98	224	15 August 1997	
5	Teza-24	235	15 September 1997	Some were transferred to Air Force
6	Total	1,242		

Source: Myanmar Gazette.

APPENDIX (3)

TABLE III (i)
The State Law and Order Restoration Council, September 1988

No.	*Serial*	*Name*	*SLORC*	*Command*	*School*
1	BC 6187	Gen. Saw Maung	Chairman	C-in-C Armed Forces	OTS -6
2	BC 6710	Lt. Gen. Than Shwe	Member	C-in-C (Army)	OTS-9
3	BN 1038	R-A Maung Maung Khin	Member	C-in-C (Navy)	
4	BAF 1127	Maj. Gen Tin Tun	Member	C-in-C (Air Force)	
5	BC 6149	Brig. Aung Ye Kyaw	Member	AG	OTS-6
6	BC 6662	Maj. Gen. Phone Myint	Member	QMG	OTS- 9
7	BC 6740	Maj. Gen. Sein Aung	Member	BSO-1	OTS-10
8	BC 6463	Maj. Gen. Chit Swe	Member	BSO-2	OTS-8
9	BC 7924	Brig. Kyaw Ba	Member	NC	OTS-21
10	BC 7600	Col. Maung Thint	Member	NEC	OTS-18
11	BC 7875	Brig. Maung Aye	Member	EC	DSA-1
12	BC 7863	Brig. Nyan Lin	Member	SEC	DSA-1
13	BC 6917	Brig. Myint Aung	Member	SWC	OTS-12
14	BC 6605	Brig. Mya Thin	Member	WC	OTS-9
15	BC 7864	Brig. Tun Kyi	Member	NWC	DSA-1
16	BC 7034	Brig. Aye Thaung	Member	CC	OTS-13
17	BC 7557	Brig. Myo Nyunt	Member	YC	OTS-18
18	BC 8468	Brig. Khin Nyunt	Secretary-1	DDSI	OTS-25
19	BC 8182	Col. Tin Oo	Secretary-2	Colonel GS	OTS-22

TABLE III (ii)
State Peace and Development Council, November 1997

No.	*Serial*	*Name*	*SLORC*	*Command*	*School*
1	BC 6710	Sen. Gen. Than Shwe	Chairman	C-in-C Armed Forces	OTS-9
2	BC 7875	Gen. Maung Aye	V-Chairman	C-in-C (Army)	DSA-1
3	BC 8468	Lt. Gen. Khin Nyunt	Secretary-1	DDSI/OSS	OTS-25
4	BC 8182	Lt. Gen Tin Oo	Secretary-2	Chief of Staff/ BSO	OTS-22
5	BC 8809	Lt. Gen. Win Myint	Secretary-3	AG	OTS-28
6	BN 1087	V-Admiral Nyunt Thein	Member	C-in-C (Navy)	DSA-3
7	BAF 1334	Lt. Gen. Kyaw Than	Member	C-in-C (Air Force)	FOC-23
8	BC 9752	M.G Aung Htwe	Member	WC	OTS-29
9	BC 10310	M.G Ye Myint	Member	CC	OTS-31
10	BC 10320	M.G Khin Maung Than	Member	YC	OTS-31
11	BC 10194	M.G Kyaw Win	Member	NC	OTS-30
12	BC 11716	M.G Sit Maung	Member	CRC	DSA-12
13	BC 11252	M.G Thein Sein	Member	TRC	DSA-9
14	BC 10337	B.G Maung Bo	Member	EC	OTS-31
15	BC 11701	B.G Tin Aung Myint Oo	Member	NEC	DSA-12
16	BC 11509	B.G Myint Aung	Member	SEC	DSA-11
17	BC 11236	B.G Tin Aye	Member	SC	DSA-9
18	BC 11534	B.G Thura Shwe Man	Member	SWC	DSA-11
19	BC 11715	B.G Soe Win	Member	NWC	DSA-12

APPENDIX (4)

TABLE IV (i)
Tatmadaw Regional and Division Commanders
(September 1988–February 2008)

Intake	*No.*	*Intake*	*No.*	*Intake*	*No.*
OTS-25	1	OTS-43	4	OTS-54	1
OTS-26	1	DSA-14	2	DSA-20	9
OTS-28	2	DSA-15	7	OTS-56	2
OTS-29	5	OTS-47	1	DSA-21	3
OTS-30	7	Teza-1	1	Teza-7	2
OTS-31	3	DSA-16	8	OTS-60	1
DSA-7	3	OTS-49	4	OTS-61	4
OTS-32	2	Teza-2	2	DSA-22	11
DSA-8	2	OTS-51	1	DSA-23	5
DSA-9	4	Teza-3	1	OTS-63	3
DSA-10	5	DSA-17	9	Teza-9	4
DSA-11	7	DSA-18	9	DSA-24	1
DSA-12	7	DSA-19	9	OTS-64	1
DSA-13	8	Teza-5	2	TOTAL	**164**

There are two exceptions in this table. First is the appointment of BG Thein Zaw. He was appointed as the commander of MOC-16 for just one day to be entitled to become a brigadier general. The second is the appointment of BG Wai Lwin. The appointment of BG Wai Lwin as the commander of Naypyitaw Command in May 2006 is an exceptional case. For the first time since 1988, a deputy regional commander with no experience in the command of a LID or MOC was promoted to the rank of regional commander. Deputy regional commanders are usually considered as the end of their promotions for a command position and are not even likely to become a commander of the LID/MOC. However, there is a possibility of getting a promotion to higher ranks with no-command positions as demonstrated by LG Min Thein (Quartermaster General) and MG San Sint (Military Appointment General). To the best of my knowledge, only BG Myo Lwin, now the Myanmar ambassador in Seoul, was a deputy regional commander for a very brief period in the Western Command before he was promoted to the MOC commander. A few ROC commanders were also promoted to LID/MOC commanders, such as BG Phone Swe (now Deputy Minister for Home Affairs), BG Nyunt Hlaing (now Ambassador in Laos), and BG Soe Nwe (now Ambassador in Serbia and Montenegro). In a recent promotion order issued on 11 August 2006, three ROC Commanders were promoted to be LID Commanders. It is noteworthy that just before the military takeover of the state in 1988, LG Myo Nyunt was promoted from Deputy Commander to Commander of the Yangon Command. Generally, to become a regional commander one must have served as the commander of either LID or MOC. In the cases of MG Aye Kyaw and MG Ket Sein, before they became Commanders of Northeast Command and Southeast Command respectively, the former was first promoted to Commander of No. 66 LID from Deputy Commander of the Central Command (present day Southern Command) based in Taungoo, whereas the latter was promoted to Commander of No. 77 LID from Deputy Commander of Yangon Command. In the case of BG Chit Than, before he became Commander of Triangle Region Command, he was promoted to the Commander of a MOC from Director of Ordnance. This is unusual in the sense that a director rarely becomes a LID/MOC commander and then the regional commander except for VSG Maung Aye who was promoted in exactly the same pattern. BG Chit Than's case was considered exceptional as he belonged to the DSA-15 intake, which was looked after by VSG Maung Aye while he was an instructor at the Defence Services Academy (DSA). Foreign Minister MG Nyan Win, Minister for Electricity-2 Col. Zaw Min, Minister for Revenue MG Hla Tun, and MG San Sint belonged to this intake.

APPENDIX (5)

A Brief History of Regional Command Headquarters at (Maymyo/Mandalay) and (Mingalardon/Taungoo)

The history of the two regional command headquarters located at either Maymyo or Mandalay and at either Mingalardon or Taungoo is complex and confusing. In order to understand these commands, we need to look at Myanmar's pre-independence period. The reoccupation of Burma was carried out by the British 14th Army under the command of General William Slim. As troops were needed to operate on the Malay peninsula, the 14th Army was assigned the duty. The 12th Army commanded by Lieutenant General Stopford took over the command on 1 June 1945. The HQ-BURMA COMAND was formed on 1 January 1946 with Lieutenant General Stopford as commander, by transforming the British 12th Army. However, on 30 January, General Briggs was appointed as the General Officer Commanding (GOC) of the HQ-BURMA COMMAND. He served in this position until the HQ-BURMA COMMAND was abolished in late 1947. No. 64 Infantry Brigade (Maymyo), North Burma Area HQ (Mandalay), and South Burma Area HQ (Yangon) were under HQ-BURMA COMMAND.

In June 1945, the Supreme Allied Command South East Asia (SACSEA) appointed Major General Thomas as Inspector General (IG) of the British Burma Army. He remained in this position until the end of April 1947. Colonel Letya and Colonel Smith Dun served under him as Deputy Inspector Generals (DIGs). When the HQ-BURMA ARMY was opened on 1 May 1947, Major General Thomas became the General Officer Commanding (GOC). He was assisted by Brigadier Smith Dun as Vice-GOC. Colonel Letya was attached to the HQ-BURMA COMMAND. No. 1 Infantry Brigade (Meikhtila) and No. 2 Infantry Brigade (Mingalardon) were under the HQ-BURMA ARMY.

In August 1947, North Burma Area HQ and No. 64 Infantry Brigade were merged as North Burma Brigade Area HQ in Maymyo, later renamed North Burma Sub-District (NBSD). No. 1 Infantry Brigade was attached to NBSD although it remained directly under the HQ-BURMA ARMY. In December 1947, South Burma Area HQ and No. 2 Infantry Brigade were merged as South Burma Brigade Area HQ in Mingalardon, later renamed South Burma Sub-District (SBSD). Now the HQ-BURMA ARMY had NBSD and No. 1 Infantry Brigade.

Beginning from 1 November 1947, the commanding officers of Burma Rifles and Burma Regiments were replaced with Myanmar citizens. Colonel Ne Win and Colonel Saw Kyar Doe were promoted to brigadier general and appointed as the commanders of NBSD and SBSD respectively on 22 December 1947. In fact, Colonel Ne Win was posted to the NBSD as understudy commander on 8 October 1947. As a result, 8 October 1947 is regarded as the birthday of the NBSD, the day a Myanmar commander took charge of the command. In the case of the SBSD, 22 December 1947 is regarded as its birthday. However, on 18 May 1950, NBSD and SBSD were reorganized and renamed the "Northern Command HQ" and the "Southern Command HQ", although their Myanmar names remained unchanged as "Myauk Paing Taing" and "Taung Paing Taing".

On 24 June 1957, the Northern Command was moved from Maymyo to Mandalay. On 1 October 1961, when the brigades were reorganized into regional command HQs, the Northern Command (NC) and the Southern Command (SC) were transformed to North West Command (NWC) and Central Command (CC) respectively. Again in 1972, when new regional commands were opened and a new command structure was introduced, the NWC was reorganized on 8 August 1972. This date is regarded as its birthday. The SC was reorganized and moved from Mingalardon to Taungoo on 18 September 1972. On the same day, the "Bago Yoma Special Operation Command HQ (Pa-Hta-Kha)" was established, on an ad hoc basis, at the Central Command HQ to oversee the "Operation Aung Soe Moe". Although the commander of the Pa-Hta-Kha was the commander of the Central Command, some staff positions were created to assist the operation. The GSO-2 of the Pa-Hta-Kha was Major Khin Nyunt, later the Secretary-1 of the State Peace and Development Council. Then on 16 March 1990, the North West Command in Mandalay was renamed the Central Command and the Central Command in Taungoo was renamed the Southern Command. The commanders who served in the two command headquarters are shown in Tables V(i) and V(ii).

TABLE V (i)
The NBSD/ NC/NWC/CC Headquarters

No.	*Serial*	*Name*	*From*	*To*
1	BC 3502	Brigadier General Ne Win	20-12-47	01-08-48
2	BC 5181	Brigadier General Lazun Tan	01-08-48	04-11-48
3	BC 3504	Brigadier General Kyaw Zaw	04-11-48	05-02-49
4	BC 3501	Colonel Letya	05-02-49	17-02-49
5	BC 3507	Lt. Colonel Maung Maung	17-02-49	20-02-49
6	BC 3722	Lt. Colonel Maung Kyin	21-02-49	13-08-49
7	BC 3582	Lt. Colonel Thein Maung	13-08-49	30-08-49
8	BC 5109	Brigadier General Blake	30-08-49	07-07-53
9	BC 3504	Brigadier General Kyaw Zaw	07-07-53	13-02-57
10	BC 3505	Brigadier General Aung Shwe	13-02-57	25-05-59
11	BC 3569	Brigadier General San Yu	25-02-59	16-10-61
12	BC 3575	Colonel Maung Shwe	16-10-61	29-11-61
13	BC 3569	Brigadier General San Yu	29-11-61	15-02-63
14	BC 3610	Colonel Lun Tin	15-02-63	21-05-65
15	BC 3576	Colonel Sein Mya	21-05-65	02-07-69
16	BC 5444	Colonel Sein Lwin	03-07-69	08-03-74
17	BC 6133	Colonel Aye Ko	08-03-74	18-03-75
18	BC 5497	Brigadier General Hla Tun	18-03-75	21-07-77
19	BC 5934	Brigadier General Aung Khin	21-07-77	04-05-79
20	BC 6356	Brigadier General Than Nyunt	04-05-79	04-11-85
21	BC 7864	Major General Tun Kyi	05-11-85	23-10-92
22	BC 8458	Major General Kyaw Than	23-10-92	18-06-95
23	BC 10310	Major General Ye Myint	18-06-95	11-12-01
24	BC 12607	Major General Ye Myint	11-12-01	28-05-05
25	BC 13242	Major General Khin Zaw	28-05-05	18-11-07
26	BC 16485	Brigadier General Tin Ngwe	18-11-07	

TABLE V (ii)
The SBSD/SC/CC/SC Headquarters

No.	*Serial*	*Name*	*From*	*To*
1	BC 5107	Brigadier General Saw Kya Doe	22-12-47	13-04-48
2	BC 5015	Brigadier General Aung Thin	14-04-48	05-02-49
3	BC 3504	Brigadier General Kyaw Zaw	05-02-49	07-07-53
4	BC 5109	Brigadier General Blake	07-07-53	25-02-59
5	BC 3505	Brigadier General Aung Shwe	25-02-59	15-02-61
6	BC 3525	Brigadier General Sein Win	15-05-61	11-10-61
7	BC 3523	Colonel Thaung Kyi	11-10-61	29-11-61
8	BC 3525	Brigadier General Sein Win	29-11-61	19-09-64
9	BC 3651	Brigadier General Tin Oo	19-11-64	20-04-72
10	BC 5605	Colonel Khin Ohn	29-04-72	08-03-74
11	BC 5581	Colonel Myo Aung	08-03-74	20-05-74
12	BC 5603	Colonel Than Tin	20-05-74	18-03-75
13	BC 6220	Colonel Yan Naung Soe	18-03-75	30-09-77
14	BC 6138	Colonel Wan Tin	30-09-77	23-03-79
15	BC 5841	Brigadier General Taung Zar Khaing	23-03-79	22-07-83
16	BC 6662	Brigadier General Phone Myint	22-07-83	04-11-85
17	BC 7034	Major General Aye Thaung	05-11-85	09-10-92
18	BC 8642	Major General Soe Myint	09-10-92	18-06-95
19	BC 10593	Major General Kyi Aung	18-06-95	16-11-97
20	BC 11236	Major General Tin Aye	16-11-97	21-12-01
21	BC 12008	Major General Aung Min	21-12-01	11-02-03
22	BC 14235	Major General Ko Ko	11-02-03	

APPENDIX (6)

TABLE VI (i)
Chiefs of Staff (or) Commanders-in-Chief of the Defence Services

No.	*Serial*	*Name*	*From*	*To*
1	BC 5106	Lt. General Smith Dun	04-01-48	31-01-49
2	BC 3502	General Ne Win	01-02-49	20-04-72
3	BC 3569	General San Yu	20-04-72	01-03-74
4	BC 3651	General Thura Tin Oo	01-03-74	06-03-76
5	BC 5331	General Thura Kyaw Htin	06-03-76	03-11-85
6	BC 6187	Senior General Saw Maung	04-11-85	22-04-92
7	BC 6710	Senior General Than Shwe	22-04-92	—

TABLE VI (ii)
Regional Commands and Infantry Division, 1958

Name	*Location*	*Year*	*Remark*
North Burma Sub-District	Maymyo	1946	Nothern Command
South Burma Sub-District	Mingaladon	1946	Southern Command
No. (1) Infantry Division	Meiktila	1958	
Naypyidaw Command Hqs	Yangon	1958	Within the War Office

TABLE VI (iii)
Infantry Brigades, 1958

Brigade	*Location*	*Year*	*Remark*
No. (1) Infantry Brigade	Sagaing/Meiktila	1947	
No. (2) Infantry Brigade	Taungoo	1950	
No. (3) Infantry Brigade	Bago/Ba An	1950	
No. (4) Infantry Brigade	Keng Taung/Taungyi	1950	
No. (5) Infantry Brigade	Mawlamyaing	1951	
No. (6) Infantry Brigade	Mandalay/Lashio	1951	
No. (7) Infantry Brigade	Myitkyina	1952	Remained until 1972
No. (8) Infantry Brigade	Pathein	1952	
No. (9) Infantry Brigade	Loilin/Keng Tung	1953	
No. (10) Infantry Brigade	Chauk	1954	
No. (11) Infantry Brigade	Mandalay/ Nyaung Laybin	1954	Later moved to Ba-An
No. (12) Infantry Brigade	Maubin	1957	
No. (13) Infantry Brigade	Pyay	1957	

APPENDIX (7)

Commanders of the Tatmadaw

TABLE VII (i)
Ministry of Defence (September 1988)

No.	*Name*	*Command*	*School*
1	Gen. Saw Maung	C-in-C Armed Forces	OTS-6
2	Lt. Gen. Than Shwe	C-in-C (Army)	OTS-9
3	R-A Maung Maung Khin	C-in-C (Navy)	
4	Maj. Gen Tin Tun	C-in-C (Air Force)	
5	Brig. Gen. Aung Ye Kyaw	Adjutant General	OTS-6
6	Maj. Gen. Phone Myint	Quartermaster General	OTS-9
7	Maj. Gen. Sein Aung	Bureau of Special Operation-1	OTS-10
8	Maj. Gen. Chit Swe	Bureau of Special Operation-2	OTS-8

TABLE VII (ii)
Regional and Division Commanders (September 1988)

No.	*Name*	*Command Position*	*Intake*
1	Brig. Gen. Mya Thin	Western Command	OTS-9
2	Brig. Gen. Myint Aung	South West Command	OTS-12
3	Brig. Gen. Aye Thaung	Central Command	OTS-13
4	Col. Kyaw Min	LID-55	OTS-14
5	Brig. Gen. Myo Nyunt	Yangon Command	OTS-18
6	Col. Maung Thint	North East Command	OTS-18
7	Brig. Gen. Nyan Lin	South East Command	DSA-1
8	Brig. Gen. Tun Kyi	North West Command	DSA-1
9	Col. Tin Aye	LID-44	DSA-1
10	Brig. Gen. Maung Aye	Eastern Command	DSA-1
11	Col. Win Zaw Nyunt	LID-99	DSA-1
12	Brig. Gen. Kyaw Ba	Northern Command	OTS-21
13	Col. Tin Oo	LID-66	OTS-21
14	Col. Hla Shwe	LID-33	OTS-22
15	Col. Soe Myint	LID-77	OTS-26
16	Col. Thein Han	LID-88	OTS-27
17	Col. Tin Hla	LID-22	DSA-3

TABLE VII (iii)
Ministry of Defence (February 2002)

No.	*Name*	*Command*	*School*
1	Sr. Gen. Than Shwe	C-in-C Armed Forces	OTS-9
2	Gen. Maung Aye	C-in-C (Army)	DSA-1
3	Lt. Gen. Khin Nyunt	Chief of Defence Services Intelligence	OTS-25
4	Maj. Gen. Thura Shwe Man	Joint Chief of Staff (Army/Navy/Air Force)	DSA-11
5	Vice Admiral Kyi Min	C-in-C (Navy)	DSA-6
6	Maj. Gen. Myint Swe	C-in-C (Air Force)	DSA-11
5	Maj. Gen. Soe Win	Air Defence Bureau	OTS-12
6	Maj. Gen. Aung Htwe	Bureau of Special Operation 1	OTS-29
7	Maj. Gen. Ye Myint	Bureau of Special Operation 2	OTS-31
8	Maj. Gen. Khin Maung Than	Bureau of Special Operation 3	OTS-31
9	Maj. Gen. Maung Bo	Bureau of Special Operation 4	OTS-31
10	Maj. Gen. Thein Sein	Adjutant General	DSA-9
11	Maj. Gen. Tin Aung Myint Oo	Quartermaster General	DSA-12
12	Maj. Gen. Kyaw Win	Chief of Armed Forces Training	OTS-30
13	Maj. Gen. Tin Aye	Chief of Ordnance Production	DSA-9
14	Maj. Gen. Tin Ngwe	Military Appointment General	OTS-32
15	Maj. Gen. Lun Maung	Inspector General	DSA-12
16	Maj. Gen. Thein Soe	Judge Advocate General	DSA-16

TABLE VII (iv)
Regional Commanders (February 2002)

No.	*Command*	*Name*	*Intake*
1	Central Command	Brig. Gen. Ye Myint	DSA-15
2	Northern Command	Brig. Gen. Maung Maung Swe	OTS-47
3	North East Command	Brig. Gen. Myint Hlaing	DSA-17
4	Eastern Command	Brig. Gen. Khin Maung Myint	OTS-49
5	South East Command	Brig. Gen. Thura Myint Aung	DSA-18
6	Southern Command	Brig. Gen. Aung Min	DSA-13
7	South West Command	Brig. Gen. Htay Oo	OTS-43
8	Western Command	Brig. Gen. Maung Oo	DSA-13
9	North West Command	Brig. Gen. Soe Naing	DSA-17
10	Triangle Region Command	Brig. Gen. Chit Than	DSA-15
11	Coastal Region Command	Maj. Gen. Aye Kyae	OTS-43
12	Yangon Command	Brig. Gen. Myint Swe	DSA-15

TABLE VII (v)
LID/MOC/ROC Commanders (February 2002)

No.	*Post*	*Name*	*Intake*
1	LID-11	Col. Ko Ko	DSA-19
2	LID-22	Col. Ngwe Thein	DSA-18
3	LID-33	Col. Tin Tun Aung	DSA-19
4	LID-44	Col. Min Aung Hlaing	DSA-19
5	LID-55	Brig. Gen. Sein Lin	DSA-14
6	LID-66	Col. Aung Tun	DSA-16
7	LID-77	Col. Than Htay	DSA-18
8	LID-88	Col. Ohn Myint	DSA-17
9	LID-99	Col. Aung Khin Soe	DSA-19
10	LID-101	Col. Khin Maung Tun	DSA-16
11	MOC-1	Brig. Gen. Soe Htay	DSA-13
12	MOC-2	Brig. Gen. Thein Lwin	OTS-43
13	MOC-3	Col. Min thein	DSA-17
14	MOC-4	Brig. Gen. Saw Hla Min	DSA-15
15	MOC-5	Brig. Gen. Kyi Thein	DSA-13
16	MOC-6	Col. Soe Maung	DSA-17
17	MOC-7	Brig. Gen. Thura Sein Thaung	OTS-49
18	MOC-8	Col. Htein Win	DSA-16
19	MOC-9	Brig. Gen. Hla Myint	DSA-13
20	MOC-10	Col. Mya Win	DSA-16
21	MOC-12	Brig. Gen. Khin Maung Soe	DSA-15
22	MOC-13	Col. Thein Htike	DSA-16
23	MOC-14	Brig. Gen. Tun Tun	DSA-16
24	MOC-15	Col. Tin Naing Thein	DSA-17
25	MOC-16	Col. Soe Oo	DSA-19
26	MOC-17	Col. Thar Aye	DSA-16
27	MOC-18	Brig. Gen. Than Aung	DSA-11
28	MOC-19	Col. Ye Win	OTS-49
29	MOC-20	Col. Khin Zaw Win	OTS-51
30	MOC-21	Col. Khin Yi	DSA-17
31	ROC (Tanaing)	Brig. Gen. Kyaw Oo Lwin	Teza-3
32	ROC (Sittwe)	Brig. Gen. Phone Swe	DSA-18
33	ROC (Pyay)	Col. Soe Nwe	DSA-19
34	ROC (Loikaw)	Brig. Gen. Nyunt Hlaing	Teza-2
35	ROC (Kalay)	Brig. Gen. Khin Maung Aye	Teza-1
36	ROC (Laukai)	Brig. Gen. Zaw Win	DSA-17
DSA (29)		OTS (4)	Teza (3)

TABLE VII (vi)
Ministry of Defence (February 2008)

No.	*Name*	*Command*	*School*
1	Sr. Gen. Than Shwe	C-in-C Armed Forces	OTS-9
2	Vice Sr. Gen. Maung Aye	C-in-C (Army)	DSA-1
3	Gen. Thura Shwe Man	Joint Chief of Staff (Army/Navy/Air Force)	DSA-11
4	Vice Admiral Soe Thein	C-in-C (Navy)	DSA-11
5	Lt. Gen. Myat Hein	C-in-C (Air Force)	DSA-17
6	Lt. Gen. Myint Hlaing	Air Defence Bureau	DSA-17
7	Lt. Gen. Ye Myint	Military Affairs Security	DSA-15
8	Lt. Gen. Maung Bo	Inspector and Controller General	OTS-31
9	Lt. Gen. Ye Myint	Bureau of Special Operation-1	OTS-31
10	Lt. Gen. Kyaw Win	Bureau of Special Operation-2	OTS-30
11	Lt. Gen. Khin Maung Than	Bureau of Special Operation-3	OTS-31
12	Maj. Gen. Thar Aye	Bureau of Special Operation-4	DSA-16
13	Lt. Gen. Myint Swe	Bureau of Special Operation-5	DSA-15
14	Maj. Gen. Khin Zaw	Bureau of Special Operation-6	OTS-49
15	Maj. Gen. Thura Myint Aung	Adjutant General	DSA-18
16	Lt. Gen. Tin Aung Myint Oo	Quartermaster General	DSA-12
17	Lt. Gen. Aung Htwe	Chief of Armed Forces Training	OTS-29
18	Lt. Gen. Tin Aye	Chief of Ordnance Production	DSA-9
19	Maj. Gen. San Sint	Military Appointment General	DSA-15
20	Maj. Gen. Thein Hteik	Inspector General	DSA-16
21	Maj. Gen. Soe Maung	Judge Advocate General	DSA-17

DSA (14) OTS (7)

TABLE VII (vii)
Regional Commanders (February 2008)

No.	*Post*	*Name*	*Intake*
1	Northern Command	Maj. Gen. Ohn Myint	DSA-17
2	North East Command	Maj. Gen. Aung Than Htut	DSA-20
3	Eastern Command	Maj. Gen. Thaung Aye	DSA-20
4	Triangle Region Command	Maj. Gen. Min Aung Hlaing	DSA-19
5	South East Command	Maj. Gen. Thet Naing Win	OTS-56
6	Southern Command	Maj. Gen. Ko Ko	DSA-19
7	Central Command	Brig. Gen. Tin Ngwe	DSA-22
8	Coastal Region Command	Maj. Gen. Khin Zaw Oo	OTS-56
9	South West Command	Brig. Gen. Kyaw Swe	DSA-22
10	Western Command	Maj. Gen. Maung Shein	DSA-20
11	North West Command	Brig. Gen. Myint Soe	OTS-61
12	Yangon Command	Maj. Gen. Hla Htay Win	DSA-20
13	Natpyitaw Command	Maj. Gen. Wai Lwin	DSA-18

DSA (10) OTS (3)

TABLE VII (viii)
LID/MOC/ROC Commanders (February 2008)

No.	*Post*	*Name*	*Intake*
1	LID-11	Brig. Gen. Hla Min	DSA-22
2	LID-22	Brig. Gen. Tun Nay Lin	OTS-61
3	LID-33		
4	LID-44	Brig. Gen. Hla Myint Shwe	DSA-22
5	LID-55	Brig. Gen. Aye Khine	OTS-63
6	LID-66	Brig. Gen. Maung Maung Aye	OTS-64
7	LID-77	Brig. Gen. Win Myint	DSA-20
8	LID-88		
9	LID-99	Brig. Gen. Khin Maung Htay	OTS-63
10	LID-101	Brig. Gen. Maung Maung Ohn	DSA-22
11	MOC-1	Brig. Gen. San Myint Oo	DSA-21
12	MOC-2	Brig. Gen. San Oo	DSA-24
13	MOC-3	Brig. Gen. Myint Hein	DSA-17
14	MOC-4	Brig. Gen. Myint Naung	Teza-7
15	MOC-5	Brig. Gen. Kaung Myat	DSA-23
16	MOC-6		
17	MOC-7	Brig. Gen. Myo Aye	DSA-22
18	MOC-8	Brig. Gen. Than Soe	DSA-23
19	MOC-9	Brig. Gen. Ye Aung	DSA-23
20	MOC-10	Brig. Gen. Ko Ko Lat	Teza-9
21	MOC-12	Brig. Gen. Ne Lin	Teza-7
22	MOC-13	Col. Min Thein Zan	DSA-23
23	MOC-14	Brig. Gen. Tin Yu	DSA-21
24	MOC-15	Brig. Gen. Aung Naing	DSA-21
25	MOC-16	Brig. Gen. Thet Oo	Teza-5
26	MOC-17	Brig. Gen. Tin Maung Win	OTS-61
27	MOC-18	Brig. Gen. Kyaw Soe Win	Teza-9
28	MOC-19	Brig. Gen. Cho Tun Aung	Teza-5
29	MOC-20	Brig. Gen. Zaw Thin Myint	OTS-61
30	MOC-21	Brig. Gen. Soe Win	DSA-23
31	ROC (Tanaing)	Brig. Gen. Khin Maung Aye	Teza-1
32	ROC (Sittwe)	Brig. Gen. Than Tun Aung	DSA-18
33	ROC (Pyay)	Brig. Gen. Sein Myint	Teza-9
34	ROC (Loikaw)	Brig. Gen. Nyunt Tin	OTS-63
35	ROC (Kalay)	Brig. Gen. Kyaw Oo Lwin	Teza-3
36	ROC (Laukai)	Brig. Gen. Win Maung	Teza-9
DSA (16)		OTS (7)	Teza (10)

APPENDIX (8)

TABLE VIII (i)
Officers Commissioned Through Training Schools
(September 1988 – December 1999)

No.	*Intake*	*D/C*	*Army*	*Navy*	*Air Force*	*Total*	*Remark*
1	OTS-76	30-09-88	84	—	—	84	
2	OTS-77	23-06-89	108	10	2	120	
3	OTS-78	24-11-89	111	—	—	111	
4	OTS-79	22-06-90	208	1	1	210	
5	OTS-80	24-08-90	167	—	—	167	
6	OTS-81	21-06-91	176	8	5	189	
7	OTS-82	09-08-91	162	7	—	169	
8	OTS-83	19-06-92	186	2	1	189	
9	OTS-84	24-07-92	245	9	3	257	
10	OTS-85	11-06-93	349	22	16	387	
11	OTS-86	02-07-93	230	—	—	230	
12	OTS-87	06-08-93	229	—	—	229	
13	OTS-88	17-06-94	162	25	10	197	
14	OTS-89	05-08-94	169	34	2	205	
15	OTS-90	09-09-94	201	—	1	202	
16	OTS-91	23-06-95	196	—	18	214	
17	OTS-92	28-07-95	187	21	—	208	
18	OTS-93	25-08-95	227	—	—	227	
19	OTS-94	26-07-96	375	—	1	376	
20	OTS-95	23-08-96	189	20	—	209	

continued on next page

TABLE VIII (i) — *cont'd*

No.	*Intake*	*D/C*	*Army*	*Navy*	*Air Force*	*Total*	*Remark*
21	OTS-96	02-05-97	67	3	12	82	
22	OTS-97	11-07-97	474	—	—	474	
23	OTS-98	15-08-97	224	12	—	236	
24	OTS-99	15-05-98	368	—	1	369	
25	OTS-100	03-07-98	185	7	—	192	
26	OTS-101	14-05-99	207	8	—	215	
27	OTS-102	24-12-99	158	7	1	166	
28	DSA-30	07-04-89	93	25	9	127	
29	DSA-31	06-04-90	91	20	9	120	
30	DSA-32	05-04-91	70	22	11	103	
31	DSA-33	03-04-92	55	21	7	83	
32	DSA-34	09-04-93	115	23	24	162	
33	DSA-35	08-04-94	85	29	16	130	
34	DSA-36	07-04-95	92	25	18	135	
35	DSA-37	05-04-96	183	25	21	229	
36	DSA-38	11-04-97	171	34	22	227	
37	DSA-39	10-04-98	177	30	—	207	
38	DSA-40	07-04-99	212	25	—	237	
39	Teza-15	23-09-88	177	—	—	177	
40	Teza-16	20-10-89	134	—	—	134	
41	Teza-17	26-10-90	109	—	—	109	
42	Teza-18	11-10-91	111	—	—	111	
43	Teza-19	23-10-92	162	—	—	162	
44	Teza-20	20-09-93	132	—	11	143	
45	Teza-21	12-09-94	191	—	—	191	
46	Teza-22	20-10-95	250	—	11	261	
47	Teza-23	11-10-96	216	—	—	216	
48	Teza-24	15-09-97	235	—	—	235	
49	Teza-25	30-10-98	240	—	—	240	
50	Teza-26	10-09-99	268	—	—	268	
51	DSIT-1	11-04-99	71	7	6	84	
52	DSIM-1	17-12-99	47	—	—	47	
	TOTAL		9,331	482	239	10,052	

Source: Myanmar Gazette.

APPENDIX (9)

Tatmadaw's Commercial Enterprises

TABLE IX (i)
(9.A) UMEHL Fully Owned Firms in 2007

Sr.	*Name of the Firm*	*Y/E*	*Line of Business/ Product*
1	Myanmar Ruby Enterprise	1996	Gems, Jewellery
2	Myanmar Imperial Jade Co. Ltd.	1996	Gems, Jewellery
3	Myanmar Rubberwood Co. Ltd.	1997	Rubberwood
4	Myanmar Pineapple Juice Enterprise	1998	Pineapple Juice Concentrate
5	Myawaddy Drinking Water	2000	Drinking Water
6	Sinmin (1/2) Cement Factory	2003	Cement
7	Ngwe Pinle Livestock and Fisheries Co. Ltd.	2001	Marine Products
8	Granite Decorative Tiles Factory	2002	Granite Tiles
9	Badonma Soap Factory	2002	Laundry/Toilet Soaps
10	Myawaddy Trading	1998	Trading
11	Myawaddy Bank Ltd.	1993	Banking
12	Bandoola Transportation	1999	Transportation
13	Myawaddy Travel and Tours	1995	Travel and Tours
14	Nawaday Hotel and Travel Ltd.	1995	Hotels
15	Myawaddy Agriculture Services Co. Ltd.	2000	Agriculture Machinery
16	Kan Bauk Palm Oil Firm	2003	Agriculture
17	Kan Bauk Palm Oil Factory	2006	Manufacturing

continued on next page

TABLE IX (i)
UMEHL Fully Owned Firms in 2007

Sr.	*Name of the Firm*	*Y/E*	*Line of Business/ Product*
18	Okkan Sugar Factory	2004	Sugar
19	Okkan Sugarcane Firm	2006	Agriculture
20	Inngakhwa Sugar Factory	2005	Sugar
21	Shar Pyin Sugarcane Firm	2006	Agriculture
22	Berger Paint Manufacturing Co. Ltd.	1997	Paint (former subsidiary)
23	Sulphuric Acid Factory	2006	Industrial Raw Material
24	Plastic Ware Factory	2007	Plastic Ware
25	Tawwin Woven PVC Bag Factory	2007	PVC Bags
26	Tatmadaw Welfare Shop Enterprise	2004	Service
27	Export Sesame Production Enterprise	2006	Export
28	Shweli Department Store	2004	Service and Trading
29	Myawaddy Trading (FE)	2001	Foreign Exchange
30	Myanma Land and Development	2005	Construction
31	Attaran Hotel Rental Service	2004	Rental Service
32	Thanintharyi Guest House Rental Service	2005	Rental Service
33	Thanintharyi Bird Nest Enterprises	2005	Production
34	X-Ray Scanning Equipment Service	2005	Service
35	Land and Building Rental Service for ILBC	2005	Rental Service

Source: UMEHL reports.

TABLE IX (ii)
UMEHL fully owned firms liquidated

Sr.	*Name*	*Y/E*	*Y/L*	*Remark*
1	Mongshu Gem Enterprise	1994	1999	Merged with Myanmar Ruby Enterprise
2	PVC Pipe Enterprise	1995	1997	Merged with Imperial Jade
3	Pyinlone Gem Enterprise	1996	1999	Merged with Myanmar Ruby Enterprise
4	Myawaddy Ice Block Factory	2000	2002	Merged with Ngwe Pinle Co. Ltd.
5	Myanmar Arh Construction	2001	2005	Construction
6	Tailor Shops Enterprise	2001	2005	Garment

Source: UMEHL reports.

TABLE IX (iii)
Subsidiary Firms of the UMEHL in 2007

Sr.	Name of the Firm	Y/E	Business	UMEHL Percentage	UMEHL Capital
1	Myanmar Segye International Ltd.	1990	Garment	40%	US$0.50
2	Myanmar Daewoo International Ltd.	1990	Garment	45%	US$0.56
3	Rothmans of Pall Mall Myanmar Pte. Ltd.	1993	Cigarette	40%	US$0.59 K 11.78
4	Myanmar Brewery Ltd	1996	Beer	45%	US$3.55
5	Myanmar Posco Steel Co. Ltd.	1997	GI Sheet	30%	US$0.96
6	Myanmar Nouveau Steel Co. Ltd.	1995	GI Sheet	35%	US$1.87
7	The First Automotive Co. Ltd.	1997	Automobile	40%	US$0.41 K 407.25
8	Hanthawaddy Golf Course and City Club	1995	Services	50%	US$8.00
9	National Development Corporation	1998	Real Estate	50%	K 50.00

Source: UMEHL reports.

TABLE IX (iv)
UMEHL subsidiary firms liquidated

Sr.	*Name*	*Y/E*	*Y/L*	*Remark*
1	Myanmar Leading Logistics Ltd.	1990	2002	
2	Myanmar Electronic System	1992	1997	
3	Ban Hock Hin Myanmar Ltd.	1992	2002	
4	Myanmar Unimax International Ltd.	1993	2002	
5	Myanmar-Macao Hotel and Tour	1995	2001	Renamed Nawaday
6	Myanmar Fair Price	1995	2001	
7	MG Ruby Co. Ltd.	1996	2001	
8	Myanmar Jade International Ltd.	1996	2002	
9	Myanmar Ayer Co. Ltd.	1996	1997	Road Construction
10	Mogoke Motel Enterprise	1996	2002	Merged with Nawaday
11	Myanmar Nouveau Co. Ltd.	1996	2003	Jewellery
12	Myanmar Cement Co. Ltd.	1996	2002	
13	Myanmar Land and Development Co. Ltd.	1997	2002	Construction
14	Myram Co. Ltd.	1997	1998	Renamed Yadana Kadekada
15	Yadana Kadekada Co. Ltd.	1998	2001	
16	Siemens Ltd. (Myanmar)	1991	2005	Electronic

Source: UMEHL reports.

TABLE IX (v)
Affiliated Firms of the UMEHL in 2007

Sr.	*Name of the Firm*	*Y/E*	*Line of Business*	*UMEHL Interest*
1	Mercury Manufacturing Co. Ltd.	1999	Plastic Wares	Land Use Premium
2	Myanmar Mamee Double Decker Ltd.	1999	Instant Noodle	Land Use Premium and 2% from Net Profit
3	Myanmar Samgong Industrial Co. Ltd.	1997	Inflatable Rubber Boats	Land Use Premium and 4% commission fees from Sales
4	Myanmar Tokiwa Corporation	1998	Pencil/Cosmetics	Land Use Premium
5	Diamond Dragon Co. Ltd.	1996	Trading	Land Use Premium
6	Myanmar Hotel & Cruises	1995	Hotel & Tourism	5% from Net Profit as Commission fees
7	Dragon State Ltd.		Garment	Land Use Premium

Source: UMEHL reports.

TABLE IX (vi)
UMEHL affiliated firms liquidated

Sr.	*Name*	*Year of Establishment*	*Year of Liquidation*	*Remark*
1	I & E Trading Pte. Ltd.	1995	1997	
2	Myanmar Triumph International Ltd.	1996	2002	Garment
3	Myanmar Kurosawa Trust Co. Ltd.	1998	2005	Jewellery
4	Myanmar Hwa Fuh International Ltd.	1995	2005	Garment

Source: UMEHL reports.

BIBLIOGRAPHY

Books and Monographs

တပ်မတော်သားသုတေသီတစ်ဦး။ *၁၉၄၈ခုနှစ်မှ ၁၉၈၈ခုနှစ်ကာလအတွင်း ဖြစ်သန်းလာသော မြန်မာ့သမိုင်း အကျဉ်းနှင့် တပ်မတော်ကဏ္ဍ* ၂တွဲ (ရန်ကုန်၊ သတင်းနှင့်စာနယ်ဇင်းလုပ်ငန်း၊ ၁၉၉၀) (A Tatmadaw Researcher. *A Brief History of Myanmar in the Period between 1948 and 1988 and The Role of the Tatmadaw*, two volumes. Yangon: News and Periodical Enterprise, 1990).

ဘဆွေ၊ ရန်ကုန်။ *ရဲဘော်တို့နှင့်အတူ* (ရန်ကုန်၊ တင်းကုတ်စာပေ၊ ၁၉၆၃) (Ba Swe. *Together with the Comrades*. Yangon: Tin Goak Sarpay, 1963).

မြန်မာ့ဆိုရှယ်လစ်လမ်းစဉ်ပါတီ ဗဟိုကော်မတီ။ *တပ်မတော်ပါတီစည်းရုံးရေးကော်မတီ၏ ဖွဲ့စည်းမှုနှင့်တာဝန်များ* (ရန်ကုန်၊ မြန်မာ့ဆိုရှယ်လစ်လမ်းစဉ်ပါတီ ပုံနှိပ်တိုက်၊ ၁၉၈၅) (Central Committee of the Burma Socialist Programme Party. *Organization and Duties of the Party Organizations within the Tatmadaw*. Yangon: BSPP Press, 1985).

စစ်သမိုင်းပြတိုက်နှင့်တပ်မတော်မော်ကွန်းတိုက်မှူးရုံး။ *တပ်မတော်သမိုင်း*၊ ၈တွဲ (ရန်ကုန်၊ စစ်သမိုင်းပြတိုက်နှင့် တပ်မတော်မော်ကွန်းတိုက်မှူးရုံး၊ ၁၉၉၄၊ ၁၉၉၄၊ ၁၉၉၅၊ ၁၉၉၆၊ ၁၉၉၇၊ ၁၉၉၈၊ ၂၀၀၀၊ ၂၀၀၂) (Defence Services Museum and Historical Research Institute. *History of the Tatmadaw*, eight vols. Yangon: Defence Services Museum and Historical Research Institute, 1994, 1994, 1995, 1996, 1997, 1998, 2000, and 2002).

ကျော်ဟန်၊ ပီ။ *သူနှင့်ကျွန်တော်* (ရန်ကုန်၊ မြဝတီစာပေတိုက်၊ ၁၉၉၇) (Kyaw Han, P. *He and Me* (Yangon: Myawaddy Press, 1997).

ကျော်ဟန်၊ ပီ။ *ကျွန်တော်ချစ်သောတပ်မတော် ၁၉၅၀-၁၉၅၂* (ရန်ကုန်၊ မျိုးဆက်သစ်စာပေ၊ ၂၀၀၇) (Kyaw Han, P. *The Tatmadaw I loved, 1950–1952*. Yangon: Myosetthit Sarpay, 2007).

မောင်မောင်၊ ဒေါက်တာ။ *ဗိုလ်ချုပ်ကြီးနေဝင်းနှင့် မြန်မာ့နိုင်ငံရေးခရီးစဉ်* (ရန်ကုန်၊ ပုဂံစာအုပ်တိုက်၊ ၁၉၆၉) (Maung Maung, Dr. *General Ne Win and Myanmar's Political Journey*. Yangon: Bagan Publishing House, 1969).

မောင်မောင်၊ ဒေါက်တာ။ *သားမောင်စစ်သည်သို့* (ရန်ကုန်၊ ဝင်းမြင့်အောင်စာပေ၊ တကြိမ်၊ ၁၉၉၉) (Maung Maung, Dr. *To My Son, A Soldier*, 3rd printing. Yangon: Win Myint Aung Sarpay, 1999).

မိုမိုတာရောစန်။ *မုန်တိုင်းကိုမမှုအံတုလေသော်* (ရန်ကုန်၊ မြဝတီစာပေ၊ ၁၉၉၄) (Momotaro-San. *In Defiance of the Storm*. Yangon: Myawaddy Press, 1994).

မိုမိုတာရောစန်။ *ပန်းခင်းသာလမ်းမဟုတ်ပါ* (ရန်ကုန်၊ မြဝတီစာပေ၊ ၁၉၉၇) (Momotaro-San. *Not a Smooth Path*. Yangon: Myawaddy Press, 1997).

မိုမိုတာရောစန်။ *ကိုယ်နှင့်သက်ကိုနှင်းဆက်အပ်မည်* (ရန်ကုန်၊ တူဒေးစာအုပ်တိုက်၊ ၂၀၀၆) (Momotaro-San. *With Body and Soul for the Nation*. Yangon: Today Press, 2006).

မြဝင်း။ *တပ်မတော်ခေါင်းဆောင်များသမိုင်းအကျဉ်းချုပ်* (ရန်ကုန်၊ သတင်းနှင့်စာနယ်ဇင်းလုပ်ငန်း၊ ၁၉၉၁) (Mya Win. *A Brief History of Tatmadaw's Leaders*. Yangon: News and Periodical Enterprise, 1991).

မြဝင်း။ *တပ်မတော်၏အမျိုးသားနိုင်ငံရေးအစဉ်အလာ* (ရန်ကုန်၊ သတင်းနှင့်စာနယ်ဇင်းလုပ်ငန်း၊ ၁၉၉၂) (Mya Win. *Tatmadaw's Traditional Role in National Politics*. Yangon: News and Periodical Enterprise, 1992).

အုံးမြင့်၊ အထောက်တော်။ *ခက်ဖွယ်ရယ်ကြုံ လက်နက်ကယ်စုံအညီနဲ့* (ရန်ကုန်၊ အင်ကြင်းမြိုင်ပုံနှိပ်တိုက်၊ ဒုကြိမ်၊ ၁၉၉၀) (Ohn Myint, Ataucktaw. *In the Face of an Armed Rebellion*, 2nd printing. Yangon: Ingyin Myaing Press, 1990).

နောင်စစ်သည်။ *သေတစ်နေ့မွေးတစ်နေ့*၊ ၂တွဲ (ရန်ကုန်၊ ပန်းမျိုးတစ်ရာစာပေ၊ ၂၀၀၆) (Naung Sitthi. *Once to be Born and Dead*, two vols. Yangon: Panmyo Tayar Press, 2006).

စည်သူအောင်နှင့်မောင်မှတ်။ *ရွှေပြည်တော်မျှော်မဝေးပြီမို့* (ရန်ကုန်၊ သတင်းနှင့်စာနယ်ဇင်းလုပ်ငန်း၊ ၁၉၉၅) (Sithu Aung and Maung Hmat. *No Longer a Distance to the Golden Land*. Yangon: News and Periodical Enterprise, 1995).

သောင်းထိုက် (ငြိမ်း)၊ ဒုဗိုလ်မှူးကြီး။ *ဂျပန်ခေတ်စစ်တက္ကသိုလ်နှင့်ဗြိတိသျှဆင်းဟတ်စစ်တက္ကသိုလ်* (ရန်ကုန်၊ ဘဝတက္ကသိုလ်စာပေ၊ ၁၉၈၅) (Thaung Htike (retired), Lieutenant Colonel. *At the Military Academy of the Japanese Occupation Period and the Britain's Sandhurst Academy*. Yangon: Bawa Thetkatho Sarpay, 1985).

သောင်းထိုက် (ငြိမ်း)၊ ဒုဗိုလ်မှူးကြီး။ *ဖို့ဒ်လီဗင်ဝပ် အမေရိကန်စစ်ဦးစီးတက္ကသိုလ်* (ရန်ကုန်၊ ဘဝတက္ကသိုလ် စာပေ၊ ၁၉၈၇) (Thaung Htike (retired), Lieutenant Colonel. *The American Staff College at Fort Leavenworth*. Yangon: Bawa Thetkatho Sarpay, 1987).

တင်မောင်၊ ဗိုလ်မှူးကြီးဟောင်း။ *တိုင်းပြည်ကနန မုန်တိုင်းကထန်ထန်* (ရန်ကုန်၊ စာပေလောက စာအုပ်တိုက်၊ ပဉ္စမအကြိမ်၊ ၁၉၉၉) (Tin Maung, Ex-Colonel. *Feeble Nation: Severe Storm*, 5th printing. Yangon: Sarpay Lawka, 1999).

တင်မောင်၊ ဗိုလ်မှူးကြီးဟောင်း။ *မုန်တိုင်းလွန်သော်* (ရန်ကုန်၊ ချစ်မြိုင်စာပေ၊ ၁၉၇၄) (Tin Maung, Ex-Colonel. *When the Storm is Over*. Yangon: Chit Myaing Parpay, 1974).

မောင်ထူး၊ တပ်ကြပ်။ *အောင်ဆန်းသူရိယလှသောင်း* (ရန်ကုန်၊ အားမာန်သစ်စာပေ၊ ဒုကြိမ်၊ ၁၉၉၉) (Maung Htoo, Tatkyet. *Aung San Thuriya Hla Thaung*, 2nd printing. Yangon: Armanthit Sarpay, 1999).

U.S. Department of Defence. *Dictionary of Military Terms*. Pennsylvania: Stackpole Books, 1995.

Min Maung Maung. *The Tatmadaw and its Leadership Role in National Politics*. Yangon: News and Periodical Enterprises, 1993.

Hart, B.H. Liddell. *Strategy*, 2nd revised edition. New York: Meridian Printing, 1991.

Warden III, John A. *The Air Campaign: Planning for Combat*. New York: Pergamon-Brassey's, 1989.

Pape, Robert. *Bombing to Win: Air Power and Coercion in War*. Ithaca and London: Cornell University Press, 1996.

Till, Geoffrey. *Seapower: A Guide for the Twenty First Century*. London: Frank Cass, 2004.

Friedman, Norman. *Seapower as Strategy: Navies and National Interests*. Annapolis, Maryland: Naval Institute Press, 2001.

Ball, Desmond. *Burma's Military Secrets: Signals Intelligence (SIGINT) from 1941 to Cyber Warfare*. Bangkok: White Lotus, 1998.

Sein Win. *The Split Story*. Rangoon: The Guardian Press, 1959.

Selth, Andrew. *Burma's Secret Military Partners*. Canberra: Strategic and Defence Studies Centre, ANU, 2000.

———. *Transforming the Tatmadaw*. Canberra: Strategic and Defence Studies Centre, ANU, 1996.

———. *Burma's Armed Forces: Power Without Glory*. Norwalk: EastBridge, 2002.

Articles and Working Papers

Ashton, William. "Burma Receives Advances from its Silent Suitors in Singapore". In *Jane's Intelligence Review*, March 1998.

———. "Burma's Armed Forces: Preparing for the 21st Century". In *Jane's Intelligence Review*, November 1998.

———. "Burma's Chemical Weapons Status". In *Jane's Intelligence Review*, June 1995.

———. "Chinese Bases in Burma: Fact or Fiction?". In *Jane's Intelligence Review*, February 1995.

———. "Myanmar and Israel Develop Military Pact". In *Jane's Intelligence Review*, March 2000.

———. "Myanmar: Foreign Military Training a Mixed Blessing". In *Asia-Pacific Defence Reporter*, February–March 1998.

———. "Myanmar's Military Links with Pakistan". In *Jane's Intelligence Review*, June 2000.

———. "Myanmar's New MiG-29s a Threat to Regional Stability?". In *Asia-Pacific Defence Reporter*, February 2002.

———. "The Burmese Air Force". In *Jane's Intelligence Review*, October 1994.

———. "The Burmese Navy". In *Jane's Intelligence Review*, January 1994.

Ball, Desmond. "SIGINT Strengths Form a Vital Part of Burma's Military Muscle". In *Jane's Intelligence Review*, March 1998.

Brooke, Micool. "Myanmar's Security Challenges for the 21st Century". In *Asian Defence Journal*, July 2001.

Haseman, John B. "Myanmar Leaders Reorganise Military, Intelligence Structures". In *Jane's Intelligence Review*, March 2002.

Selth, Andrew (with Yeshua Moser-Puangsuwan). "Myanmar's Forgotten Minefields". In *Jane's Intelligence Review*, October 2000.

Selth, Andrew. "Burma Develops Its Ability to Build Arms". In *Jane's Intelligence Review*, May 1996.

———. "Landmines in Burma: The Military Dimension". In *Burma Debate*, vol. VII, no. 4, Winter 2000/2001.

———. *Assisting the Defence of Australia: Australian Defence Contacts with Burma, 1945–1987*. Canberra: Strategic and Defence Studies Centre, ANU, 1990.

———. "Australia Defence Contact with Burma". In *Modern Asian Studies*, vol. 26, no. 3, 1992.

———. "Australian Contacts with Colonial Myanmar". In *Myanmar Historical Research Journal*, vol. 6. Yangon: UHRC, December 2000.

———. *Australia's Relations with Colonial Burma, 1886–1947*. Melbourne: Centre of Southeast Asian Studies, Monash University, 1994.

———. "Burma and Exotic Weapons". In *Strategic Analysis*, vol. 19, no. 3, June 1996.

———. "Burma and the Strategic Competition between China and India". In *Burma/Myanmar in the Twenty-First Century: Dynamics of Continuity and Change*, edited by John J. Brandon. Bangkok: Thai Studies Section, Chulalongkorn University, 1997.

———. "Burma and the Strategic Competition between China and India". In *The Journal of Strategic Studies*, vol. 19, no. 2, June 1996.

———. *Burma and Weapon of Mass Destruction*. Canberra: Strategic and Defence Studies Centre, ANU, 1999.

———. "Burma's Armed Forces under Civilian Rule: A Return to the Past?". Technical Advisory Network of Burma, Working Paper 02/01, May 2001.

———. *Burma's Arms Procurement Programme*. Canberra: Strategic and Defence Studies Centre, ANU, 1995.

———. *Burma's Defence Expenditure and Arms Industries*. Canberra: Strategic and Defence Studies Centre, ANU, 1997.

———. "Burma's Expanding Armed Forces: National Defence or National Disgrace". In *Current Affairs Bulletin*, October/November 1996.

———. *Burma's Intelligence Apparatus*. Canberra: Strategic and Defence Studies Centre, ANU, 1997.

———. "Burma's Intelligence Apparatus". In *Burma Debate*, vol. 4, no. 4, September/October 1997.

———. "Burma's Intelligence Apparatus". In *Intelligence and National Security*, vol. 13, no. 4, Winter 1998.

———. "Burma's Military Expansion Program: Plans and Perception". In *Journal of Contemporary Asia*, vol. 26, no. 4, 1996.

———. *Burma's Order of Battle: An Interim Assessment*. Canberra: Strategic and Defence Studies Centre, ANU, 2000.

———. "Can Burma's Military Regime Survive?". In *Australian Quarterly*, vol. 68, no. 3, 1996.

———. "Landmines in Burma: Forgotten Weapons in a Forgotten War". In *Small Wars and Insurgencies*, vol. 12, no. 2, Summer 2001.

———. *Landmines in Burma: The Military Dimension*. Canberra: Strategic and Defence Studies Centre, ANU, 2000.

———. "The Armed Forces and Military Rule in Burma". In *Burma: Prospect for a Democratic Future*, edited by Robert I. Rotberg. Washington D.C.: Brooking Institution Press, 1998.

———. *The Burma Air Force*. Canberra: Strategic and Defence Studies Centre, ANU, 1997.

———. *The Burma Navy*. Canberra: Strategic and Defence Studies Centre, ANU, 1997.

———. "The Burma Navy Under the SLORC". In *Journal of Contemporary Asia*, vol. 29, no. 2, 1999.

———. *The Burmese Armed Forces Next Century: Continuity or Change?* Canberra: Strategic and Defence Studies Centre, ANU, 1999.

———. "The Burmese Army". In *Jane's Intelligence Review*, November 1995.

———. "The China-Burma-India Triangle". In *India Looks East: An Emerging Power and Its Asia-Pacific Neighbours*, edited by Sandy Gordon and Stephen Henningham. Canberra: Strategic and Defence Studies Centre, ANU, 1995.

———. "The Future of the Burmese Armed Forces". In *Burma-Myanmar: Strong Regime, Weak State?*, edited by Ron May, Morten Pedersen, and Emily Rudland. Adelaide: Crawford House Publication, 2000.

———. "The Myanmar Air Force since 1988: Expansion and Modernization". In *Contemporary Southeast Asia*, vol. 19, no. 4, March 1998.

———. "The Myanmar Army since 1988: Acquisition and Adjustments". In *Contemporary Southeast Asia*, vol. 17, no. 3, December 1995.

Stepan, Alfred. "The New Professionalism of Internal Warfare and Military Role Expansion". In *Authoritarian Brazil: Origins, Policies, Future*, edited by Alfred Stepan. Yale University Press, New Haven, 1973.

မောင်လှပေါ်(မန္တလေး)။ "မှန်ကြည့်ပါဦးမည်" *ငွေတာရီမဂ္ဂဇင်း* (အမှတ် ၄၅၈၊ စက်တင်ဘာ ၁၉၉၈) (Maung Hla Paw (Mandalay). "I Will Look at the Mirror". *Ngwe Taryi Magazine*, no. 458, September 1998).

ဆလိုင်းနွယ်။ "အရာရှိကောင်းများမွေးထုတ်ပေးနေသော တက္ကသိုလ်" *ပြည်သူ့တပ်မတော်စာစဉ်* (အတွဲ ၃၅၊ အမှတ် ၈။ ၁၅ ဩဂုတ် ၁၉၉၉) (Salaing Nwe. "The Academy that Produces Good Officers". *Pyithu Tatmadaw Sarsin*, vol. 35, no. 8, 15 August 1999).

အမည်မပါ၊ "နိုင်ငံတော်ကာကွယ်ရေးသည် အရေးကြီးသည်" *ပြည်သူ့တပ်မတော်စာစဉ်* (အတွဲ ၁၆၊ အမှတ် ၂။ ၁၅ ဖေဖော်ဝါရီ ၁၉၇၉) (Anno. "National Defence is Important". *Pyithu Tatmadaw Sarsin*, vol. 16, no. 2, 15 February 1979).

အမည်မပါ၊ "လူငယ်နှင့်အခြေခံစစ်ပညာသင်တန်း" *ပြည်သူ့တပ်မတော်စာစဉ်* (အတွဲ ၁၇၊ အမှတ် ၁၂။ ၁၅ ဒီဇင်ဘာ ၁၉၇၉) (Anno. "Youth and Basic Military Training". *Pyithu Tatmadaw Sarsin*, vol. 17, no. 2, 15 December 1979).

Journals and Magazines

Jane's Intelligence Review
Jane's Defence Weekly
Asian Defence Journal
Asian Military Review
Myanmar Today (Ministry of Information)
စစ်ပညာဂျာနယ်များ (*Journal of Military Affairs*)
ပြည်သူ့တပ်မတော်စာစဉ်များ (*People's Armed Forces Journal*)
တပ်မတော်(လေ)နှစ်ပတ်လည်မဂ္ဂဇင်းများ (*Myanmar Air Force Annual Magazines*)
တပ်မတော်(ရေ)နှစ်ပတ်လည်မဂ္ဂဇင်းများ (*Myanmar Navy Annual Magazines*)
စစ်တက္ကသိုလ် နှစ်ပတ်လည်မဂ္ဂဇင်းများ (*Defence Services Academy Annual Magazines*)
တပ်မတော် ဆေးတက္ကသိုလ် နှစ်ပတ်လည်မဂ္ဂဇင်းများ (*Defence Services Medical Academy Annual Magazines*)
ဆေးတပ်ဖွဲ့သမိုင်းစာစောင်များ (Publications on History of Defence Services Medical Services)
နိုင်ငံတော်ကာကွယ်ရေးတက္ကသိုလ် နှစ်ပတ်လည်မဂ္ဂဇင်းများ (*National Defence College Anniversary Magazines*)
တပ်မတော်(ကြည်း)တိုက်ခိုက်ရေးသင်တန်းကျောင်း နှစ်ပတ်လည်မဂ္ဂဇင်းများ (*Myanmar Army Combat Forces School Anniversary Magazines*)
တပ်မတော် နည်းပညာတက္ကသိုလ် နှစ်ပတ်လည်မဂ္ဂဇင်းများ (*Defence Services Technological Academy Annual Magazines*)

Documents from DSHMRI

CD. 14, Matters relating to Brigadier General Kyaw Zaw.

CD. 99, Documents distributed at the Tatmadaw Conference held in September 1954.

CD. 349, Minutes of the Commanding Officers Conference held at the War Office on 28–30 March 1951.

CD. 350, Minutes of the COs' Conference held in January and February 1950.

CD. 351, Minutes of the Commanding Officers' Conference held on 21 July 1951.

CD. 883-4, The 1969 CO Conference.

CD. 884-4, The 1968 CO Conference.

CD. 875, Diary of Colonel Maung Maung.

DR. 497, The 1948 CO's Meeting.

DR. 859, 1949 COs' Meeting.

DR. 876, The 1953 Tatmadaw Conference.

DR. 1535, Burma Army List 1952.

DR. 8556, History of the Tatmadaw-Lei.

DR. 8559, History of the Tatmadaw-Yay.

DR. 9349, Medical Corps Centre.

DR. 9447, Nurses Training Wing.

DR. 9453, Interview with Colonel Chit Myaing for the History of the Tatmadaw.

DR. 9653, Burma Army Combat Forces School.

DR. 9656, Command and General Staff College.

DR. 9692, History of the Directorate of Military Training.

DR. 10600, The National Defence College.

DR. 10266, Land/Air Warfare and Paratroops School.

Unpublished Material

Maung, Aung Myoe. Counterinsurgency in Myanmar: The Government's Response to the Burma Communist Party. Unpublished Ph.D. dissertation, Australian National University, 1999.

INDEX

E

L

M

N

About the Author

Maung Aung Myoe received his B.A in International Relations from University of Mandalay and M.A in the same discipline from International University of Japan, and Ph.D in Political Science and International Relations from Australian National University. He was a visiting fellow at the Institute of Defence and Strategic Studies (IDSS), Nanyang Technological University (NTU) and a postdoctoral fellow at the Asia Research Institute (ARI), National University of Singapore. His research interests cover Myanmar politics and foreign relations as well as regionalism, security and strategy, and civil-military relations. He teaches Southeast Asian Politics and International Relations at Inha University in Korea.

www.ingramcontent.com/pod-product-compliance
Lightning Source LLC
LaVergne TN
LVHW091341110826
845155LV00043B/4
* 9 7 8 9 8 1 2 3 0 8 4 8 1 *